A Grower's Choice

A Grower's Choice

Professional Tips on Plant Selection & Care for the Pacific Northwest

MICHAEL K. LASCELLE

RAINCOAST BOOKS

The photograph on the dedication page is of the author's grandmother, Patricia
Plementos, and great-grandmother, May Sherwood, Stanley Park, 1938.

First published in 2001 by

Raincoast Books
9050 Shaughnessy Street
Vancouver, B.C.
V6P 6E5

www.raincoast.com

1 2 3 4 5 6 7 8 9 10

Canadian Cataloguing in Publication Data
Lascelle, Michael Kenneth, 1961–
    A grower's choice

    Includes index.
    ISBN 1-55192-428-5

    1. Gardening — Northwest, Pacific. I. Title.
SB453.2.N83L37 2001   635.9'09795   C2001-910157-0

THE CANADA COUNCIL | LE CONSEIL DES ARTS
FOR THE ARTS | DU CANADA
SINCE 1957 | DEPUIS 1957
Raincoast Books gratefully acknowledges the support of the
Government of Canada, through the Book Publishing Industry Development
Program, the Canada Council for the Arts and the Department of Canadian
Heritage. We
also acknowledge the assistance of the Province of British Columbia, through
the British Columbia Arts Council.

Printed and bound in Canada

For all those who have ever loved a garden
enough to share it with another

Contents

Acknowledgements

Writing, like gardening, is an acquired skill and, without the people who have allowed me the opportunity to pursue these interests, this book would have never been possible. First and foremost on my thank you list would be my wife Pauline, followed very closely by my daughters Nicole, Rochelle and Madeleine — who have put up with my late nights of writing and "family outings" to various botanical gardens for longer than I care to mention.

As a professional gardener of 20 years, I have many people to acknowledge — beginning with Wim Hunfeld, the head gardener of the estate where I began my career — as well as the many people who later entrusted their gardens to my care during my time with Sierra Landscaping of North Vancouver. More to date, I would like to thank my regular customers at Amsterdam Garden Centre, who continue to share both their garden problems and triumphs with me and who always manage to leave with a new plant in hand. Special thanks to Kim Kamstra for helping me to "paste" together the initial book proposal and Todd Major of Park & Tilford Gardens, who is always there to give me his frank but honest opinion.

In regard to writing, I would like to mention Leonard Wexler of Build & Green, who gave me my first gardening column and Mary Mills, who subsequently took me on at what was then *Island Grower* magazine. I would also like to thank Lorri Espeseth of the VanDusen Botanical Garden education department, who allowed me the opportunity to share my experience with others through teaching. Lastly, I want to acknowledge the many contributors who are the substance of *A Grower's Choice*, and the staff at Raincoast, for patiently guiding me through this, my first book.

Introduction

I have been involved in the business of horticulture for about two decades. In my various occupations as estate gardener, landscaper, nursery manager and garden designer, I have always been keenly aware that without quality plant stock, there is no way for me to do a good job. We are all indebted, to some extent to the professional gardeners, commercial and retail growers, designers and landscapers who are responsible, either directly or indirectly, for much of the new plant material we see each spring in our local garden centres. *A Grower's Choice* is simply my way of recognizing the people responsible for producing and promoting some of our favourite plants.

These new introductions do not just happen. There is a lengthy process of finding or breeding the plants, test growing them, propagating enough stock for commercial production and finally marketing them to the retail sector. The first part of this process is usually the exclusive domain of the growers, while the marketing often occurs incidentally when landscape gardeners and designers incorporate these plants into our public parks and private residences. I do not pretend to represent the whole of the horticultural community with this book but, with more than 50 different contributors, *A Grower's Choice* will certainly give the gardener an insider's view of the past, present and future of gardening in the Pacific Northwest ... and beyond.

About This Book

How This Book Was Written
The contributors were asked to submit 10 selections, along with some relevant cultural notes, pertaining to a specific plant group. Many of the chapters came to me fully written and, for the most part, were only lightly rearranged to conform to format. Others originated as notes or catalogue descriptions that I transcribed into chapter form on behalf of the contributor.

The Chapter Format
Basically, the first two paragraphs introduce the plant group in general terms and provide some background on the contributor. This is followed by the 10 plant choices and some cultural notes specific to the plant group.

The Plant Choices
The individual selections were left entirely to the contributors' discretion and are by no means a complete representation of the plant group. For the most part, 10 plants are fully described in each chapter, but in a few instances this number was extended to give a broader perspective. Even at that, more than 500 main selections with an additional 700 companion plants or alternate choices are listed in the cultural notes — so this book is certainly not short on options.

Height and Spread
Heights and widths of trees are averaged over 15 to 20 years and will vary with site conditions. Heights and widths of shrubs are averaged over eight to 10 years.

Flowering Period
The flowering period has been included in many of the plant choices, with the exception of foliage shrubs or those with insignificant blooms. As with any act of nature,

flowering is much influenced by seasonal changes, sun exposure and hardiness zone, or it may vary somewhat depending on the weather and planting location. The flowering period is either expressed in terms of a general season (i.e., early spring) or as a specific monthly period (i.e., June–July).

Plant Hardiness

A lot of factors determine plant hardiness. The most limiting is perhaps the minimum winter temperature a plant will endure. Plant hardiness may be expressed as hardiness zones (1 to 9) or minimum temperatures (i.e., hardy to -29°C / -20°F). The following chart has been included so you can cross-reference these figures against the hardiness zone in which you live. If you are unsure about your hardiness zone, contact your local garden centre — they should be able to give you a good approximation and show you which plants will thrive where you live. Temperatures are approximate.

	FAHRENHEIT	CELCIUS
ZONE 1	BELOW -50°	BELOW -46°
ZONE 2	-50° TO -40°	-45° TO -40°
ZONE 3	-40° TO -30°	-40° TO -35°
ZONE 4	-30° TO -20°	-35° TO -29°
ZONE 5	-20° TO -10°	-29° TO -23°
ZONE 6	-10° TO 0°	-23° TO -18°
ZONE 7	0° TO 10°	-18° TO -12°
ZONE 8	10° TO 20°	-12° TO -6°
ZONE 9	20° TO 30°	-6° TO -1°

Sidebars — Cultural Notes

The "cultural notes" are an eclectic grouping of short pieces of gardening advice and plant lists relevant to the plant group. Many of the contributors have included alternate or companion plants in this section, while others have chosen to concentrate on specific procedures such as pruning, planting and fertilizing. Rather than adhere to a strict format in this section, I thought it was more important to reflect the grower's interests and concerns — so expect the cultural notes to vary considerably from chapter to chapter.

Trees

I have been a great admirer of trees since I was a young boy growing up on air force bases across western Canada. The only constant in the otherwise bleak residential landscape was that mature shade trees regularly tempted me with their lower limbs. Not one to resist temptation, I would gladly climb the smooth grey branches of the trembling aspens to sit in the crown and listen to the gentle rustling of the leaves. Much later, while working as a landscaper, I was able to continue this tradition and so I learned to appreciate trees from both the inside and out.

While the average homeowner may not have the same affection for trees as I have, as some of the largest plants in our landscapes, they deserve more than just a passing thought about planting site and appropriate cultivars. A poorly placed specimen may quickly obscure a choice view or clog underground storm drains with an invasive root structure.

On the other hand, the rewards of a well-placed shade tree greatly outweigh the few detriments, with cooling shade, privacy screening and season after season of flowers and autumn foliage awaiting the wise gardener.

Shade Trees

John Alexander
(Sandy) Howkins
Specimen Trees Wholesale
Nurseries Ltd.
Pitt Meadows, B.C.

Shade trees are the backbone of most landscapes and in many cases will grow on to outlive the people who planted them. We have all been graced by their presence at one time or another — be it a row of maples planted down the street, the solitary horse chestnut raining down "**conkers**" on the schoolyard or a clump of paper birch, with its white bark gleaming in the winter sun. Quite often we take this beauty for granted, but perhaps the shade tree's greatest contribution to the urban landscape is simply its quiet presence — giving us a sense of stability in an ever-changing world.

Alexander (Sandy) Howkins has been interested in horticulture ever since his first endeavour in gardening, as a child of five in eastern Africa. This interest carried him through various gardens and eventually resulted in a bachelor of science degree from the University of Guelph. Sandy continued to serve in various horticultural positions in eastern Canada until landing his current position of operations manager at Specimen Trees Wholesale Nurseries, where his knowledge of propagation techniques and tree cultivars is highly valued.

Acer rubrum "Red Sunset"

HEIGHT: 15 M / 50 FT	SPREAD: 3 M / 10 FT	ZONE: 4

This is the most beautiful and versatile of all the red maple varieties. *Acer rubrum* "Red Sunset" is planted more often than any other residential or commercial street tree in North America and is well known for its symmetrical growth pattern. The dark green foliage is palm-sized with a shiny upper surface, and the cultivar name is derived from the tremendous fall display composed of brilliant red and orange.

Cercidiphyllum japonicum

HEIGHT: 15 M / 50 FT	SPREAD: 18 M / 60 FT	ZONE: 5

The katsura tree has a beautiful, open canopy when mature but is quite upright in growth when young. Very fine, delicate branches carry heart-shaped leaves that flush a purple-red and gradually change to a bluish-green on the top of the leaf. The foliage gives off a delicious toffee aroma on warm summer days and, in autumn, it turns to shades of golden-yellow and apricot. Katsura will tolerate partial shade.

Fagus sylvatica "Purple Fountain"

HEIGHT: 8 M / 26 FT	SPREAD: 3 M / 10 FT	ZONE: 6

This is a very unusual, upright tree with a tight, cascading branch pattern. "Purple Fountain" stands like an obelisk in the landscape, as this tree is very seldom seen with more than one leader. It features smooth grey bark, typical of most European beech and 5-cm / 2-in long leaves that remain dark purple throughout the growing season.

Paulownia tomentosa

HEIGHT: 15 M / 50 FT	SPREAD: 12 M / 40 FT	ZONE: 5
FLOWERING PERIOD: APRIL –MAY		

It is no wonder that this species is called the empress or princess tree, as this native of China produces huge leaves (25 cm / 10 in across) on graceful branches that form a beautiful specimen. Flowering occurs very early in the year before the foliage begins to emerge. The fragrant pale violet blossoms are borne in terminal clusters and are similar to foxglove flowers in appearance. This tree is often mistaken for catalpa at a distance, and it produces pecan-like pods (5 cm / 2 in long) that persist for most of the season.

Planting a Specimen Tree

1. Remove any string from around the trunk of the tree to prevent girdling.

2. Large trees may come in wire baskets with burlap liners that are usually laced through the wire loops, away from the trunk. While it is important to leave the root ball intact, be sure to cut any rope or twine around the tree trunk.

3. Once the tree has established itself (rooted) after one growing year, you may cut any exposed string or wire.

4. The depth of the planting hole should be the same as the depth of the root ball to ensure that the tree does not shift when settling. Never plant any deeper, as it can suffocate the roots or cause bark damage, particularly in wet areas.

5. If you are planting in a wet area, be sure to elevate the planting area by creating a berm in which to plant the tree.

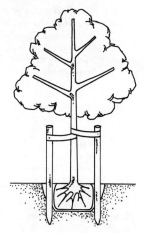

6. The diameter of the planting hole in the top third to half of the root zone should be one-third larger than the root ball. The bottom portion of the hole should form fit to give the tree support.

7. All trees should be staked above the mid-point of the trunk — two two-by-twos are ideal as stakes on each side of the tree, but be sure to place them out of the root zone. The strapping material should be as wide as possible to prevent damage to the tree.

8. To establish strong rooting, top dress with a low nitrogen, high phosphate fertilizer (i.e., 10–52–10) at the suggested rate. Apply the fertilizer away from the trunk and foliage to prevent burning.

9. In the second year of growth, fertilize with a 21–7–10 at a rate of 100 g per cm / 9 oz per in of **caliper***.*

Low-Growing Maples
This genus of ornamental trees is particularly useful for its many compact species and cultivars, which are good specimens in small urban areas or beneath power lines.
Acer palmatum *"Bloodgood" / Bloodgood Maple (6 m / 20 ft)*
A. griseum / Paperbark Maple (6–9 m / 20–30 ft)
A. palmatum "Shojo"/ Red Japanese Maple (3–5 m/10–16 ft)
A. platanoides "Globosum" / Globe Norway Maple (5 m / 16 ft)
A. ginnala "Flame" / Flame Amur Maple (5 m / 16 ft)
A. palmatum "Trompenburg" / Trompenburg Maple (5 m / 16 ft)

Stewartia pseudocamellia

HEIGHT: 15 M / 50 FT	SPREAD: 12 M / 40 FT	ZONE: 5
FLOWERING PERIOD: JUNE–JULY		

Japanese stewartia is a tree for all seasons, and this single- to multi-stemmed species is a must for collectors. The bark is a patchwork of shapes and colours — with hints of polished browns, silvers and ochre. In mid summer, the tree is covered in white camellia-like blooms (5 cm / 2 in across) that contrast well against the dark green leaves. It produces outstanding orange and yellow autumn foliage.

Aesculus x *carnea* "Briotii"

HEIGHT: 15 M / 50 FT	SPREAD: 10 M / 33 FT	ZONE: 5
FLOWERING PERIOD: MAY		

This cultivar of the red horse chestnut (*Aesculus pavia* x *A. hippocastanum*) is best appreciated in an open landscape. "Briotii" features deeper rose-crimson flower **panicles**, better disease resistance to the common leaf disorders and a more compact growth habit. The deep green, **palmately** compound foliage is also quite large.

Liquidambar styraciflua "Worplesdon"

HEIGHT: 20 M / 66 FT	SPREAD: 10 M / 33 FT	ZONE: 4

Of all the sweet gum cultivars, this selection is the best. "Worplesdon" is an excellent boulevard specimen due to its upright form and narrow-lobed leaves, which resemble those of maple. This shade tree holds its foliage late into the season and features outstanding wine red to apricot-orange autumn colours.

Cladrastis lutea

HEIGHT: 10 M / 33 FT	SPREAD: 12 M / 40 FT	ZONE: 4
FLOWERING PERIOD: MAY–EARLY JUNE		

American yellow-wood is a small, attractive flowering tree with smooth grey bark resembling polished steel. The common name refers to the colour of the heartwood, and the **pinnately** compound foliage also changes to a bright yellow in the fall. White, fragrant flowers are borne in wisteria-like terminal clusters in May to early June. *Cladrastis lutea* is native to limestone regions and is quite tolerant of soils with a high pH.

Robinia pseudoacacia "Frisia"

HEIGHT: 25 M / 82 FT	SPREAD: 20 M / 66 FT	ZONE: 4

A favourite of all the golden-leafed trees, "Frisia" is a great choice for the West Coast. This black locust cultivar is a tough, drought-tolerant tree with upright branches and deeply furrowed bark. The compound, chartreuse foliage gives nicely dappled shade and turns a striking golden-yellow in the fall. "Frisia" tolerates poor soil conditions.

Parrotia persica

HEIGHT: 13 M / 43 FT	SPREAD: 10 M / 33 FT	ZONE: 4
FLOWERING PERIOD: FEB–MARCH		

Persian ironwood is a real focal point, with many outstanding characteristics. The trunk sweeps gracefully as it curves upward and the exfoliating bark gives way to white, green and mahogany blotches. The leaves flush reddish-purple, changing to an attractive medium green, while the fall colours are a medley of yellows, oranges and reds. Insignificant flowers bloom in late winter, giving an overall reddish hue to the tree canopy. *Parrotia persica* may be trained as a multi-stem or standard.

A. tataricum / *Tatarium Maple*
(*7 m / 23 ft*)

A. circinatum / *Vine Maple*
(*6 m+ / 20 ft+*)

A. palmatum *"Osakazuki"* /
Osakazuki Maple (6 m / 20 ft)

Removing a Large Branch
Occasionally, a mature tree will require the removal of a large limb for disease control or just for aesthetic reasons. It is important to use proper pruning techniques in order to avoid torn bark or further damage to the tree.

1. Make a partial bottom cut 30 cm (1 ft) away from the trunk.

2. Make a second cut on top of the branch, 1 cm / 1/2 in out from the first cut.

3. The final cut should be just beyond the branch bark ridges or collar.

4. Never make a flush cut, as this creates a larger wound surface.

5. In the case of a limb with enclosed bark, lighten the branch as described in the first two steps above.

6. Cut upward toward the top of the branch and trunk union.

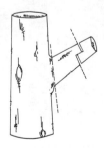

Flowering Trees

Geoff Anderson
Cannor Nurseries Ltd.
Chilliwack, B.C.

We have all grown up with one flowering tree or another, whether it was a row of ornamental cherries lining the street or that solitary dogwood planted in the front yard. Many homeowners like to have at least one flowering tree on the property, and while most provide a spectacular show of blooms for several weeks, quite a few of them also serve as excellent shade trees for the balance of the growing season.

Cannor Nurseries is one of the largest wholesale shrub and tree growers in the Fraser Valley. Their Chilliwack-based field and container operation supplies many retail nurseries with a diverse selection of ornamental plants and fruit trees. As Cannor's main sales representative, Geoff Anderson uses his intimate knowledge of flowering trees to help his retail clients choose a variety of species and cultivars to satisfy the needs of West Coast gardeners.

Styrax japonicum "Japanese Snowbell"

HEIGHT: 6–8 M / 20–25 FT	SPREAD: 6–8 M / 20–25 FT	ZONE: 5
FLOWERING PERIOD: MAY–EARLY JUNE		

A delicate tree, Japanese Snowbell bears fragrant, pure white, bell-shaped flowers that hang along the length of the branches from May to early June. It is best placed where one can enjoy the blooms from below, as well as the light shade of the small **ovate** leaves. Interesting coffee bean-shaped seeds hang on for much of the winter.

Cercis canadensis "Eastern Redbud"

HEIGHT: 6–8 M / 20–25 FT	SPREAD: 8–9 M / 25–30 FT	ZONE: 4
FLOWERING PERIOD: MAY–JUNE		

This low-branched or multi-stemmed tree has medium green, heart-shaped leaves that open with a slight reddish cast. The flowers appear in tight clusters along the stems and are purplish-red in bud, opening to a rosy-pink. "Forest Pansy" is a cultivar of eastern redbud that features shiny, deep burgundy new foliage, which matures to bronze.

Syringa reticulata "Ivory Silk"

HEIGHT: 6–8 M / 20–25 FT	SPREAD: 4.5 M / 15 FT	ZONE: 4
FLOWERING PERIOD: MAY–JUNE		

This tree form of lilac really deserves to be planted more often. The large creamy-white flowers are typical of lilacs, but are not as tight as the French hybrids *(Syringa vulgaris)*. Its Zone 3 hardiness should make it popular with homeowners in difficult, exposed sites.

Prunus s. "Kwanzan" / Ornamental Cherry

HEIGHT: 9 M / 30 FT	SPREAD: 8 M / 25 FT	ZONE: 5
FLOWERING PERIOD: APRIL–MAY		

"Kwanzan" has been a standard boulevard tree for decades — much in part to its excellent upright, vase form. The leaves emerge copper-bronze and mature to a dark green, with autumn tints of orange to reddish-purple. The April to May display of large, double pink blossoms is one of the highlights of the season.

The Flower and Form of Ornamental Japanese Cherries

Prunus "Kwanzan" — *deep pink double flowers / vase-shaped, upright form*

P. "Shirotae" — *semi-double white flowers / horizontal form, flat top*

P. "Akebono" — *light pink single flowers / robust spreading form*

P. "Shirofugen" — *pale pink to white double flowers / wide, spreading form*

P. "Amanogawa" — *pale pink semi-double flowers / columnar form*

P. subhirtella "Pendula" — *single pale pink blooms / weeping form*

P. "Ukon" — *greenish-yellow semi-double blooms / spreading form*

P. "Accolade" — *semi-double pink flowers / spreading form*

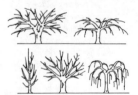

***Choosing a Flowering
Tree for the Garden***
*Quite often, homeowners choose
a flowering tree in bloom at
their local nursery with little
consideration of its ultimate size.
Consequently, many of these
specimens need to be removed
when they are in their prime
(usually 10 to 15 years after
planting), leaving little behind
except the stump. This can easily
be avoided by carefully selecting
a tree that will not overwhelm its
allotted growing space.*

Amelanchier x *grandiflora* "Autumn Brilliance"

HEIGHT: 6–8 M / 20–25 FT	SPREAD: 4.5 M / 15–25 FT	ZONE: 3
FLOWERING PERIOD: MAY–APRIL		

A tree-sized relative of the Saskatoon berry, "Autumn Brilliance" has small bluish-green leaves and an abundance of tiny white **panicles** that hang from the branches. The fall foliage colours of bright orange to red are truly spectacular. This tree attracts birds with its edible purple-black berries.

Laburnum x *watereri* "Vossii" / Golden Chain Tree

HEIGHT: 8 M / 25 FT	SPREAD: 6 M / 20 FT	ZONE: 5
FLOWERING PERIOD: MAY		

The quintessence of spring beauty is best expressed with the many pendulous trusses of bright yellow blooms, which the golden chain tree brings each spring. "Vossii" features a vase-shaped form and is best used as a background planting, as it is rather undistinguished for the rest of the season. All parts of this tree are highly toxic if ingested.

Prunus x *blireana* / Flowering Plum

HEIGHT: 6 M / 20 FT	SPREAD: 6 M / 20 FT	ZONE: 5
FLOWERING PERIOD: APRIL		

This flowering plum features reasonably small leaves that emerge a deep reddish-purple in spring and fade to a bronze-green as the summer progresses. "Blireana" bears an abundance of slightly fragrant, double pink blooms that are approximately 2.5 cm / 1 in across.

Crataegus × *mordensis* "Toba" / Hawthorn

HEIGHT: 4.5–6 M / 15–20 FT	SPREAD: 4–4.5 M / 12–15 FT	ZONE: 3
FLOWERING PERIOD: MAY		

A hybrid hawthorn that was developed at Morden, Manitoba, in the 1950s, "Toba" is quite disease-resistant and is not subject to leaf spot or summer defoliation. The double flowers open white, changing to pink as they mature.

Acer griseum / Paperbark Maple

HEIGHT: 6–8 M / 20–25 FT	SPREAD: 4–6 M /15–20 FT	ZONE: 5
FLOWERING PERIOD: FLOWERS INSIGNIFICANT		

This is not exactly a flowering tree but, as one of Geoff's favourites, it certainly deserves a place in his chapter. *Acer griseum* is still a highly ornamental species with **trifoliate** leaves and reddish-brown **exfoliating** bark, which looks great on newly fallen snow. This slow-growing tree is highly recommended as a winter feature.

Franklinia alatamaha / Franklinia

HEIGHT: 6–9 M / 20–30 FT	ZONE: 6
FLOWERING PERIOD: SEPT–OCT	

A very rare tree that was once native to regions of the southern United States, but is now extinct in the wild, Franklinia has many ornamental features, including orange to scarlet fall foliage, attractive reddish-brown bark and large, single white flowers accented with a cluster of yellow **stamens**. It is slow-growing.

"Standard" refers to a tree that has been trained to a single stem, with the branches removed for the first 1.5–2 m / 5–6 ft (or less for slower growing trees). With flowering bushes specifically, "standard" refers to large shrubs that are trained into a standard form, rather than left to grow as large multi-stemmed bushes.

Small (3–6 m / 10–20 ft)

Malus "Red Jade" / Weeping Crabapple
Crataegus "Paul's Scarlet" / Red Flowering Hawthorn
Oxydendrum arboreum / Sourwood

Medium (6–9 m / 20–30 ft)

Catalpa bignonoides / Indian Bean Tree
Sorbus h. "Pink Pagoda" / Pink Mountain Ash
Prunus c. "Pissardi Nigra" / Purple Leaf Flowering Plum

Large (over 9 m / 30 ft)

Liriodendron tulipifera / Tulip Tree
Prunus sargentii / Sargent Cherry

Magnolias

Bruce Rutherford
Piroche Plants
Pitt Meadows, B.C.

The magnolia family, Magnoliaceae, includes some of the oldest known flowering plants still in existence. It encompasses many species of trees and shrubs that are admired for their opulent flowers and attractive foliage. This family is constantly growing due to newly discovered species and many recently introduced varieties. Genetic information suggests that there are really only two **genera**, *Magnolia and Liriodendron* — although many botanists have long thought that there were several.

Piroche Plants is fortunate to be on the forefront of introducing new magnolias into North America, largely due to its joint venture with a nursery in China, which is home to perhaps several hundred species. As a busy international wholesale nursery, we often see many new and old varieties, as well as previously unknown species. Piroche Plants also has an exciting magnolia hybridization program, which is producing never-before-seen crosses.

This list of 10 magnolias includes both new and established varieties, which demonstrate the wide range of horticultural possibilities that this family has to offer for the West Coast and beyond. The botanical names used include the original multi-generic nomenclature, the new reclassified names and several common references.

Magnolia grandiflora "Victoria" / Southern Magnolia

HEIGHT: 6–10 M / 20–30 FT	SPREAD: 6–10 M / 20–30 FT	ZONE: 7–8
FLOWERING PERIOD: SUMMER–FALL		

This evergreen tree, native to the southern United States, is perhaps the most sought-after magnolia — mostly in part to its large tropical leaves and huge, fragrant white flowers (to 15 cm / 6 in wide). Of the many selections of this species available, one of the best and most cold hardy varieties is "Victoria," which was selected in British Columbia. It features lustrous foliage with striking brown pubescent undersides.

Magnolia officinalis / Medicinal Magnolia

HEIGHT: 10 M / 30 FT	SPREAD: 8 M / 26 FT	ZONE: 6–7
FLOWERING PERIOD: LATE SPRING		

A large, deciduous tree native to China that is sparsely branched when young, this magnolia produces large, exotic-looking leaves up to 40 cm / 15 in long. It features purple-brown buds that open to huge, ivory-coloured fragrant flowers (to 18 cm / 7 in across). Throughout history, all parts of this tree have been used medicinally, but today it has become endangered in its native habitat despite commercial propagation. *Magnolia officinalis* is quite a hardy species and a good choice for gardeners looking for a tropical feature.

Magnolia sieboldii / Oyama Magnolia

HEIGHT: 4 M / 13 FT	SPREAD: 5 M / 16 FT	ZONE: 6
FLOWERING PERIOD: LATE SPRING–SUMMER		

One of the smaller deciduous magnolias, *M. sieboldii* is native to Japan and Korea, and attains the dimensions of a large vase-shaped shrub or small multi-stemmed tree. It has broad, pointed leaves and downward facing, lightly fragrant white blooms with prominent burgundy stamens. Bright red twisted fruits follow the flowers, adding summer colour.

Magnolia x *soulangiana* / Saucer Magnolia

HEIGHT: 5–8 M / 16–26 FT	SPREAD: 5–8 M / 16–26 FT	ZONE: 4–5*
FLOWERING PERIOD: MID SPRING	*Depending on cultivar	

Generally a small multi-stemmed tree, this deciduous group of cultivars originally of *M. denudata* x *M. liliflora* parentage, includes varieties with flower colours ranging from white to pink to red, through to dark purple. Some

Transplanting Magnolias
Some magnolia varieties can be sensitive when transplanted, and may languish until they become adjusted to their new home. This is especially evident with field-dug plants that are not relocated immediately or have small root balls, but even containerized specimens can take time to settle in. It is important to prepare the site well and not to plant the root ball too deeply, as the roots are susceptible to suffocating. In any case, choose your planting site well, as magnolias do not like being shuffled around the garden.

popular cultivars include "Lennei" (dark magenta-purple), "Rustica Rubra" (rosy-red), "Burgundy" (reddish-purple) and "Brozzonii" (white).

Manglietia insignis (Magnolia insignis) / Red Lotus Tree

HEIGHT: 6–10 M / 20–33 FT	SPREAD: 5–7 M / 16–23 FT	ZONE: 7
FLOWERING PERIOD: EARLY SUMMER		

This evergreen tree from China was virtually unknown in the early 1990s, but can now be found in many public and private gardens. It has an upright habit and can be trained as a standard or multi-stemmed specimen. The olive green leaves are long, narrow and quite tough. Flower colour may vary on seedling-raised plants, but they are generally deep red before the bud opens — revealing nine petals in three layers of three petals each. The outer layer is primarily red, but it successively changes to a mostly white inner layer. Flowers are 8–10 cm / 3–4 in across and they emit a fresh scent.

Magnolia denudata (M. heptapeta) / Yulan Magnolia

HEIGHT: 6–10 M / 20–33 FT	SPREAD: 6–10 M / 20–33 FT	ZONE: 5
FLOWERING PERIOD: EARLY TO MID SPRING		

Magnolia denudata has long been cultivated in its native China and has been used extensively in breeding programs since it was first introduced to the West, some 200 years ago. Like many of its relatives, it can be quite incestuous, readily hybridizing with any nearby species that are pollinating at the same time. Seed-grown plants are quite variable, but it generally develops into a well-branched young tree, which blooms after about five years. White, scented flowers can then be expected as this magnolia matures to a broad, medium-sized specimen.

Michelia maudiae *(Magnolia maudiae)* / Smiling Lily Tree

HEIGHT: 5–10 M / 16–33 FT	SPREAD: 3–5 M / 10–16 FT	ZONE: 7
FLOWERING PERIOD: MID SPRING		

Another evergreen species from China unknown in Western cultivation until the late 1990s, *Michelia maudiae* features flowers that bloom along the length of the branches rather than just at the tips, as do all *Michelias*. The pure white blooms are variable in size (averaging 10–12 cm / 4–5 in across), but they emit an elegant fragrance often described as a combination of ginger and wintergreen. Foliage tends to be a sea-green colour on top with silvery-green undersides.

Magnolia "Yellow Fever"

HEIGHT: 8–12 M / 26–40 FT	SPREAD: 5–8 M / 16–26 FT	ZONE: 4
FLOWERING PERIOD: LATE SPRING		

A deciduous hybrid of *M. acuminata* x *M. denudata*, "Yellow Fever" will eventually become a medium to large, well-branched tree. It produces fragrant yellow flowers up to 15 cm / 6 in across.

Parakmeria lotungensis *(Magnolia lotungensis)* / Eastern Joy Lotus Tree

HEIGHT: 8–10 M / 26–33 FT	SPREAD: 4–7 M / 13–23 FT	ZONE: 7
FLOWERING PERIOD: LATE SPRING		

A third evergreen Chinese species introduced only recently to cultivation, it is considered rare and endangered in its native habitat. The smooth, shiny foliage emerges a copper red, then matures to a dark olive with powdery green undersides. It bears 7–10 cm / 3–4 in wide creamy-yellow flowers that produce small, red, oblong potato-like fruits.

Pruning

Most magnolias are vigorous growers in the Pacific Northwest and the majority of the pruning they require will be to maintain size, once they are established. Make sure you know the growth habits of the variety you are planting, as many shrubby types can grow quite wide in 10 to 15 years. One option is to prune outlying branches back to an upward facing bud, just after flowering. Upright magnolias should be regarded as medium-sized trees and will require little pruning, other than removing the lower limbs so people can walk underneath.

General Care

Most magnolia relatives are native to areas with higher summer precipitation — so they prefer additional water during dry periods, especially when young. While they can tolerate wet climates, all require well-drained sites. Magnolias perform well in acidic, loamy soil and will benefit from the addition of an iron supplement if **chlorosis** should occur. Avoid placing young plants near established trees, where their roots will have to compete for both nutrients and water. Most are tolerant of some shade when young, but will eventually need access to more sunlight as they mature and flower. Early-blooming varieties are susceptible to damage from frost — so if you are situated in a frost pocket, consider using later flowering cultivars.

Magnolia campbellii var. lanarth / Campbell's Magnolia

HEIGHT: 10–15 M / 33–50 FT	SPREAD: 8–12 M / 26–40 FT	ZONE: 7
FLOWERING PERIOD: MID SPRING		

This deciduous magnolia produces large, deep pink blooms (to 25 cm / 10 in wide) that are "heavenly" scented. The broad leaves are up to 20 cm / 8 in long and nearly as wide. It can quickly become a large tree and really deserves the space to display its grace and beauty.

Japanese Maples

Typically, a gardener's interests evolve over the many years of nurturing a landscape. Newcomers tend to focus on flowers but, as their enthusiasm for plants grows, they inevitably develop an eye for foliage. Flowers then seem to take second place or, more precisely, the seasoned gardener perceives as much beauty in a leaf as in a blossom. This is indeed a fortunate progression, since about 90 percent of our gardens are foliage.

Japanese maples are among the most favoured "foliage plants" used by West Coast gardeners and designers. These trees — *Acer palmatum*, *Acer japonicum* and *Acer shirasawanum* — have a range of use to fit virtually any landscape need. The spectrum of leaf colour is truly remarkable, ranging from spring tones of shrimp pink and chartreuse to dramatic autumn displays of reds, purples and golds. Japanese maples are equally at home as a focal point in the lawn, in the mixed border planted with bold shrubs or in larger containers as patio specimens.

All of the following choices only suggest the incredible diversity of this group of plants. To put it in perspective, the Japanese have been selecting choice cultivars for more than 300 years and there are currently more than 250 varieties in use today, each with its own charm. Heights and widths are average over 15 to 20 years and will vary with site conditions.

Don and Bev MacWatt
Island Specialty Nursery
Chemainus, B.C.

Japanese maples are well suited to our Pacific Northwest climate and thrive with good cultural practices and careful siting. Nevertheless, they do have problems at times — as does almost every important group of garden plants — so care in planting and culture is very important. The following is information we have gathered from our experience growing Japanese maples. We hope that by sharing it, you will have continued enjoyment from these worthy trees.

Choosing a Planting Site
To remain healthy, small deciduous trees like Japanese maples require excellent drainage. Poor drainage will put immediate stress on these trees and seriously compromises their ability to fend off disease. Unless the soil drainage is near perfect, the following methods are recommended.
1. Raise the root ball above the normal ground level and form a mound of soil around the plant.
2. Plant on a slope with drainage material such as coarse rock trenched from below the root zone out to the soil surface, to allow excess water to drain off.
Avoid placing Japanese maples where they may be exposed to harsh, drying winds. This is particularly important for dissected varieties and forms with long narrow leaves, as these desiccate very quickly in wind.

Acer japonicum / Full-moon Maple

HEIGHT: 6 M / 20 FT	SPREAD: 6 M / 20 FT	ZONE: 5

This species is outstanding in all seasons, with a strong form and bold leaves. *Acer japonicum f. aconitifolium* has multi-divided foliage which is deeply cut, giving it a fern-like texture reminiscent of *Aconitum* (monkshood). The leaves are deep green through spring and summer, turning to intensive shades of flaming red (with splashes of orange and purple) as autumn arrives. Full-moon maple is usually multi-stemmed in character.

Acer shirasawanum "Aureum" / Golden Full-moon Maple

HEIGHT: 3 M / 10 FT	SPREAD: 3 M / 10 FT	ZONE: 5

The wide "full-moon" leaves emerge a pale yellow-green, and these chartreuse tones hold well into the season, turning to oranges and reds in the fall. *Acer shirasawanum* "Aureum" definitely needs shade to preserve the delicate green foliage. Unfortunately, this cultivar has a limited availability, as it is difficult to propagate and slow to establish.

Acer palmatum "Sango-kaku" / Coral Bark Maple

HEIGHT: 6 M / 20 FT	SPREAD: 4.5 M / 15 FT	ZONE: 5

This cultivar of Japanese maple, occasionally referred to as the Senkaki maple, is revered for its brilliant red bark, which contrasts perfectly against the soft green leaves. Fall foliage is a bright yellow with tones of orange and red, after which the highly coloured bark lights up the winter landscape. Sadly, this cultivar seems more prone to deadly fungal bark disease, so it is very important to pay extra attention to cultural practices to relieve any stress.

Acer palmatum "Katsura" / **Wig Maple**

HEIGHT: 4 M / 12 FT	SPREAD: 2.5 M / 8 FT	ZONE: 5

This is one of the loveliest smaller maples, bursting into spring with orange and yellow **palmate** leaves, which turn to a rich green during the summer. The dense foliage reverts to shades of yellow and orange in the fall. "Katsura" needs some shade from the intense summer sun and may appear a bit stunted in warmer climates.

Acer palmatum "Okagami" / **Mirror Maple**

HEIGHT: 4 M / 12 FT	SPREAD: 3 M / 10 FT	ZONE: 5

This unusual and attractive lawn specimen has seven-lobed leaves that are broader than the typical *palmatum* leaf. Purplish-red new foliage matures to a shiny black-red, then to fiery vermilion and finally scarlet in autumn.

Another seven-lobed maple is the classic "Osakazuki," which is best known for its intense crimson fall colour and rich green leaves in summer. "Ichigyoji" is identical to "Osakazuki" save one aspect — its autumn colour is a brilliant yellow-orange. They are both highly recommended as companion plants for a dazzling fall display.

Acer palmatum "Omurayama"

HEIGHT: 4.5–6 M / 15–20 FT	SPREAD: 5.5–6.5 M / 18–22 FT	ZONE: 5

This choice variety has graceful, cascading branches reminiscent of weeping willow. Brilliant green summer colour gives way to gold, orange and crimson autumn foliage. The leaves are deeply divided, with each lobe separated all the way into the centre of the leaf, giving a lacy, light-textured effect.

Sun or Shade?
The red and green forms of the broader-leafed Japanese maples are reasonably happy with a full sun exposure in our West Coast climate where moisture is sufficient. A light canopy of taller trees is perfect and most appreciate a respite from the very hot early afternoon sun. The pale green, golden, variegated and pink forms really need some shade to be at their best. It is surprising to see how well older specimens adapt to open conditions, but younger plants with these lighter foliage tones will suffer by summer's end.

Watering Needs
Japanese maples need regular watering throughout the growing season. They are stressed by soil saturation or by drying out. A little on the drier side is better than too wet. Constancy is the key here. It sounds a bit tricky but in fact, once they are established, maples are content with most regimes, save extremes. Watering should be reduced in September (not to the point of wilt) to help the plant harden off late season growth — by October, all watering should be stopped completely. Regular mulching also helps to retain soil moisture and allows surface roots to exist in a well-aerated, humus-rich environment.

Acer palmatum "Kasagayama"

HEIGHT: 4.5 M / 15 FT	SPREAD: 4.5 M / 15 FT	ZONE: 5

A rare and very unusual cultivar with distinctive colouring, this maple's deeply divided leaves are brick red with an undertone of green; veins are dark. It will make a somewhat open-growing shrub or small tree.

A similar effect is displayed by "Aka shigitatsu sawa," which sports deeply divided **reticulated** leaves. In the cultivar name, "Aka" means red, referring to the green tones being overlaid with pink and red. "Shigitatsu sawa" is the green counterpart to the above. Its lime-green foliage with white veining is particularly handsome early in the season before it darkens. This cultivar appreciates more shade than most Japanese maples.

Acer palmatum "Villa Taranto"

HEIGHT: 2.5 M / 8 FT	SPREAD: 1.8 M / 6 FT	ZONE: 5

This representative of the "Linearilobum" group of Japanese maples is characterized by deeply divided, long, narrow leaves with smooth margins. Lacy and delicate, the green foliage is tinged with pink early in the season and changes to clear yellow in autumn. With age, it exhibits a dome-shaped form.

"Red Pygmy" is another worthy cultivar with thread-like, deep maroon foliage that turns to lovely purplish tones in the fall. "Beni Otaki" is a striking, small upright tree with distinctive purple-red leaves reminiscent of bamboo.

Acer palmatum dissectum / Weeping Japanese Maple

This group of Japanese maples usually has seven-lobed leaves that are deeply serrated and divided to the base, giving a very fern-like texture. They are, without exception, all weeping in form. Here are a few of our favourite cultivars:

"Viridis"

HEIGHT: 1.8 M / 6 FT	SPREAD: 2.75 M / 9 FT	ZONE: 5

A vibrant, green-leafed variety that changes to a vivid gold in autumn.

"Tamukeyama"

HEIGHT: 2.5 M / 8 FT	SPREAD: 3.5 M / 12 FT	ZONE: 5

This excellent red-leafed cultivar has strongly cascading foliage that emerges crimson-red, deepens to dark purple-red during the summer and changes to scarlet in autumn.

"Ornatum Variegatum"

HEIGHT: 1.8 M / 6 FT	SPREAD: 2.5 M / 8 FT	ZONE: 5

The very appealing variegation of tawny, pink, cream and subdued green all blends wonderfully in this graceful variety.

Acer palmatum "Orido nishiki"

HEIGHT: 4.5 M / 15 FT	SPREAD: 3.5 M / 12 FT	ZONE: 5

This is a fairly vigorous shrub with variegated foliage that seldom reverts. The **palmate** leaves are a rich, shiny green with pink and cream markings. Totally pink or white leaves are not uncommon — the new bark is also often streaked with pink and white. "Orido nishiki" is the best of the brightly variegated Japanese maples.

Acer palmatum "Mikawa yatsubusa"

HEIGHT: 90 CM / 3 FT	SPREAD: 90 CM / 3 FT	ZONE: 5

One of the rarest and choicest of Japanese maples is this dwarf, primarily cultivated for its fascinating growth habit. The light green leaves tend to overlay each other, much like "shingles on a roof." It is multi-branched, with short new shoots densely covered in leaves that are uncommonly large for a dwarf.

Fertilizer Needs

Japanese maples are not heavy feeders, preferring to be kept on the lean side. Feeding is always much better in an organic form, although maples will respond to chemical fertilizers applied lightly in early spring, before the leaves emerge. Their requirements are similar to that of rhododendrons, including their water needs. It is very important to harden off maples early in the fall, especially since they can be otherwise encouraged into late growth with long, warm days and residual nitrogen fertilizer. An early frost can easily kill this late growth, allowing the introduction of harmful fungi. So, do not apply nitrogen past the beginning of July and use a light application of a phosphorus-potash fertilizer in early September to aid in the hardening process.

Shrubs

When you think about it, the word "shrubs" hardly does justice to the beautiful and varied melange of flowers, foliage and texture these plants bring to our gardens. They form the backbone of many landscape designs, providing foliar substance below the vertical elements of vines and trees. Quite often, flowering shrubs such as hydrangea and heather — with their long lasting displays of brightly coloured blooms — will actually garner more attention than the summer flowers. Broadleaf evergreens play a much subtler role in the garden, providing year round coverage, which is most welcome in winter and many come with the added bonus of attractive flower clusters.

Heaths & Heathers

David Wilson
The Heather Farm
Sardis, B.C.

Few evergreen shrubs can offer us the diversity of flower colour and foliage texture that heaths and heathers bring to our landscapes. Although these plants have long been valued in their native Europe, gardeners in North America are just starting to realize their design potential. The many cultivars of *Erica* and *Calluna vulgaris* make excellent ground covers, container specimens or accents in the conifer garden.

The Heather Farm is a Fraser Valley mail-order nursery that specializes in growing these plants and offering them to the public. Its owner, David Wilson, is often contacted by heather enthusiasts from across the globe — in search of the many elusive varieties that he propagates.

Erica x *stuartii* "Irish Lemon"

HEIGHT: 25 CM / 10 IN	SPREAD: 50 CM / 20 IN	ZONE: 5
FLOWERING PERIOD: MAY–SEPT		

Erica x *stuartii* is a cross between *E. mackaiana* and *E. tetralix*, with brightly coloured spring foliage. "Irish Lemon" in particular features a bold display of large, mauve flowers (May to September) that contrast well against the brilliant yellow new growth. It forms a tidy, rounded shrub and is also quite hardy.

Erica x *darleyensis* "Kramer's Red"

HEIGHT: 35 CM / 14 IN	SPREAD: 60 CM / 2 FT	ZONE: 5
FLOWERING PERIOD: NOV–MAY		

This winter-flowering heath is a recent introduction from Germany, yet it has quickly become a favourite among gardeners. The deep ruby blooms of this cultivar seem to almost glow against the dark, bronze-green foliage.

"Kramer's Red" is quite easy to grow, like most of the Darley heath varieties, including "Furzey" (dark pink) and "White Perfection."

Calluna vulgaris "Silver Queen"

HEIGHT: 45 CM / 18 IN	SPREAD: 60 CM / 2 FT	ZONE: 4
FLOWERING PERIOD: AUG–SEPT		

The first thing you will notice when looking at "Silver Queen" is the unique silvery-grey foliage. This variation in foliar colour can make an impressive impact in the garden, if it is placed with some care. "Silver Queen" has a spreading habit and spikes of lavender flowers during late summer.

Erica tetralix "Pink Glow"

HEIGHT: 20 CM / 8 IN	SPREAD: 45 CM / 18 IN	ZONE: 4
FLOWERING PERIOD: JUNE–SEPT		

Erica tetralix is one of the hardier heaths and grows wild in many regions of northern and central Europe. As the name implies, "Pink Glow" bears deep magenta-pink blooms over a long period and features tidy yet vigorous grey-green foliage. Once established, its drought tolerant nature makes it an ideal choice for low maintenance landscapes.

Daboecia cantabrica "Atropurpurea"

HEIGHT: 40 CM / 16 IN	SPREAD: 65 CM / 26 IN	ZONE: 6
FLOWERING PERIOD: JUNE–OCT		

Irish bell heath is a much underused shrub, yet this native of Ireland and Spain has plenty to offer, including large urn-shaped blooms, partial shade and drought tolerance, as well as a long flowering season. The shrub itself has large leaves for a heath and is generally erect and open, when not sheared. "Atropurpurea" features deep purple flowers and dark green foliage.

Heath or Heather?
All of the species discussed in this chapter are members of the heath or Ericaceae *family, and while most are commonly referred to as heathers, there was a time when they had distinct common names. Heath was once used exclusively for* Erica *species and heather for* Calluna vulgaris *(or Scotch heather), but you will find that this strict terminology has broadened over the years to include other species, such as* Daboecia cantabrica.

Heather in Bloom —
All Season Long
Quite literally, there is at least one species or cultivar of heather in bloom for every month of the year. Here is a short list of the major species and the extent of their flowering period:

Spring
Erica x darleyensis / *Dec–May*
Erica erigena / *Nov–June**

Summer
Erica x stuartii / *May–Sept*
Calluna vulgaris / *July–Oct*
Erica cinerea / *June–Nov*
Erica tetralix / *June–Nov*

Autumn
Erica x watsonii / *June–Oct*
Daboecia cantabrica / *June–Nov*
Erica vagans / *Aug–Nov*

Winter
Erica carnea / *Dec–May*

**This species is becoming quite popular, particularly "Irish Dusk" (strictly Zone 7)*

Erica carnea "Golden Starlet"

HEIGHT: 15 CM / 6 IN	SPREAD: 40 CM / 16 IN	ZONE: 4
FLOWERING PERIOD: DEC–APRIL		

Another recent German introduction that is a cross of "Foxhollow" and "Snow Queen," this heather has absolutely glowing winter foliage of golden-yellow that fades to a lime-gold toward late summer. Its compact growth habit, white flowers and moderate spread has made it a very popular cultivar.

Erica vagans "Mrs. D. F. Maxwell"

HEIGHT: 30 CM / 1 FT	SPREAD: 45 CM / 18 IN	ZONE: 5
FLOWERING PERIOD: AUG–OCT		

Discovered in Cornwall, England, this cultivar of Cornish heath is perhaps one of the single most popular varieties grown anywhere. "Mrs. D. F. Maxwell" bears deep rose-pink blooms from August to October, contrasted against dark green foliage. It tolerates hard pruning quite well and can be used as a reliable ground cover.

Calluna vulgaris "Spring Torch"

HEIGHT: 40 CM / 16 IN	SPREAD: 60 CM / 2 FT	ZONE: 4
FLOWERING PERIOD: AUG–OCT		

A Scotch heather that lives up to its name, this heather's growth tips of vibrant red and cream-yellow could almost be mistaken for flowers at a distance. "Spring Torch" is a vigorous plant with deep green mature leaves and attractive mauve blooms in late summer. It is very popular with gardeners looking to make an impact with both foliage texture and colour.

Erica cinerea "Velvet Night"

HEIGHT: 25 CM / 10 IN	SPREAD: 55 CM / 18 IN	ZONE: 6
FLOWERING PERIOD: JUNE–SEPT		

The dark red blooms of "Velvet Night" are very unusual for an *Erica*. This summer-flowering bell heath blooms fairly early (starting in June) and has dark green foliage. "Atrosanguinea" (magenta), "Purple Beauty" (deep purple) and "P. S. Patrick" (upright purple blooms) also provide very showy flowers for this species.

Erica x watsonii "Pink Pacific"

HEIGHT: 40 CM / 16 IN	SPREAD: 35 CM / 14 IN	ZONE: 5
FLOWERING PERIOD: JULY–OCT		

This exciting new introduction from The Heather Farm features striking orange-red spring foliage and clear pink flowers. A similar cultivar, "Pink Pearl," also introduced by this nursery has a slightly more compact growth habit. "Pink Pacific" may be a little hard to find, but another variety, "Dawn," is usually available.

Heaths and Heathers by Colour

Dark Purple /	Erica cinerea "Purple Beauty"
Purple /	Calluna vulgaris "Easter Bonfire"
Lavender /	Calluna vulgaris "Boskoop"
Heliotrope /	Erica carnea "Adrienne Duncan"
Mauve /	Calluna vulgaris "Spring Glow"
Lilac /	Calluna vulgaris "Arina"
Deep Red /	Daboecia cantabrica "Waley's Red"
Crimson /	Calluna vulgaris "Corbett's Red"
Bright Magenta /	Erica cinerea "C.D. Eason"
Dark Pink /	Erica x darleyensis "Ghost Hills"
Salmon Pink /	Erica erigena "Irish Dusk"
Rose Pink /	Erica vagans "Birch Glow"
Shell Pink /	Erica carnea "Prince of Wales"
White /	Erica carnea "Springwood White"

Broadleaf Evergreens

Lyle Courtice
Pickett's Nurseries Ltd.
Pitt Meadows, B.C.

Broadleaf evergreens are an important component of any landscape, as these shrubs retain their foliage throughout the year, adding structure and interest during the winter months when many areas of the garden are otherwise vacant. Most of them produce beautiful flowers or attractive fruit that can be used as a focal point to draw attention to a particular landscape feature. Others provide a dazzling array of leaf types and variegation patterns, which are continually present as the seasons of colour pass by.

Lyle Courtice began his gardening career back in 1983 and went on to earn an associates degree in horticulture, after which he worked many years in both the retail and wholesale trade. He is currently with Pickett's Nurseries of Pitt Meadows and also dabbles in importing rare plants — with his small townhouse in Maple Ridge serving as the testing ground for his most recent findings. Lyle's keen interest in new introductions and collectors' plants is quite evident in this chapter on broadleaf evergreens.

Choisya ternata "Aztec Pearl"

HEIGHT: 1 M+ / 3¼ FT+	SPREAD: 1 M+ / 3¼ FT+	ZONE: 7
FLOWERING PERIOD: MAY, LATE SUMMER		

This is an elegant selection of Mexican orange with deeply divided foliage that forms a dense, rounded shrub. The slender, emerald green leaves are a good foil for the fragrant white (flushed pink) flowers that are borne in May and again in late summer. It tolerates full sun to partial shade but is best located in a sheltered site with good drainage.

Gaultheria mucronata "Variegata"

HEIGHT: 1 M / 3¼ FT	SPREAD: 1 M+ / 3¼ FT+	ZONE: 7
FLOWERING PERIOD: LATE SPRING		

A variegated form of prickly heath with small sharp-pointed leaves arranged in whorls, "Variegata's" glossy, dark green foliage is finely edged in cream and contrasts well against the juvenile reddish stems. Masses of small bell-shaped flowers are followed by lilac-coloured berries, if a male plant is present for pollination ("Variegata" is a female clone). These shrubs form low, compact mounds that perform best when placed in full sun. It is formerly known as *Pernettya mucronata*.

Mahonia x *media* "Charity"

HEIGHT: 3 M+ / 10 FT+	SPREAD: 2 M+ / 6½ FT+	ZONE: 7
FLOWERING PERIOD: JAN–MARCH		

This handsome shrub makes a definite statement in any garden, with its large, spiny compound leaves that emerge bronze-red and mature to a glossy, dark green. Fragrant yellow flowers emerge in large **terminal** clusters from January to March — followed by spikes of small blue berries. These shrubs mature into huge clumps that make an excellent backdrop for finely textured plants.

Buxus sempervirens "Variegata"

HEIGHT: 3 M+ / 10 FT+	SPREAD: 2 M+ / 6½ FT+	ZONE: 6
PRIMARILY A FOLIAGE PLANT		

English boxwood is a sturdy and reliable shrub for hedging and topiary, adding a formal presence to any landscape. This form has glossy dark green leaves edged in creamy-white and, like most *Buxus*, tolerates full sun to partial shade. When grown naturally, they form tall airy pyramids, making a good variegated backdrop for those dull corners in the garden.

Care and Maintenance

As most broadleaf evergreens tend to be shallow rooted, water is essential until the plants are well established. This could take up to two or three years, during which time they should receive frequent watering when rainfall is sparse and especially during the hot summer months. A 5-cm / 2-in deep mulch of fine bark or well-rotted compost is advisable to help retain moisture. Overwatering can also present its own complications, often resulting in root or stem rot. Pruning new growth by a maximum of two-thirds is done only to keep the plants in check. Flowering plants such as rhododendron should be pruned within four to six weeks after flowering — foliage types (i.e., boxwood) can be pruned any time from spring into late summer.

Companion Plants

Be it wispy blades of ornamental grasses or contrasting purple-leaf deciduous shrubs, many of the following plants will complement the dense foliage and textures of broadleaf evergreens.

Acer palmatum *"Red Pygmy"* / *Dwarf Japanese Maple*

Brunnera macrophylla *"Langtrees"* / *Siberian Bugloss*

Cimicifuga ramosa *"Black Negligee"* / *Purple Bugbane*

Cotinus coggygria *"Rhenella Mist"* / *Purple Smokebush* *

Fothergilla gardenii *"Blue Mist"* / *Dwarf Witch Alder*

Helleborus x hybridus / *Lenten Rose*

Miscanthus sinensis *"Cosmopolitan"* / *Variegated Silver Grass*

Ophiopogon nigrescens / *Black Mondo Grass*

Paeonia lactiflora *"Harkaway Lemon Embers"* / *Chinese Peony* *

Physocarpus opulifolius *"Diabolo"* / *Purple Ninebark*

Tiarella *"Mint Chocolate"* / *Foamflower*

* *Lyle's own introductions, available 2001–2002.*

Daphne x *burkwoodii* "Carol Mackie"

HEIGHT: 1.25 M+ / 4 FT+	SPREAD: 1.25 M+ / 4 FT+	ZONE: 4–5
FLOWERING PERIOD: MAY		

What garden would be complete without the elegance and refinement that a daphne brings, with its fragrant clusters of pale pink flowers in May? This particular selection is one of the easiest daphnes to grow, although excellent drainage and shelter from cold winter winds is required. When grown in full sun, the foliage will be dark green edged in pale yellow, and the plants keep a rounded, compact habit — in shade the form is more open and the variegation fades to cream.

Lonicera nitida "Red Tips"

HEIGHT: 1.25–1.75 M+ / 4–6 FT	SPREAD: 1.25–1.75 M+ / 4–6 FT	ZONE: 6
PRIMARILY A FOLIAGE PLANT		

This boxleaf honeysuckle forms a loose, open mound with bright cerise new growth that changes to a glossy dark green with age. These plants adapt well to shearing and produce their most intense colouring in full sun — but will tolerate shaded areas. Small white flowers appear in spring, and cuttings of the new growth make an attractive accent in floral arrangements.

Gardenia jasminoides "Kleim's Hardy"

HEIGHT: 1 M+ / 3¼ FT+	SPREAD: 1 M+ / 3¼ FT+	ZONE: 7–8
FLOWERING PERIOD: ALL SUMMER		

This amazingly hardy gardenia has tolerated temperatures as low as 0°F, yet still closely resembles its indoor cousins — with lush, dark green foliage backing single ivory-coloured blooms. The abundant flowers are short-lived but continue to bloom throughout the summer. Be sure to place this plant where you can enjoy its intoxicating fruity fragrance, preferably in a sheltered site with sharp drainage.

Abelia x *grandiflora* "Confetti"

HEIGHT: 1 M+ / 3¼ FT+	SPREAD: 1 M+ / 3¼ FT+	ZONE: 7
FLOWERING PERIOD: MAY–FROST		

An exciting introduction that forms a low mound, "Confetti" is useful as a cascading shrub or in the foreground where its airy appearance can soften the border. The foliage consists of small glossy green leaves edged in cream, accented with small white to pale pink flowers from May until frost. This plant will often take on a reddish-pink blush when planted in full sun and exposed to colder weather.

Yucca *gloriosa* "Variegata"

HEIGHT: 60 CM+ / 2 FT+	SPREAD: 60 CM+ / 2 FT+	ZONE: 7
FLOWERING PERIOD: SUMMER		

This variegated yucca has stiff, upturned leaves held in a somewhat upright, round clump — useful as a strong architectural form in the garden. The foliage is a deep green edged in creamy-yellow with a slight reddish cast to the crown. These single- or multi-trunked plants bear tall spikes (1.25 m / 4 ft) of white flowers in summer and work well with bold-leaf tropicals (i.e., hardy banana) or in desert-like plantings. Tolerates most soil types but prefers sandy, well-drained sites with full sun exposure.

Osmanthus *heterophyllus* "Tricolour"

HEIGHT: 1.5 M+ / 5 FT+	SPREAD: 1.5 M+ / 5 FT+	ZONE: 6–7
PRIMARILY A FOLIAGE PLANT		

Multi-coloured foliage and a tidy, compact habit are the main features of this showy false holly. The leaves emerge a bronze-pink colour and mature to a dark green marbled with pale yellow and white. This is a slow-growing shrub that requires minimal pruning — it can be trained into an attractive hedge. It is tolerant of most soil types but adequate drainage is essential.

Planting Broadleaf Evergreens
Spring and early fall are the ideal planting seasons, when cooler weather and adequate moisture limit any risk of the young plants drying out. Broadleaf evergreens are quite variable in their needs — with some types thriving in partial or dappled shade, needing only early morning or late afternoon sun. Others do quite well in a full sun exposure, which helps to maintain a more compact growth habit and intense leaf colouration (refer to the individual descriptions to determine which plants suit your needs). To avoid damaged foliage, give shelter from winter or prevailing winds by planting near buildings or in protected corners. Proper drainage is also quite important, especially on the West Coast where rain is ever present — most types prefer sharp drainage, but not to the point where the roots become too dry. Soil in general should be rich in organic matter with a pH around 5.5. Take special care not to plant too deeply — the original soil line should be level or slightly above the existing grade.

Hydrangeas

Vicki Cousins
Van Belle Nursery Inc.
Abbotsford, B.C.

Hydrangeas have been a garden standard for well over 100 years, and their continued popularity is much in part to their lavish flower display — often lasting from mid summer into autumn. Many of us have some sort of memory associated with this plant ... be it a vase full of cut flowers, a mass display in the local public park or as a reliable shrub in one corner of the garden. Hydrangeas are all these things.

Vicki Cousins has been working for more than a decade with Van Belle Nursery — one of the leading suppliers of vines and shrub liners in the Fraser Valley. She currently supervises the nursery's hydrangea department and is responsible for raising hydrangeas that will eventually be distributed to retail nurseries across North America.

Hydrangea macrophylla "Blaumeise"

HEIGHT: 2 M / 6½ FT	SPREAD: 2 M / 6½ FT	ZONE: 7
FLOWERING PERIOD: JUNE–FROST		

This robust "**lacecap**" hydrangea is better known in North America as "Teller's Blue." The sterile **florets** often take on a rich indigo blue when grown in acid soil and encircle the tiny fertile flowers in the centre — creating large 20-cm / 8-in wide blossoms. Like most of the "Teller's" hydrangeas, it is rather sensitive in colder climates.

Hydrangea paniculata "Unique"

HEIGHT: 3 M / 10 FT	SPREAD: 2 M / 6½ FT	ZONE: 3
FLOWERING PERIOD: JULY–FROST		

This very hardy shrub has huge, 40-cm / 15-in long **panicles** that are initially white and gradually change to a bronze-pink toward the fall. This attribute, coupled with the flower's unusual conical shape, make this hydrangea a unique addition to any landscape.

Hydrangea macrophylla "Ayesha"

HEIGHT: 1.5 M / 5 FT	SPREAD: 1.5 M / 5 FT	ZONE: 5–6
FLOWERING PERIOD: JUNE–FROST		

This cultivar has distinctive fleshy blooms composed of sterile **florets** with **sepals** in the form of tiny spoons, reminiscent of lilac flowers. The blossoms are globose in shape and scented, which is very rare for a hydrangea. Flower colour may be light blue, pale mauve or light pink — depending on the soil pH. "Ayesha" is not recommended for cold winter areas.

Hydrangea x "Preziosa"

HEIGHT: 1.2 M / 4 FT	SPREAD: 1.2 M / 4 FT	ZONE: 5
FLOWERING PERIOD: JUNE–FROST		

This *H. macrophylla* x *H. serrata* cross has attractive purplish-red stems bearing dainty **mophead** flowers that emerge light pink and mature to a bright rose, with even darker pink splotches as they age. This shrub features russet-coloured foliage in the fall. "Preziosa" will actually tolerate direct sun quite well if care is taken to keep the roots moist.

Hydrangea macrophylla "Kluis Superba"

HEIGHT: 1.75–2.5 M / 4 FT	SPREAD: 2 M / 6½ FT	ZONE: 5
FLOWERING PERIOD: JUNE–FROST		

This free-flowering **mophead** hydrangea has 16–18-cm wide blossoms composed of sterile **florets** that conceal the fertile flowers underneath. This particular cultivar is quite sensitive to soil pH, producing deep purple-blue flowers in acid soil and rich cherry blooms in alkaline conditions. "Kluis Superba" is generally listed as a compact hydrangea.

Bluing Hydrangeas
The variable flower colour in Hydrangea macrophylla has to do with the plant's ability to absorb aluminum and the pH of the surrounding soil. The more acidic the conditions (pH of 6.5 or less), the bluer the flowers of the changeable cultivars will be. More alkaline soil helps to encourage the pinks and reds to stay true and not stray into shades of mauve or lilac. Apply a heavy application of lime around the root system, before and during the flowering season — the lime will raise the pH, hindering the plant's uptake of aluminum. A treatment to encourage bluing would be a solution of 7 g / ¼ oz of aluminum sulphate and 7 g / ¼ oz of sulphate of iron mixed into one gallon of water. Apply up to 10 L / 2 g in the spring and fall, but do not exceed the recommended dosage, as damage to the roots can be fatal.

Drying Hydrangea Flowers
Drying hydrangea flowers is a real challenge for some people, with the most common advice being to wait for a light frost before cutting a flower for drying. Others take cuttings only when the bloom feels papery to the touch or when the *floret* in the centre has opened. The most effective method is to place the cut stem in 2.5 cm / 1 in of water and let stand — the flower will dry naturally once the water has evaporated. A spray of anti-stress gel is also very effective to keep the flower colour.

Other Recommended Hydrangeas

Hydrangea arborescens *"Annabelle"* — *white flowers / sun tolerant, very hardy*

H. paniculata "Kyushu" — cream panicles / glossy foliage, very hardy

H. serrata "Bluebird" — blue lacecap flowers / shade tolerant

H. macrophylla "Forever Pink" — reliable pink blooms / hardy

H. aspera — attractive species / blue lacecap flowers

H. macrophylla "Nikko Blue" — reliable blue flowers / prolific

H. anomala ssp. petiolaris / Climbing Hydrangea — white blooms

H. paniculata "White Moth" — attractive airy white flowers

H. macrophylla "Piamina" — extreme dwarf (5 cm / 2 in) pink-red blooms

Pruning Hydrangeas

H. macrophylla and H. serrata require little pruning other than to thin established plants that are more than three years old by removing old, woody canes in late winter before the new buds begin to swell. Shortening the stems will result in the loss of flowers, as they develop from vigorous buds formed the previous season. Many gardeners leave the old flower heads on all winter to protect the upper buds, but be sure to deadhead them the following spring.

H. arborescens can be hard pruned to 30 cm / 12 in tall once it is established, as the flowers buds are borne on new wood and growth is rapid with feeding.

Hydrangea quercifolia "Alice"

HEIGHT: 2.4 M / 8 FT	SPREAD: 2 M / 6½ FT	ZONE: 5
FLOWERING PERIOD: LATE JUNE–FROST		

This particular cultivar of the oakleaf hydrangea is more vigorous and bushy than the species (or other available varieties). As the common name implies, it bears leathery oak-shaped leaves that change to autumn tints of reddish-purple when planted in a sunny location. The conical white flower heads fade to pink with age and often reach a length of 30 cm / 12 in.

Hydrangea "Lemon Wave"

HEIGHT: 2 M / 6½ FT	SPREAD: 2 M / 6½ FT	ZONE: 6
FLOWERING PERIOD: JUNE–FROST		

It is not often that a shrub is collected for its foliage colour alone — "Lemon Wave" is one of those exceptions which features deep sea-green leaves edged in a creamy-white with yellow highlights. It bears white **lacecap** flowers up to 20 cm / 8 in wide that turn pink as they mature. An excellent choice for the coastal garden.

Hydrangea macrophylla "Tovelit"

HEIGHT: 80 CM / 2½ FT	SPREAD: 1 M / 3¼ FT	ZONE: 5–6
FLOWERING PERIOD: JUNE–FROST		

This dwarf hydrangea, which is sometimes known as "Tofelil," originated from Denmark. This closely packed shrub features narrow, tapered foliage. The small **mophead** flowers have a distinctive fringed appearance and average 11 cm / 4½ in wide. This particular cultivar is not recommended for bluing (see sidebar).

Hydrangea macrophylla "Adria"

HEIGHT: 1 M / 3¼ FT	SPREAD: 1 M / 3¼ FT	ZONE: 5
FLOWERING PERIOD: JUNE–FROST		

The cultivar name of this dwarf hydrangea is an abbreviated form of "Adriatic." The highly packed **inflorescence** are approximately 18 cm / 7 in across and are a rich blue in acid soil. "Adria" is a very dependable and heavy-flowering shrub, with blossoms that are ideal for drying.

Hydrangea serrata "Blue Billows"

HEIGHT: 2 M / 6½ FT	SPREAD: 1 M / 3¼ FT	ZONE: 5
FLOWERING PERIOD: JUNE–FROST		

This shade-tolerant hydrangea has light blue **lacecap** flowers that almost seem to glow, making it a good choice for brightening a dull corner. "Blue Billows" features attractive fall foliage on sturdy stems.

H. paniculata forms a large shrub, and most people prune the branches back lightly to several sets of buds, resulting in an abundance of smaller flowers. Others will hard prune the previous year's growth, leaving only one pair of buds for each stem and resulting in large panicles.

H. anomala ssp. petiolaris needs only be pruned for containment and to deadhead the spent flowers.

Sun Exposure
Most Hydrangea serrata and H. macrophylla do not like to be planted in full sun but can be adapted (with patience) if their roots are kept moist. They prefer morning and late afternoon sun. Hydrangea arborescens and H. paniculata are much more tolerant of full sun exposures.

Ornamental Shrubs

Rick Sorenson
Pride of Place Plants Inc.
Sidney, B.C.

Mike Lascelle
Amsterdam Garden Centre
Pitt Meadows, B.C.

There is an ornamental shrub to suit any landscape and, with the many new hybrids and species introductions, gardeners have a dazzling array of choices at their local garden centre. These plants can be as bold or as subtle as the flowers they bear, and many provide the additional interest of attractive berries or brilliant autumn foliage.

"Ornamental shrubs" is one of two co-authored chapters in this book — with Rick Sorenson of Pride of Place Plants Inc. making the first five plant selections and me choosing the other five plants. Between the two of us, we have selected some of the most recent introductions as well as a few old standards that have been gracing landscapes for decades now.

Cornus alba "Cream Cracker"

HEIGHT: 80 CM / 2½ FT	SPREAD: 1 M / 3¼ FT	ZONE: 3
FLOWERING PERIOD: MAY		

This deciduous shrub has year-round interest, with prominent reddish-purple stems in winter, foliage accented with golden yellow margins in spring and small creamy-white flowers in late spring and summer. The leaves eventually mature to deep green with cream edges on this medium-sized plant. "Cream Cracker" is somewhat similar to "Elegantissima" in appearance, but is actually a **sport** of *Cornus alba* "Gouchaultii."

Lonicera "Honey Baby"

HEIGHT: 2 M / 6½ FT	SPREAD: 2 M / 6½ FT	ZONE: 4
FLOWERING PERIOD: JULY–OCT		

This hybrid between *Lonicera japonica* "Halliana" and *L. periclymenum* "Belgica Select" can be used as a shrub or small vine. "Honey Baby" features an extended flowering period with fragrant blooms of creamy-yellow emerging from purplish-red buds — the blossoms also show some orange as they mature on stocky branches. This dwarf honeysuckle is suitable for containers or can be integrated into a mixed border.

Malva sylvestris "Marina R. Dema"

HEIGHT: 1.5 M / 5 FT	SPREAD: 1.5 M / 5 FT	ZONE: 4
FLOWERING PERIOD: APRIL–OCT		

This robust perennial is closely related to lavatera, and both can be grown much like a shrub in the landscape. "Marina R. Dema" is a broad, upright selection with bluish-green leaves that diminish in size on the upper portions of the plant. The soft violet-blue flowers are a very welcome addition to any garden and quite similar to "Primley Blue." This mallow will need some support, particularly during rainy weather.

Hydrangea serrata "Golden Sunlight"

HEIGHT: 60 CM / 2 FT	SPREAD: 60CM / 2 FT	ZONE: 5
FLOWERING PERIOD: JUNE–AUG		

This hydrangea has already made quite a name for itself since its introduction just a few years ago. "Golden Sunlight" is a natural mutation of *Hydrangea serrata* "Intermedia" and features brilliant yellow foliage in spring that deepens to an attractive light green. The **lacecap** flowers are composed of white to pale pink petals surrounding the darker pink fertile flowers. As with most hydrangeas, it prefers morning or evening sun, as the foliage may suffer from scorch if placed in a hot afternoon exposure — this is particularly important for container specimens.

About New Eden
New Eden is a cooperative effort between Pride of Place Plants Inc. of Sidney, British Columbia, and a Dutch-based company, Novitas Plantae — each working to increase the exchange of new plant material between North America and Europe. The focus of New Eden is to adequately represent and compensate plant breeders for their new introductions, so that the end goal of bringing these exciting plants to the retail market can be achieved more efficiently. Here are a few other introductions New Eden is currently offering:

Clematis serratifolia *"Kugotia"* *("Golden Tiara")* — attractive, nodding yellow flowers

Campsis *"Indian Summer"* — deep orange-red trumpet blooms from July to October.

Clematis *"Blue Light"* — pale violet-blue double flowers in spring and autumn

Clematis *"My Angel"* — nodding blooms, yellow inside, reddish-purple outside

Symphoricarpos x *doorenbosii* "Marleen"

HEIGHT: 1.5 M / 5 FT	SPREAD: 1.2 M / 4 FT	ZONE: 4

FLOWERING PERIOD: JUNE–SEPT

Although this is a relatively new introduction to North America, "Marleen" has already received an award of merit from the Royal Boskoop Horticultural Society. This spontaneous seedling of "Mother of Pearl" differs greatly from its parent — featuring bright, purple-pink berries that are held through the fall and into the winter, long after the shrub's leaves have dropped. The berries are borne on long, arching branches that can be cut for indoor flower arrangements.

Abeliophyllum distichum / White Forsythia

HEIGHT: 1.5–1.8 M / 5–6 FT	SPREAD: 90 CM–1.2 M / 3–4 FT	ZONE: 5

FLOWERING PERIOD: FEB–EARLY MARCH

Abeliophyllum can be a little hard to find at your local nursery, mainly because of its unruly form and sometimes sparse foliage. The pure white flowers (pink in bud) of the species are generously borne along the length of the dark burgundy stems and emit a potent fragrance of jasmine, with just a hint of almond. This deciduous shrub's moderate size and early bloom period make white forsythia an interesting choice for the mixed border,

Camellia "Jury's Yellow"

HEIGHT: 2.5–3 M / 8–10 FT	SPREAD: 1.8–3 M / 6–8 FT	ZONE: 7

FLOWERING PERIOD: SPRING

"Jury's Yellow" is my favorite camellia, and the soft creamy-yellow "anemone" blooms are the perfect foil for its glossy, deep green foliage. This hybrid of *Camellia saluenensis* and *C. japonica* "Gwenneth Morey" lineage is of fairly recent origin, having been introduced in the late 1970s. A broadleaf evergreen, it features an upright, yet compact growth habit.

Enkianthus campanulatus / Pagoda Bush

HEIGHT: 1.8–3 M / 6–10 FT+	SPREAD: 1.25–1.5 M / 4–5 FT	ZONE: 5
FLOWERING PERIOD: MAY		

It is hard to understand why this deciduous shrub has not gained more widespread favour, as it embodies the perfect balance of foliage, flowers, structure and autumn colour. *Enkianthus* begins the year with pendulous clusters of pale yellow bell-shaped blooms that are faintly streaked in red. The shrub itself has whorls of foliage near the branch ends and a distinctly tiered appearance. Pagoda bush thrives under the same conditions as rhododendron and features vibrant red foliage when grown in the sun.

Hibiscus syriacus "Blue Bird"

HEIGHT: 2.5–3 M / 8–10 FT+	SPREAD: 1.8–3 M / 6–8 FT	ZONE: 6
FLOWERING PERIOD: JULY–OCT		

This old-fashioned flowering shrub has retained its popularity since its introduction back in the early 1960s. "Blue Bird" was originally named "Oiseau Bleu" and features striking violet-blue single flowers, contrasted with a deep red centre. Full sun and near perfect drainage are essential, but this hardy hibiscus will reward you with a profusion of colour from late summer until the first frosts. Also, remember to be patient with these plants, as they are one of the last shrubs to leaf out in spring.

Fothergilla major / Witch Alder

HEIGHT: 1.8–2.75 M / 6–9 FT+	SPREAD: 1.2–2 M / 4–7 FT	ZONE: 5
FLOWERING PERIOD: APRIL–MAY		

Witch alder is a very tolerant deciduous shrub, thriving in full sun or partial shade — provided it is planted in evenly moist, acidic soil. The fragrant, white bottlebrush flowers are borne in April to May, just as the leaves are emerging. *Fothergilla major* finishes the growing season in a blaze of autumn colour ranging from yellow to orange to deep burgundy-red.

Ornamental Shrubs for Shade
Many people are under the impression that no ornamental shrubs will thrive in the shaded corner of their garden. Actually, quite a few plants will provide an ample display of flowers or foliage in shade to partial shade, including the following:

Fatsia japonica /
Japanese Aralia — shade

Mahonia aquifolium /
Oregon Grape — partial shade

Lonicera nitida /
Box Honeysuckle — partial shade

Symphoricarpos albus /
Snowberry — shade

Kalmia latifolia /
Mountain Laurel — light shade

Sarcococca ruscifolia /
Christmas Box — shade

Skimmia japonica /
Skimmia — shade

Choisya ternata /
Mexican Orange — light shade

Camellia japonica /
Camellia — light shade

Ribes sanguineum /
Flowering Currant — light shade

Rhododendrons & Azaleas

The genus *Rhododendron* is one of the few shrub group-ings that can be enjoyed equally by novice gardeners as well as the most sophisticated landscape designers. Perhaps this widespread interest has something to do with the plant's natural geographic diversity, which ranges from the Arctic tundra and exposed mountain alpines, to the sheltered understory of subtropical forests. Rhododendrons are equally diverse in flower colour, plant form and leaf texture — some of which are coated beneath with a thick, woolly layer of chestnut brown **indumentum**.

Few shrubs have also been so avidly sought after throughout the world, with many species still bearing the names of such noted plant collectors as Ernest Wilson, Sir Joseph Hooker and Robert Fortune. Rhododendrons were also the subject of intensive hybridization, which began in earnest in the late 1800s and continues to this day. So whether your interest lies with rhododendrons proper, deciduous azaleas or evergreen Japanese azaleas — there is no shortage of choices is waiting for you at your local garden centre.

Rhododendrons

Les Clay
Clay's Nurseries
Langley, B.C.

Rhododendrons are a diverse **genus** of woody plants noted for their spectacular flowers and attractive foliage. Most are native to mountainous regions, with about 30 species being found in North America — much of the remainder is indigenous to various parts of Asia. This member of the heath family (*Ericaceae*) can range in height from a few centimetres to more than 25 m / 80 ft, but mainly the shrubby species and hybrids have captured the imagination of gardeners throughout the world.

Clay's Nurseries has been involved in horticulture for 45 years, pioneering the tissue culture of rhododendrons in Canada, raising almost 300 cultivars by this method. Les was a little taken a-back by having to choose only 10 rhododendrons for his chapter. Once he explained that more than 20,000 registered hybrids and hundreds of known species were involved, I realized that a few additional choices were needed to assure that both these categories were well represented.

The ratings system has three digits (e.g., 4/4/4), representing flower quality, plant and foliage performance, respectively. The ratings are from one to five in each category.

Species Rhododendrons

R. augustinii

HEIGHT: 1.8–4.5 M / 6–15 FT	SPREAD: 1.2–1.8 M / 4–6 FT	ZONE: 6
FLOWERING PERIOD: APRIL–MAY	HARDY TO: -20° C/ -5° F	RATED: 4/3/4

This species rhododendron has an unusually wide spectrum of flower colours, with year-to-year variations occurring occasionally on individual plants. The lax **trusses** of two to six **florets** range from violet, lavender blue and rose-pink to pastel shades of pale lavender and white-tinged pink. It features narrow, dark green leaves with scaly undersides and an upright growth habit. *R. augustinii* is a native of high elevations in China through south Tibet and was named after Augustine Henry, a medical officer in Chinese Customs, who later became a professor of forestry in Dublin, Ireland.

R. litangense

HEIGHT: 30–45 CM / 12–18 IN	SPREAD: 38 CM / 15 IN	ZONE: 5
FLOWERING PERIOD: APRIL	HARDY TO: -26° C / -15° F	RATED: 3/4/4

Another native rhododendron from the high elevations of southwest Szechuan, China, this very small shrub is similar in appearance to *R. impeditum,* but is much more compact. The overall appearance of the foliage is **glaucous** and slightly scaly, with individual leaves up to 1.25 cm / ½ in long. *R. litangense* buds quite heavily and bears plum-coloured blossoms in April. Situate in full sun for the best flower production.

R. yakushimanum

HEIGHT: 1.5 M / 5 FT	SPREAD: 1.5 M / 5 FT	ZONE: 4–5
FLOWERING PERIOD: MAY	HARDY TO: -32° C / -25° F	RATED: 5/5/4

This slow-growing shrub features glossy, dark green leaves with woolly brown **indumentum** on the undersides. The new growth is covered in white felt, complementing the delicate bell-shaped blooms, which are rose in bud and open to white or blush pink. This native of Yakushima Island in Japan is quite hardy, withstanding very low temperatures.

Fertilizing Rhododendrons
Rhododendron fertilizers currently on the market do not contain sufficient nitrogen, so I suggest a slow-release 19–5–8, plus minor element Osmocote (eight- to nine-month formulation) should be applied in late March or April. In most instances, this keeps the plants in a healthy growing state for the entire growing season.

Pruning Rhododendrons
The best time to prune rhododendrons is immediately after flowering — earlier pruning results in the loss of the current season's flowers. On young plants that may not be flowering yet, removing the terminal growth buds will cause the **axillary buds** to break and develop a fuller plant. Cut back older specimens to a growth joint, which is the place where the previous season's growth commenced. After flowering, **deadheading** is recommended, as it enables the plant's energy to go into bud production for the next year, rather than producing seed. On older shrubs, it is best to remove some of the weak growth and any twigs that may be dead, as this better aerates the plant.

Growing Conditions

Rhododendrons grow best in a friable soil that is lightly acidic (pH 5–6), with even moisture during the summer months to keep the plants vigorous. Poor drainage may result in the loss of plants — so be sure to add some organic matter (humus or moist peat moss) to improve the planting soil. In very wet conditions, you may have to consider building raised beds or berms to allow for proper drainage. After planting, apply several inches of mulch over the soil (but away from the stem) as this conserves moisture and keeps the roots cool in summer, while insulating during winter.

In our coastal climate, most cultivars will tolerate a full sun exposure, with the exception of some yellow varieties, which sometimes suffer from sunburn on the foliage, especially if they do not receive sufficient water.

R. bureauii

HEIGHT: 1.2–3 M / 4–10 FT	SPREAD: 2.5 M / 8 FT	ZONE: 6
FLOWERING PERIOD: APRIL–MAY	HARDY TO: -23° C / -10° F	RATED: 3/5/3

This collector's plant has unusual foliage, with both the new shoots and the undersides of the deep green leaves being covered in a thick, rusty brown **indumentum**. The lance-shaped leaves are contrasted with trusses of flushed rose blooms that fade to white, with crimson spots. This particular species is prone to root rot in wet areas, so provide sharp drainage and some shade for the best results.

R. sutchuense

HEIGHT: 4.5–6 M / 15–20 FT	SPREAD: 3.5–4.5 M / 12-15 FT	ZONE: 6
FLOWERING PERIOD: MARCH–APRIL	HARDY TO: -23° C / -10° F	RATED: 4/3/4

This native of China forms a large shrub or small open tree and has foliage to match these proportions. Individual leaves can grow to 30 cm / 1 ft long and are a deep matte green on top and slightly paler underneath. The 7-cm / 3-in long, bell-shaped flowers are featured in medium trusses (averaging eight to 12 **florets**) and vary in colour — from white tinged pink to rose-pink to pale lilac, with some spotting possible.

Hybrid Rhododendrons

R. "Blue Boy" ("Blue Ensign" x "Purple splendor")

HEIGHT: 1.5 M / 5 FT	SPREAD: 1.5 M / 5 FT	ZONE: 5–6
FLOWERING PERIOD: MAY	HARDY TO: -26° C / -15° F	RATED: 4/3/4

A well-shaped rhododendron with medium, dark green leaves and an upright growing habit, "Blue Boy" is a prolific bloomer featuring unusual violet-blue flowers marked with an almost black blotch. Individual blossoms up to 6 cm / 2½ in wide are held in large, upright trusses.

R. "Nancy Evans" ("Hotei" x "Lem's Cameo")

HEIGHT: 90 CM / 3 FT	SPREAD: 90 CM / 3 FT	ZONE: 6
FLOWERING PERIOD: APRIL–MAY	HARDY TO: -20° C / -5° F	RATED: 5/4/4

This cultivar features a metamorphosis of flower colour with orange-red buds that open to a rich yellow, accented with just a hint of amber on the edges of newly opened blooms. "Nancy Evans" is also quite free-flowering, and its unusually large flower **calyx** helps to accentuate the many lax **trusses**. The bronzed juvenile foliage matures to a bright green, eventually forming a rounded, compact plant.

R. "Patty Bee" (R. kiskei "Yaku Fairy" x R. fletcherianum)

HEIGHT: 45 CM / 18 IN	SPREAD: 60 CM / 2 FT	ZONE: 5–6
FLOWERING PERIOD: LATE MARCH–APRIL	HARDY TO: -26° C / -15° F	RATED: 5/4/4

This densely branched shrub features very fine green foliage that takes on a plum tint during the winter months. "Patty Bee" is probably one of the best dwarf yellow rhododendrons, with attractive pale lemon blossoms held in lax **trusses** of four to six **florets**. The compact habit and sun tolerance make it a good choice for the rockery.

R. "Conroy" (R. cinnabarinum x R. concatenans)

HEIGHT: 1.2 M / 4 FT	SPREAD: 90 CM / 3 FT	ZONE: 7
FLOWERING PERIOD: MARCH–APRIL	HARDY TO: -15° C / 5° F	RATED: 3/3/3

This rhododendron has unusual blue-green foliage covered in a waxy sheen. Add to that the trumpet-shaped blooms of pale orange (flushed in red), and you have a real collector's plant. "Conroy," quite an old cultivar, was hybridized in 1937 and introduced to the public in 1950.

Companion Plants for Rhododendrons

Pieris japonica /
Lily-of-the-Valley Shrub

Cornus kousa /
Chinese Dogwood

Kalmia latifolia /
Mountain Laurel

Corylopsis pauciflora /
Winter Hazel

Vaccinium ovatum /
Evergreen Huckleberry

Vinca minor /
Periwinkle ground cover

Cornus florida /
Eastern Dogwood

Viburnum davidii /
Evergreen Viburnum

Camellia japonica /
Japanese Camellia

Hosta cultivars /
Plantain Lily

R. "Dopey" (*R. ereogynum* hybrid x "Fabia") x (*R. yakushimanum* x "Fabia Tangerine")

HEIGHT: 90 CM / 3 FT	SPREAD: 90 CM / 3 FT	ZONE: 6
FLOWERING PERIOD: APRIL–MAY	HARDY TO: -20° C / -5° F	RATED: 4/4/4

One of the "Seven Dwarfs" series that was introduced in 1971 by Waterer and Crisp, "Dopey" features waxy red flowers that fade toward the edges and are usually borne in May. The shrub itself is fairly upright with dark green leaves, forming a compact plant.

R. "Phyllis Korn" ("Diane" x "Gomer Waterer")

HEIGHT: 1.5–1.8 M / 5–6 FT	SPREAD: 1.5–1.8 M / 5–6 FT	ZONE: 5–6
FLOWERING PERIOD: APRIL–MAY	HARDY TO: -26° C / -15° F	RATED: 4/4/4

Glossy, dark green leaves cover this vigorous rhododendron, which eventually forms a dense shrub with sturdy, upright branches. The large **trusses** of cream blossoms are accented in the throat with small, currant-red blotches. Expect "Phyllis Korn" to become as wide as it is tall.

R. "Noyo Brave" ("Noyo Chief" x *R. yakushimanum* "Koichiro Wada")

HEIGHT: 1.2–1.5 M / 4–5 FT	SPREAD: 1.8–2.5 M / 6–8 FT	ZONE: 6
FLOWERING PERIOD: APRIL–MAY	HARDY TO: -20° C / -5° F	RATED: 4/4/4

"Noyo Brave" features beautiful bright pink blooms held in a ball-shaped **truss** of up to 22 flowers. The buds are actually a dark rose, and the mature blossoms will fade somewhat with age. This shrub has a spreading growth habit with thick, medium green foliage accented with some light orange **indumentum** on the underside.

R. *"Apricot Fantasy"* ("Hotei" x "Tropicana")

HEIGHT: 1.5 M / 5 FT	SPREAD: 1.5–1.8 M / 5–6 FT	ZONE: 6
FLOWERING PERIOD: APRIL–MAY	HARDY TO: -20° C / -5° F	RATED: 4/4/4

Another offspring of the ever popular "Hotei," this particular cultivar features deep orange buds that give way to fragrant clusters of pale orange-pink blooms, highlighted with dark red spots. This medium-sized, spreading shrub has dusky green leaves that cover the plant quite well. "Apricot Fantasy," a fairly recent introduction, was hybridized in 1987.

R. "Mrs. Furnival" (R. *griffithianum* hybrid x R. *caucasicum* hybrid)

HEIGHT: 1.2 M / 4 FT	SPREAD: 90 CM–1.2 M/ 3–4 FT	ZONE: 5–6
FLOWERING PERIOD: MAY–JUNE	HARDY TO: -20° C / -5° F	RATED: 5/4/4

The medium-sized flower **trusses** are upright in habit and bear light rose-pink blooms accented with a striking strawberry blotch. This highly rated rhododendron was first hybridized in 1920 and has retained its reputation with many generations of gardeners. "Mrs. Furnival" is quite hardy, and the shrub itself is best described as dense and well branched, with matte green foliage.

R. "Point Defiance" ("Anna" x "Marinus Koster")

HEIGHT: 1.8–2 M / 6–7 FT	SPREAD: 2 M / 6½ FT	ZONE: 6
FLOWERING PERIOD: APRIL–MAY	HARDY TO: -20° C / -5° F	RATED: 5/4/4

"Point Defiance" is probably best known for its huge, dome-shaped **trusses** of succulent white blossoms (fading from pale pink) with rose-pink, **picoteed** edges. It is a fairly vigorous shrub with large, dull green leaves and an upright growing habit that can round with age.

Evergreen Azaleas

Hart Wellmeier and
Tiina Turu
Wrenhaven Nursery
Surrey, B.C.

Predominantly native to Japan, evergreen azaleas, often called Japanese azaleas, have been a part of North American gardens since the mid-1800s. They are typically low, spreading plants that in spring erupt into a profusion of blooms in a multitude of colours except for yellow and "true" orange. Evergreen azaleas are noted for their ease of care and as such, are a natural choice for the "casual" West Coast garden.

Hart Wellmeier of Wrenhaven Nursery has 20 years experience as a grower of rhododendrons and azaleas. Along with his wife, Tiina Turu, Hart is committed to using time-honoured field growing methods to produce a wide selection of these slow-growing shrubs. The nursery is situated on several acres of park-like grounds, which transform into a dazzling kaleidoscope of colour each year.

All height and spread figures are based on a 10-year growing period (in average conditions with annual pruning).

Azalea "Hino Crimson"

HEIGHT: 45 CM+ / 18 IN+	SPREAD: 60 CM+ / 2 FT	ZONE: 6
FLOWERING PERIOD: APRIL	HARDY TO: -20° C / -5° F	

Quite possibly one of the most familiar evergreen azaleas around, and for good reason, this azalea's vivid, cerise-red single blooms literally contour the entire surface of the compact shrub. Late autumn finds this azalea developing brilliant bronze-red foliage, which remains throughout the cold weather. One of the older varieties, it was introduced to the United States from Japan in the early 1900s.

Azalea "Rosebud"

HEIGHT: 60 CM+ / 2 FT+	SPREAD: 75 CM+ / 2½ FT+	ZONE: 6
FLOWERING PERIOD: LATE MAY	HARDY TO: -20° C / -5° F	

A distinctive shrub with medium pink double flowers, which certainly resemble rosebuds, this late-blooming azalea features good plant form and is well clothed with fresh green foliage. "Rosebud" is a *Kurume* hybrid.

Rhododendron obtusum var. "Amoenum"

HEIGHT: 50 CM+ / 20 IN+	SPREAD: 75 CM+ / 2½ FT+	ZONE: 6
FLOWERING PERIOD: LATE APRIL	HARDY TO: -20° C / -5° F	

Native to Japan, this variety was introduced to England from a Shanghai garden around 1850. A truly stunning azalea in both form and colour, its small leaves and "electric magenta" blossoms make it a suitable bonsai specimen. It has a tendency to send out long shoots in summer, which can easily be sheared.

Azalea "Mucronatum"

HEIGHT: 60 CM+ / 2 FT+	SPREAD: 90 CM+ / 3 FT+	ZONE: 6
FLOWERING PERIOD: MAY	HARDY TO: -20° C / -5° F	

This vigorous azalea has been cultivated in Japan for more than 300 years. It features luscious white flowers up to 6 cm / 2½ in wide and quite hairy leaves. "Mucronatum" just gets better with age and is absolutely lovely as a mature specimen.

Azalea "Orange Favorite"

HEIGHT: 45 CM+ / 18 IN+	SPREAD: 60 CM+ / 2 FT+	ZONE: 5–6
FLOWERING PERIOD: MAY	HARDY TO: -23° C / -10° F	

A handsome shrub with glossy foliage on a compact, dense plant, this azalea's blooms are not exactly orange as the name implies, being much closer to salmon-orange. This award-winning cultivar is a good choice for colder regions.

Fertilizing Evergreen Azaleas
Feed twice a year, once in early spring before the bloom and then immediately after flowering. Any granular rhododendron and azalea fertilizer is fine but, as a rule of thumb, use only 5 ml per 30 cm / 1 tsp per ft of height or spread, per feeding.

Planting Evergreen Azaleas
The best time to plant evergreen azaleas is either in the spring or fall — but be sure to avoid planting in the heat of summer. Despite common belief, these plants will tolerate exposures from shade to full sun, if they are planted in well-drained acidic soils with even moisture. As these shrubs are shallow rooted, it is important to provide consistent watering throughout the dry months. Also, take care not to mound soil up the stem, as this reduces the root's access to oxygen from the air. Creating a shallow saucer of soil around the base of the azalea will help direct water toward the root zone.

Soil Preparation

Amend the planting area with moistened peat moss to acidify the soil — a small amount of well-rotted steer manure or garden compost would also be beneficial. Avoid mushroom or poultry manures, as they tend to be "hot" or slightly alkaline.

Evergreen Azaleas by Colour

Pure White /	"Hino White"
White with Green Throat /	"Palestrina"
Salmon-Pink /	"Blaauw's Pink"
Dark Pink / "Louise Gable"	
Reddish-Purple /	"Purple Splendor"
Violet-Blue /	"Blue Danube"
Rose Red /	"Mother's Day"
Bright Red /	"Vuyk's Scarlet"
Orange-Red /	"Buccaneer"
Flame Orange /	"Bengal Fire"

Azalea "Keremesina Rose"

HEIGHT: 40 CM+ / 16 IN+	SPREAD: 55 CM+ / 22 IN+	ZONE: 5–6
FLOWERING PERIOD: EARLY MAY	HARDY TO: -23° C / -10° F	

One of the few hardy bicolour azaleas with charming (albeit small) pink-and-white striped blossoms, this variety has been known to withstand winter temperatures in central Ontario. The shrub itself features a flat, spreading habit.

Rhododendron kiusianum "Album"

HEIGHT: 30 CM+ / 12 IN+	SPREAD: 45 CM+ / 16 IN+	ZONE: 5–6
FLOWERING PERIOD: EARLY MAY	HARDY TO: -23° C / -10° F	

This native from the island of Kyushu, Japan, is very slow to establish and should only be considered a semi-evergreen azalea. "Album," the white form of this species, holds many flowers per bud. The shrub itself is also quite interesting, with a wonderful branch structure.

Azalea "Herbert"

HEIGHT: 60 CM+ / 2 FT+	SPREAD: 90 CM / 3 FT+	ZONE: 5–6
FLOWERING PERIOD: LATE APRIL	HARDY TO: -23° C / -10° F	

"Herbert" was hybridized specifically for the hardiness requirements of eastern North America and does extremely well there. This cultivar features attractive mid-green foliage and unusual, bright reddish-purple blossoms that are ruffled. It is more vigorous in growth than most evergreen azaleas.

Azalea "Diamant Salmon"

HEIGHT: 40 CM+ / 16 IN+	SPREAD: 55 CM+ / 22 IN+	ZONE: 5–6
FLOWERING PERIOD: LATE MAY	HARDY TO: -23° C / -10° F	

A German hybrid that was introduced in 1969, this durable shrub develops into a low, wide mat completely blanketed in hot pink flowers when in bloom. It has proven to be hardy in the Okanagan and central Ontario.

Azalea "James Gable"

HEIGHT: 55 CM+ / 22 IN+	SPREAD: 70 CM+ / 28 IN+	ZONE: 6
FLOWERING PERIOD: EARLY MAY	HARDY TO: -20° C / -5° F	

This evergreen azalea has a more open structural growth habit than most. "James Gable" is also much appreciated for its rich red flowers, which are among the darkest of the azalea **cultivars**.

Azalea or Rhododendron?
While all azaleas are listed botanically as members of the Rhododendron genus, several characteristics distinguish them.
1. Azaleas have hair on the leaf surface lying parallel to the main vein — if there is hair on a rhododendron leaf, it is only on the outside edge.
2. All azalea flowers are composed of five lobes.
3. Most azaleas have only five **stamens**, while rhododendrons average 10 or more.

Deciduous Azaleas

Mike Cuthbertson
Shiloh Nurseries
Pitt Meadows, B.C.

Shiloh Nurseries has been a family business for 30 years and is situated on six hectares / 15 acres in the heart of Pitt Meadows. Mike Cuthbertson currently manages this wholesale operation, along with owner Glen Boese. Together with their staff, they produce more than 300 varieties of rhododendrons and deciduous azaleas, all propagated by tissue culture.

From May until July, very few ornamental shrubs can equal deciduous azaleas for their flower show or colour range. During this time, brilliant hues of orange, red, white, pink and yellow smother these plants — many with fragrant blooms. While they may seem a bit subdued for the balance of the summer, the cool touch of autumn brings them to life once more, transforming the foliage to shades of gold and purple.

Rhododendron "Gibraltar"

HEIGHT: 1.8–2.5 M / 6–8 FT	SPREAD: 90 CM–1.5 M / 3–5 FT	ZONE: 5–6
FLOWERING PERIOD: MAY–JUNE	HARDY TO: -25° C / -15° F	

"Gibraltar" is probably one of the best known of the deciduous azaleas, with flame-red buds that open to vivid orange blossoms. The clustered flowers are funnel-shaped with frilled petals and are borne in profusion. "Gibraltar" is a mid season bloomer and has good mildew-resistant foliage.

Rhododendron schlippenbachii / Royal Azalea

HEIGHT: 2.5–3 M / 8–10 FT	SPREAD: 1.25–1.5 M / 4–5 FT	ZONE: 5
FLOWERING PERIOD: APRIL–MAY	HARDY TO: -25° C / -15° F	

An early-flowering species azalea with unique whorled foliage and good autumn colours ranging from crimson to orange to yellow, the "Royal Azalea" bears large, white-tinged pink blooms that are star-shaped. As this is an undergrowth plant in the wild, be sure to locate this shrub in light shade with no afternoon sun.

Rhododendron "Homebush"

HEIGHT: 1.2–2 M / 4–7 FT	SPREAD: 1.25–1.5 M / 4–5 FT	ZONE: 6
FLOWERING PERIOD: MAY–JULY	HARDY TO: -20° C / -5° F	

"Homebush" is an azalea developed by the Knap Hill Nursery of Surrey, England, that has unusual deep pink blooms held in double **truss** shapes, forming almost round flower heads. The abundant blossoms are sweetly fragrant on this medium to late season flowering shrub. "Homebush" does best when situated in full sun.

Rhododendron "Orchid Lights"

HEIGHT: 90 CM–1.2 M / 3–4 FT	SPREAD: 90 CM / 3 FT	ZONE: 2
FLOWERING PERIOD: MAY–JUNE	HARDY TO: -45° C / -49° F	

This member of the "Northern Lights" series was bred for prairie hardiness, yet still manages to bear a profusion of lilac pink flowers in the mid to late season. It is quite a dense shrub with a compact growing habit. "Orchid Lights" is extremely hardy and does well in full sun.

Rhododendron "Klondyke"

HEIGHT: 1.2–1.8 M / 4–6 FT	SPREAD: 1–1.5 M / 3–5 FT	ZONE: 6
FLOWERING PERIOD: MAY–JULY	HARDY TO: -20° C / -5° F	

"Klondyke" is undoubtedly one of the finest Exbury hybrids ever produced. It features very fragrant, orange-peach blossoms and foliage of an unusual burgundy-bronze tint that is mildew resistant. This mid to late season deciduous azalea was developed at Exbury around 1947.

Deciduous Azalea Groups
Much breeding has been done with deciduous azaleas, both by individuals and nurseries selecting different species and cultivars for specific characteristics. This has resulted in many distinct groups. Of the more than 200 cultivars available, the most common are as follows:

Ghent: includes crosses of R. viscosum, R. calendulaceum and R. nudiflorum (R. periclymenoides) from Ghent, Belgium / Zone 5

Knap Hill: raised by the Knap Hill Nursery of Surrey, England / Zone 6

Exbury: includes crosses of Knap Hill azaleas by Lionel de Rothschild / Zone 6

Mollis: originate from a cross of R. molle and R. japonicum / Zone 5

Occidentale Hybrids: originate from crosses of R. occidentale with Mollis and Ghent azaleas / Zone 5

Viscosum Hybrids: includes crosses of R. viscosum and Mollis azaleas / Zone 5

"Northern Lights" Series: bred at the University of Minnesota for prairie hardiness / Zone 2–3

Powdery Mildew

Powdery mildew, a fungal disease, is the most common problem with deciduous azaleas — often showing as a white, powdery cast on the foliage and shoots. Providing good air circulation around your plants is the best solution, although with our wet coastal weather you may still experience some powdery mildew. This unsightly damage is not permanent, as the leaves eventually drop off — but be sure to remove the infected foliage once it has fallen. Your other choices are to plant resistant cultivars or use the fungicide benomyl, which will provide control if applied at the first sign of fungus.

Rhododendron "Popsicle"

HEIGHT: 2.5 M / 8 FT	SPREAD: 2.5 M / 8 FT	ZONE: 5
FLOWERING PERIOD: JUNE–JULY	HARDY TO: -25° C / -15° F	

An *R. occidentale* hybrid with very large, deep pink flowers that are delicately fragrant, "Popsicle" forms a broad, open shrub. This offspring of the species native to California blooms in late June with foliage that colours well in the fall.

Rhododendron luteum

HEIGHT: 1.8–2.5 M / 6–8 FT	SPREAD: 1.8–2.5 M / 6–8 FT	ZONE: 5
FLOWERING PERIOD: MAY–JUNE	HARDY TO: -25° C / -15° F	

This species azalea from eastern Europe has some of the finest fragrance you will experience from any flowering plant. The single, lemon-yellow blossoms are tubular in shape, quite sticky and strongly resemble honeysuckle flowers. *Rhododendron luteum* forms a tall, fairly open shrub and is an excellent choice for naturalizing in an open woodland setting.

Rhododendron "Lemon Drop"

HEIGHT: 1.5–1.8 M / 5–6 FT	SPREAD: 1.5–1.8 M / 5–6 FT	ZONE: 5–6
FLOWERING PERIOD: JUNE–JULY	HARDY TO: -15° C / 5° F	

"Lemon Drop" is a hybrid of the swamp honeysuckle or *Rhododendron viscosum*. It forms sticky pink buds that open to extremely fragrant yellow, funnel-shaped flowers. Probably the best feature of this deciduous azalea is the late blooming period, June to July.

Rhododendron "Northern Hi-Lights"

HEIGHT: 1.8–2.5 M / 6–8 FT	SPREAD: 1.2–1.8 M / 4–6 FT	ZONE: 2–3
FLOWERING PERIOD: MAY–JUNE	HARDY TO: -45° C / -49° F	

Another introduction from the "Northern Lights" series, "Northern Hi-Lights" grows a little taller than most rhododendrons. The white-blotched yellow blossoms are borne on a robust shrub with mildew-resistant foliage. As with the rest of the series, it is extremely hardy.

Rhododendron "Yellow Cloud"

HEIGHT: 1.5 M / 5 FT	SPREAD: 90 CM–1.2 M / 3–4 FT	ZONE: 5–6
FLOWERING PERIOD: JUNE–JULY	HARDY TO: -25° C / -15° F	

This Knap Hill azalea features large **trusses** of fragrant yellow flowers, borne in profusion late in the season.

Suggestions for Landscape Uses

Deciduous azaleas thrive in slightly acidic, fertile loamy soil that is evenly moist, yet well drained. They prefer an exposure with morning sun and afternoon shade but will tolerate less ideal circumstances, including lower light levels, high heat, poor soil and low moisture. It is this tolerance of a wide variety of growing conditions that makes these plants so useful in residential landscapes. Here are a few planting suggestions for your garden. Plant deciduous azaleas:

En masse in odd-numbered groups of three, five, seven or nine in complementing or contrasting colour schemes.

As a single specimen among dwarf conifers or evergreen shrubs.

With cascading perennials and annuals in containers for patios and decks.

In a woodland garden area mixed with hostas, ferns or native plants.

Interplanted with assorted-sized rhododendrons or evergreen azaleas.

Pruning Deciduous Azaleas

Deciduous azaleas require pruning only when they outgrow their space in the garden. They can be pruned anywhere on the stem length and will develop new buds and branch out from below that point. The best time to prune is when flowering has finished, which will leave enough time to set buds for the following year.

Roses

I have to admit that when this book was in the planning stages, I had thought that one or two rose chapters would be sufficient. This illusion was quickly put to rest when I started contacting potential contributors, who were nothing short of appalled at my blatant attempt to narrow the field. What I hadn't anticipated was the passion that **rosarians** have for their plants and, to be quite honest, this was the driving force behind an expanded rose section.

Aside from the enthusiasm of the numerous contributors, roses have enjoyed a prominent place throughout many cultures, past and present. Roses were favoured during ancient Greek, Roman and Persian civilizations and later represented opposing English houses — the red rose of Lancaster and the white rose of York — during the War of the Roses from 1455–1485. Roses also gained "royal" prominence centuries later during the time of Napoleon as a favourite pastime of Empress Josephine, who sought to collect every known variety in her vast rose gardens.

Some of these same antique or species roses are just now being discovered by a whole new generation of gardeners, while David Austin's English roses bring an Old World charm of fragrance and flower form through selective breeding techniques. The Meidiland landscape roses are quickly becoming a standard of many commercial landscapes by virtue of their low maintenance requirements and floriferous nature — much the same qualities that floribundas provide for homeowners looking for an "easy-care" rose.

Hybrid teas are constantly being improved for aesthetic qualities as well as overall vigour but are still favoured for their large, well-formed blooms that make perfect cut flowers. Miniature roses are increasingly in demand for use in urban areas where garden space is limited and on larger, rural properties. Shrub roses are finding favour as informal hedges that provide both beauty and some security. Lastly, ramblers and climbers — many of which have been with us for a century or more — are again adorning our fences and outbuildings with generous sprays of flowers and fragrance. So whatever your needs may be, our rose experts are bound to have suggested at least one plant to beautify your landscape.

Hybrid Teas & Floribundas

Roses are the "princesses" in everyone's garden — few shrubs garner the constant attention and praise that these plants have lavished on them. With a flowering period ranging from early summer until frost, hybrid teas and floribundas are some of the most gratifying ornamentals that one can have in the landscape. All they ask for in return is well-drained loamy soil, regular fertilizing and a minimum of six hours of sun for flower production. Having walked through Jan Verschuren's rose fields in the middle of summer, I can tell you that his plants receive all of these. What they do not get is a great deal of "fussing," as Jan will grow only rose cultivars that hold their own for beauty as well as disease resistance. This simple process of selection has been the basis of his success, and I am sure that you will not be disappointed with Jan's choices for hybrid teas and floribundas.

Jan Verschuren
Roses and Roses
Aldergrove, B.C.

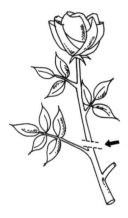

Floribundas by Flower Colour

Dark Red /	"Lavaglut"
Medium Red /	"Showbiz"
Orange-Red /	"Melody Maker"
Orange-Pink /	"Anisley Dickson"
Apricot Blend /	"Pensioner's Voice"
Light Pink /	"English Miss"
Medium Pink /	"Wishing"
Pink Blend /	"Valentine Heart"
Medium Yellow /	"Mountbatten"
Deep Yellow /	"Mary Cave"
White /	"Margaret Merrill"
Mauve /	"Heirloom"

Rosa "Lavaglut" (1978 — Floribunda)

With a name that translates as "Lavaglow," you can be assured that this rose's deep red to nearly black-red blooms live up to their reputation. Although this **floribunda** has very little scent, the evenly spaced flower clusters are prolific and borne on a dense shrub with purple-tinged, glossy green foliage. "Lavaglut" is also known as "Intrigue," but should not be confused with the reddish-purple rose of the same name introduced by Warriner.

Rosa "Timeless" (1996 — Hybrid Tea)

AARS WINNER 1997

This exciting hybrid tea was bred from the red florist rose "Kardinal," with flowers that open deep pink and mature to a vivid red. This rose is a repeat bloomer and will keep flowering from early summer through to fall. While there is only slight fragrance, the large, symmetrical blooms will open very slowly for your enjoyment.

Rosa "Princess of Wales" (1997 — Floribunda)

This rose was originally presented to Princess Diana. A Harkness introduction, "Princess of Wales" bears subtle cream buds that open to outstanding pure white flowers, contrasting well against the dark green foliage. The fragrant blooms are freely borne and held quite close to the dense, compact shrubs.

Rosa "Sunset Celebration" (1994 — Hybrid Tea)

AARS WINNER 1998

This multiple award-winning **hybrid tea** was named to celebrate the hundredth anniversary of *Sunset* magazine. It features exquisite salmon to apricot blooms that are quite large and moderately fruity in fragrance. This extremely healthy shrub colours better in regions with cooler summers. The flowers are good for cutting and are relatively unaffected by wind or rain. "Warm Wishes" is the European name for this rose.

Rosa "Mary Cave" (1995 — Floribunda)

Gorgeous bright yellow flowers borne in generous clusters are just one reason to have this rose in your garden. This hybrid of "Rosemary Harkness" and "Golden Years" also features glossy, bright green foliage on a disease-resistant plant. "Mary Cave" has a very subtle but nonetheless pleasant spicy fragrance.

Rosa "Stephen's Big Purple" (1985 — Hybrid Tea)

Strong fragrance with the deepest purple flowers make this New Zealand introduction one of the best hybrid teas available. The blooms are carried on long stems well above the healthy, matte green foliage below. An offspring of "Purple Splendor," this upright shrub flowers best in cooler weather.

Rosa "Valentine Heart" (1990 — Floribunda)

The perfect "buttonhole" rose with tightly formed, sparkling pink blooms emerging from pale scarlet buds, "Valentine Heart" produces clusters of fragrant flowers right through the growing season and well into autumn. This **floribunda** rose, also known as "St. Andrews," features healthy, dark green foliage and a dense, spreading growth habit.

Rosa "High Sheriff" (1992 — Hybrid Tea)

Fragrant bronze-orange to red blossoms are the main attraction of this rose. The flowers are very full and more deeply tinted toward the edge of the petals. "High Sheriff" is a vigorous shrub with glossy foliage, few thorns and good disease resistance. It is multiflowering and high-growing — although it is not as tall as some **hybrid teas**.

Rootstocks

The rose rootstock used primarily by growers in the United States (the Dr. Huey rootstock) results in shrubs that will thrive in hot, desert-like climates but are totally unfit for cool West Coast or subzero temperatures. Roses for the Pacific Northwest should be grown on seedling (multiflora or canina) not cutting rootstock, as cutting rootstock will die from winter damage long before the budded variety will. The R. canina "Pfander" seedling rootstock that Jan uses for his tree roses will be the last to suffer from winter damage.

Hybrid Teas by Flower Colour

Dark Red / "Schwarze Madonna"
Medium Red / "Loving Memory"
Orange-Red / "Victor Borge"
Orange-Pink / "Ave Maria"
Apricot Blend / "Alpine Sunset"
Light Pink / "New Zealand"
Medium Pink / "The McCartney Rose"
Pink Blend / "Chicago Peace"
Medium Yellow / "Berolina"
Deep Yellow / "Sunburst"
Mauve / "Paradise"

Variety Selection
Apart from the rootstock, rose cultivars are also subject to local climatic conditions. With species originating from such diverse geographic locations as Iran, Southern France, China, Turkey and Siberia, it is understandable that not every variety is suited for the Pacific Northwest. Many **hybrid tea** *and* **floribunda** *roses will have larger blooms with better colour in cool temperatures, while others are the exact opposite. The last factor is disease resistance and, with our coastal weather, varieties subject to* **black spot** *or* **powdery mildew** *might best be avoided. I still recommend an occasional spraying with* **Funginex** *(a* **systemic fungicide***) as a preventive measure.*

Rosa "Tournament of Roses" (1988 — Hybrid Tea)

AARS WINNER 1989

An extremely easy-to-grow rose with abundant clusters of porcelain pink, bicolour blooms, this vigorous **hybrid tea** is classified as a **grandiflora** in North America and features shiny, dark green foliage and good disease resistance. The flowers are fully double and lightly scented.

Rosa "City of London" (1988 — Floribunda)

With "New Dawn" as one of its parents, it is to be expected that one of the chief attributes of this **floribunda** is the production of stunning soft pink flowers, which fade to blush. The shrub itself bears healthy foliage with few thorns and can be trained as a small climber with some support. Add to that its continual blooming period and the New Zealand fragrance award in 1993, and you have a rose worthy of any garden.

Rambling & Climbing Roses

Rambling roses originated in the wild and have been hybridized to create flowing vines with large fragrant clusters of small flowers in summer. The more modern climbing roses generally have larger blooms, flower longer and are shorter in stature, with stiffer, upright canes.

Carol Martin Quin
Old Rose Nursery
Hornby Island, B.C.

Old Rose Nursery specializes in "own-root" rambling and climbing roses, as well as many other classes, including David Austin, Antique and Rugosa. Located on Hornby Island in the Strait of Georgia, Tony and Carol Quin's cottage garden is surrounded by more than 600 rose plants, from which they propagate new stock from cuttings. In business since 1987, Old Rose Nursery has been featuring varieties that are fragrant, reliable and disease resistant in our West Coast climate, as well as hardy roses for the colder regions of Canada and the U.S.

Rosa "Dortmund" (1955 — Climber)
HEIGHT: 4 M / 13 FT

This classic climber from northern Germany is related to the hardy *Rosa kordesii* and shares its brilliant red colour and glossy foliage. The large, single red flowers of this variety are accented with white centres and borne in clusters throughout the summer into early winter, when its lovely **hips** gain prominence.

Rosa "Bleu Magenta" (1900 — Rambler)
HEIGHT: 4.5 M / 15 FT

An exquisite rose for its unique flower colour, "Bleu Magenta" bears clusters of small, fully double blossoms of dark magenta-blue during the summer. This vigorous shrub looks best when interplanted with contrasting white climbers such as "Rambling Rector," "Iceberg" or "Kiftsgate." The long-reaching growth habit of this rambling rose makes it an excellent choice for covering tall fences, archways and pergolas, as does its shade tolerance and disease resistance.

Rosa "Aloha" (1949 — Climber)
HEIGHT: 3.5 M / 12 FT

A thoroughly modern rose in size and appearance, "Aloha" pairs outstanding fragrance with lovely shades of rose-pink blossoms. This is not a tall climber but is well suited for training on pillars or small fences and can even be treated as a free-standing shrub, if so pruned. "Aloha" will continue to bloom all summer but, like all heavy blooming roses, it will benefit from a manure mulch, deadheading and regular watering in dry periods.

Rosa "Crimson Shower" (1951 — Rambler)
HEIGHT: 5 M / 16 FT

This rambler provides a veritable waterfall of deep pink, double pompom flowers held in large clusters. As with many of the popular older ramblers, "Crimson Shower" (and its relatives "Excelsa" and "Dorothy Perkins") puts all its energy into providing massive clouds of colour in a once-blooming, mid summer display — although this variety will provide a few autumn flowers.

Rosa "Albertine" (1921 — Rambler)
HEIGHT: 4.5 M / 15 FT

A vigorous rambler with a "just plant it and stand back" reputation, "Albertine" is also known for its big show of large salmon-coloured flowers, which are well scented. This is a wonderful rose for cottage garden trellises and deer fences, even though it flowers only in June and July.

Rosa "Compassion" (1973 — Climber)

HEIGHT: 2.5 M / 8 FT

A medium-sized climber that bears lovely apricot-pink, double flowers in true rose form, "Compassion's" large, fragrant blooms are almost continuously produced. This rose is relatively disease-resistant and vigorous, making it a good choice for growing on pillars, trellises or walls. Try it in combination with deep blue, large-flowered clematis such as "The President" or "Jackmanii."

Rosa "Kiftsgate" (1908 — Rambler)

HEIGHT: 8 M / 26 FT

A well-known white rose with small flowers borne in huge clusters, the extremely vigorous "Kiftsgate" can take over if it is not carefully located. Like similar roses of this type ("Paul's Himalayan Musk" and "The Garland"), it is quite fragrant and often covered in masses of tiny orange **hips** during the winter — to the delight of many varieties of wild birds. This shade-tolerant rambler is closely related to its species or wild rose parent and will easily cover an old building with its nearly 4 m /12 ft of new canes each season.

Rosa "Alberic Barbier" (1900 — Rambler)

HEIGHT: 5 M / 16 FT

With glossy semi-evergreen leaves, this fragrant rose provides an almost ivy-like background for its fully double, creamy-white flowers, which bloom throughout the summer. *"Alberic Barbier"* is disease-free and shade-tolerant.

Rosa "Dublin Bay" (1976 — Climber)

HEIGHT: 2.5 M / 8 FT

Vivid red double flowers are borne on a healthy plant that is not overwhelming in its growth habit and therefore is useful as a pillar rose or for covering short fences. This cultivar can be treated as a tall shrub and is continuously

---

Pruning Climbing Roses

Climbing and rambling roses need pruning in the fall to early spring only to shape them, keep them under control or to cut out old canes.

Ramblers: Rambling roses bloom on seasoned wood. Do not cut them back severely or you will prevent flowering the following year.

Climbers: Continuously flowering climbers will appreciate deadheading and a pruning back of lateral branches in spring — while fanning the canes out will encourage more blooms.

Fragrant Ramblers and Climbers

"Constance Spry" /
pink climber
"Mme. Alfred Carriere" / white climber
"Paul's Himalayan Musk" / light pink rambler
"Mermaid" /
single yellow climber
"Coral Dawn" /
deep pink climber
"Moonlight" /
creamy-white rambler
"Etoile de Hollande" /
red climber
"Royal Sunset" /
peach climber
"Veilchenblau" /
mauve rambler
"La France" / pink climber

Disease Resistance
*The past few decades have seen a trend toward planting more modern and readily available roses such as the **hybrid teas**, which were developed for their large, perfect blooms and continuous flowering ability rather than for their disease resistance. Since then, roses in general have developed a reputation as being difficult to grow, because quite a few of the newer introductions were prone to black spot and **powdery mildew**. This is most unfortunate, as many of the older plants, including ramblers and a large number of shrub, rugosa, floribunda and even modern English roses, are far easier to grow — without the constant fussing and spraying.*

blooming but, like "Dortmund," it has little fragrance. Carol and her husband were able to enjoy some "Dublin Bay" flowers (with several other varieties) in their huge 1999 Christmas table arrangement.

Rosa "New Dawn" (1930 — Rambler)

HEIGHT: 4 M / 13 FT

Perhaps one of the greatest ramblers, "New Dawn" is loved by old rose enthusiasts and amateur gardeners alike. This variety is a continuously flowering **sport** of its famous look-alike father, the summer-flowering "Dr. Van Fleet." With its fragrant, pale pink flowers, "New Dawn" is the most requested climbing rose at Old Rose Nursery and is gorgeous in combination with red and magenta roses or blue clematis. Also, be sure to look for "Awakening," a "New Dawn" **sport** featuring **quartered** flowers, a headier fragrance and a compact growing habit.

David Austin's English Roses

Robin Dening
Brentwood Bay
Nurseries Ltd.
Brentwood Bay, B.C.

English roses are an extremely useful and very versatile group of plants — a delicate blend of old rose charm and the reliability of modern floribundas. All are the result of David Austin's vision to bring together the best of both worlds, and his excellent breeding program has produced many fine roses to date.

Brentwood Bay Nurseries is a small specialty nursery located on Vancouver Island's Saanich Peninsula, that Robin and Betsy Dening have owned and operated since 1991. They specialize in perennials and roses — but also carry an extensive selection of uncommon trees, shrubs and vines. Their objective is to grow rare and unusual plants not only for the avid gardener, but for anyone who might pick up a gardening magazine and wonder where the featured plants can be found.

The following is a list of 10 David Austin roses that are doing quite well in Brentwood Bay's garden. Robin and Betsy have never sprayed them for **black spot** or mildew, and aphid control is left in the capable hands of ladybugs and their ugly larvae. Brentwood Bay Nurseries is fortunate to have a licence agreement with David Austin, so is able to propagate English roses on site.

David Austin's book *English Roses* and his catalogues have been used as a source of descriptions for these roses.

Rosa "Golden Celebration"
("Charles Austin" x "Abraham Darby" / 1992)

HEIGHT: 1.2 M / 4 FT	SPREAD: 1.2 M / 4 FT

"Golden Celebration" has exceptionally large, in-curved, cup-shaped flowers that have a rich golden-yellow colour and are almost continually in bloom. A very powerful fragrance starts out as a tea scent but then develops into "a wonderful combination of sauterne wine and strawberry." This is one of the few roses I actually cut for the house, as the heavy blooms tend to hang their heads at the ends of slightly arching canes.

Rosa "Molineux"
(1994 — "Golden Showers" seedling x seedling)

HEIGHT: 75 CM / 2½ FT	SPREAD: 60 CM / 2 FT

"Molineux" has become a very popular English rose around Victoria and on Vancouver Island. The continuous flowers are a rich yellow colour with a good tea rose fragrance. "Molineux" has very healthy dark green leaves and forms an attractive small, upright shrub, making it a good choice for bedding or containers.

Rosa "Lucetta" (1983 — breeding unknown)

1.2 M / 4 FT	SPREAD: 1.2 M / 4 FT

"Lucetta" is an absolute delight in the garden. It is very similar to "Heritage" with large, soft pink flowers that are saucer-like in shape and almost semi-double. As the very fragrant blooms age, they fade to near white. "Lucetta" flowers almost continually, with tremendous flushes of blooms weighing heavily on the strong canes.

Rosa "Charlotte" (1993 — seedling x "Graham Thomas")

HEIGHT: 75 CM / 2½ FT	SPREAD: 90 CM / 3 FT

"Charlotte" has medium-sized, cup-shaped flowers of soft yellow accented with a delicate tea rose fragrance. The specimen planted by our front path emits a delightful scent every time we walk by. David Austin describes this as one of the most beautiful of his yellow English roses. Pair this shrub with geranium "Anne Fokkard" (yellowish leaves and magenta flowers) and let them bloom together, all summer long.

Rosa "Abraham Darby"
(1985 — "Yellow Cushion" x "Aloha" modern climber)

HEIGHT: 1.5 M / 5 FT   SPREAD: 1.5 M / 5 FT

This cross between two modern roses is not a typical David Austin hybrid; however, it has many characteristics of an old rose. The large, coppery-apricot flowers have a very rich, fruity fragrance and are cupped with outer petals that are close to pink in colour. "Abraham Darby" is a repeat bloomer and forms a healthy, well-rounded shrub.

Rosa "Heavenly Rosalind"
(1995 — "Shropshire Lass" x "Heritage")

HEIGHT: 1.2 M / 4 FT   SPREAD: 1.25 M / 4½ FT

David Austin describes this rose as an *Alba* hybrid, which repeats well. In our garden it seems to be almost continually in bloom from June to frost. "Heavenly Rosalind" has delightful masses of single, medium-sized flowers that open pink and turn to a soft salmon-pink with age. After the petals fall off, the prominent pink **stamens** remain, giving an interesting effect. The blooms have a light musk fragrance.

Rosa "The Pilgrim"
(1991 — "Graham Thomas" x "Yellow Button")

HEIGHT: 1 M / 3¼ FT   SPREAD: 90 CM / 3 FT

"The Pilgrim" seems to have been a little underrated, as we have found it to be a superb rose that is almost continually in bloom. The large flowers are pure yellow in the centre, paling toward white on the outside, with a fragrance described as a "perfect balance between a classic tea scent and the English rose, myrrh fragrance."

Rootstocks

We have found that many roses from the United States are on rootstock that is not always hardy in the Canadian winters. However, this is starting to change and a few U.S. growers are beginning to provide some roses on their own roots. The main reason for producing roses by grafting or budding is that larger volume can be achieved — each bud on a stem can produce one saleable plant. Own-root roses from cuttings need a piece of stem with about four buds, so they produce only one quarter the volume. Whenever possible, Brentwood Bay Nurseries grows roses on their own roots, as these plants perform better in the long run.

Some Other Worthy English Roses

"Mary Rose" / rose-pink
"Gertrude Jekyll" / rich pink
"Leander" / deep apricot
"The Alexandra Rose" / copper-pink, pale yellow
"Winchester Cathedral" / white tinted in yellow
"Constance Spry" / soft pink
"The Herbalist" / deep pink to rose
"Belle Story" / delicate pink
"L.D. Braithwaite" / deep red
"Evelyn" / apricot to pink

English Roses in the Home Landscape
At Brentwood Bay Nurseries we do not have a designated English rose bed — they are interplanted throughout the garden. Taller varieties like "Graham Thomas" or "Chianti" may be used as short climbers or pillar roses in the centre of a more formal bed or as a focal point instead of a fountain or piece of statuary. Perennials and small vines are allowed to weave through them at will. The medium-sized varieties (roses in the 90 cm – 1.5 m / 3 – 5 ft range), such as "Heritage" and "Kathryn Morley," may be used as individual shrubs or in borders, blended with perennials. David Austin suggests planting his roses in groups of three of the same variety about 45 cm / 18 in apart, in a triangular shape. The shorter varieties (roses under 90 cm / 3 ft) such as "Radio Times" and "Molineux" can be used as bedding roses in the front of borders, or in pots and planters for the patio.

Rosa "Heritage"
(1984 — seedling x ["Iceberg" x "Wife of Bath"])

HEIGHT: 1.2 M / 4 FT	SPREAD: 1.2 M / 4 FT

This wonderful rose has perfectly cupped, medium-sized blooms with a "beautiful fragrance, with overtones of fruit, honey and carnation on a myrrh background." The flowers have a soft, clear pink colouring at the centre, with the outer petals fading to almost white or pale blush pink. This shrub has healthy, smooth, mid-green foliage with strong stems.

Rosa "Graham Thomas"
(1983 — "Charles Austin" x ["Iceberg" x seedling])

HEIGHT: 1.2 M / 4 FT	SPREAD: 1.2 M / 4 FT

"Graham Thomas" is not only one of the best and beautiful of the English roses, it is also one of the most popular. If you are looking for a small climber or large shrub, this is a good choice. The foliage is healthy with shiny, pale green leaves and long climbing shoots. This rose has rich, pure yellow blooms that are cupped and scented. "Graham Thomas" is named after the famous **rosarian** and plantsman, Graham Stuart Thomas.

Rosa "Pat Austin"
(1995 — "Graham Thomas" x "Abraham Darby")

HEIGHT: 1 M / 3½ FT	SPREAD: 1.2 M / 4 FT

This rose is named after David Austin's wife, who is an amazing sculptor. The flower colour is a most unusual combination of copper, pink and orange. For companion plants, we grow *Phygelius* "Moonraker," *P.* "Leaping Salmon" and Hopley's purple oregano with "Pat Austin." The new growth has a bronze hue and the foliage is shiny mid-green in colour.

Miniature Roses

Miniature roses are versatile garden plants that bear all the attributes of larger roses in reduced proportions. Despite their delicate appearance, they withstand cold temperatures and adverse conditions better than many large roses. With the vast selection available, one can find a mini-rose to suit almost any garden situation — be it a miniature climber on an apartment balcony or a vigorous shrub form in the foreground of a mixed border.

Brad Jalbert has been dabbling in roses since about 1986 — three years later his hobby became a serious business venture, after he earned a certificate in ornamental horticulture and built his first greenhouse with the help of his father. Since then, a simple policy of hard work and long hours has allowed Select Roses to become one of the most popular destination nurseries in the Fraser Valley. Brad currently produces many of his own rose hybrids and, to date, has 10 varieties on the market, with an average of two new introductions planned per season.

Brad Jalbert
Select Roses
Langley, B.C.

Rosa "Rainbow's End"

HEIGHT: 30 CM / 1 FT	SPREAD: 30 CM / 1 FT
FLOWERING PERIOD: ALL SUMMER	

"Rainbow's End" has been Brad's firm favourite since he first started growing miniature roses. A superb rose for containers or the garden, it features a compact growth habit coupled with a fast blooming cycle. The colour is truly remarkable and continually changing, with every bloom seeming a little different than the one before it. Flowers usually start out yellow with a slight reddish edge, which turns a deeper shade of red and begins to spread down each petal as the flower matures.

Pruning Miniature Roses
Pruning is the easiest part of rose growing, yet it is often the most feared. The time to prune varies by region but is usually around February or March, later in cold winter areas. While different pruning methods work equally well, never fear a rose will die by pruning. Start by first taking out any diseased or damaged wood.
Cut the tops of the average miniature rose back by about one-half, or even more after a severe winter. Just remember that a healthy miniature rose will always bounce back with plenty of new growth.

Rosa "Green Ice"

HEIGHT: 30 CM / 1 FT	SPREAD: 60 CM / 2 FT
FLOWERING PERIOD: ALL SUMMER	

Truly unique in flower form, colour and growth habit, this spreading cultivar is perfect for hanging baskets or rockeries. The blossoms are very double, much like old-fashioned roses, and hang in large clusters. Easily appreciated for its subtle flower colour, "Green Ice" shifts from ivory-white to the palest green. Brad has seen specimens of this little rose flourishing in poor conditions for many years without care, which is why it is one of his top picks.

Rosa "Glowing Amber"

HEIGHT: 45 CM / 18 IN	SPREAD: 30 CM / 1 FT
FLOWERING PERIOD: ALL SUMMER	

Hybridized by George Mander of Coquitlam, B.C., "Glowing Amber" has become one of the great success stories in Canadian rose breeding. It is constantly gaining popularity throughout the world as a top exhibition-style rose. Each flower on this upright-growing shrub is perfectly shaped and borne one to a stem. The blossoms are deep red with a golden-yellow reverse, making it a striking bicolour specimen.

Rosa "Sandalwood"

HEIGHT: 30 CM / 1 FT	SPREAD: 30 CM / 1 FT
FLOWERING PERIOD: ALL SUMMER	

If you appreciate plants of unique beauty and quality of flower, then "Sandalwood" will be your favourite miniature rose. The blooms are best described as terra cotta but will exhibit a slight dusty rose pink tint in some weather conditions. They are of **hybrid tea** form and quite large for the compact nature of this plant. "Sandalwood" is winter tender and appreciates some extra protection in colder regions, but has still proven to be my most successful introduction to date.

Rosa "Pink Petticoat"

HEIGHT: 60 CM / 2 FT	SPREAD: 30 CM / 1 FT
FLOWERING PERIOD: ALL SUMMER	

Although an older variety, "Pink Petticoat" still deserves to be mentioned, as it is one of the easiest roses to grow. The plant is exceptionally strong and produces blossoms in wonderful bouquets. Flower colour is a delicate cream with coral pink edges, making it a good choice for the vase. It is very disease resistant and also slightly fragrant.

Rosa "Sun Chariot"

HEIGHT: 60 CM / 2 FT	SPREAD: 30 CM / 1 FT
FLOWERING PERIOD: ALL SUMMER	

This is a rose Brad bred using "Pink Petticoat," and it has inherited all of the strengths of its parent, with some improvements. The colour is a bright sunshine yellow with a slight salmon shade to the edges in cool weather — these open to show a boss of gold **stamens** and emit a sweet scent, reminiscent of wild roses. Foliage is very glossy and healthy.

Rosa "Laura Ford"

HEIGHT: 2.5 M / 8 FT
FLOWERING PERIOD: ALL SUMMER

One of the most useful roses to grow, "Laura Ford" is part of the new generation of climbing miniatures from England that thrives in our climate. The flowers are yellow, with orange shadings to the edges of the petals as they age. It grows well with only four hours of sun per day and produces blooms all summer long. To enjoy rose **hips**, simply leave the late flowers on and they will produce a good display.

Planting Miniature Roses

Miniature roses are very easy plants to grow and winter hardy in outside areas, provided you give them reasonable care. They are grown all over Canada and the US, and survive harsh winters if the proper varieties are chosen and extra protection is given. It is important to note that cultural conditions and hardiness will vary considerably if you are planning to grow your roses in containers. For garden applications, start by choosing a site with fertile, well-drained soil. If soil quality is poor, add some compost or other organic matter to improve it. Miniature roses thrive best with four hours of sun per day or more, but some varieties will do fine in partial shade.

Rosa "Warm Welcome"

HEIGHT: 2.5 M+ / 8 FT+

FLOWERING PERIOD: ALL SUMMER

Everyone who grows this climbing rose loves it! They start wondering if they appreciate the unusual flower colour — the blossoms are a single burnt orange with yellow centres — but soon realize that "Warm Welcome" has become one of the highlights of their garden. Very winter hardy and free-blooming, the plant itself is easy to train.

Rosa "Jeanne Lajoie"

HEIGHT: 3 M+ / 10 FT+

FLOWERING PERIOD: ALL SUMMER

When in full bloom, a mature specimen of this climbing miniature rose will show more than a thousand blossoms. In fact, you will never be able to count how many flowers "Jeanne Lajoie" will give you in a season. The perfect little rosebuds are a pleasing shade of pink and grow in clusters, like grapes. The plant is fast-growing and very winter hardy. Somewhat prone to **black spot,** but who cares — it will still continue to flower and grow despite it.

Rosa "Cupcake"

HEIGHT: 30 CM / 1 FT   SPREAD: 30 CM / 1 FT

FLOWERING PERIOD: ALL SUMMER

As the name suggests, "Cupcake" is a rich shade of pink and truly looks good enough to eat. The flowers have tightly packed petals with a pleasant **hybrid tea** shape. The plant is sturdy and blooms freely. Introduced back in 1981, "Cupcake" is still one of the best pink miniature roses for garden performance.

Meidiland Landscape Roses

Meilland of France is a venerable name in the international rose trade, and they have produced many famous hybrids, including "Peace" (1946), "Christian Dior" (1962) and "Miss All-American Beauty" (1968). Locally, they are probably best known for their durable landscape roses, which are commonly found in both residential and commercial settings.

Brian Christie
Christie Nursery Ltd.
Pitt Meadows, B.C.

Christie Nursery Ltd. began in 1979 as a family affair, created by Brian and Margaret Christie, along with their sons Blair and Brian Jr. They were the first nursery to bring Meidiland landscape roses to the Vancouver market, and their wholesale operation in Pitt Meadows continues to specialize in these plants, as well as hardy ground covers. Meidiland roses have become popular with landscapers for their long displays of colour, good disease resistance and minimal maintenance requirements — with most needing little or no pruning.

Rosa cv. "Meipoque" / Pink Meidiland

HEIGHT: 1.2 M / 4 FT	SPREAD: 75 CM / 2 FT	ZONE: 4
FLOWERING PERIOD: SPRING–FROST		

This is an upright landscape rose with a vigorous growth habit, suitable for hedges. "Meipoque" is a dependable repeat bloomer, flowering throughout the summer and finishing the season with orange-red **hips**. Although the large flowers are single, they are a beautiful bright pink accented with a white eye and are borne in clusters.

Rosa cv. "Meidomonac" / Bonica

HEIGHT: 90 CM–1.5 M / 3–5 FT	SPREAD: 1.3–1.5M / 4½–5 FT	ZONE: 4
FLOWERING PERIOD: SPRING–FROST		

Bonica was the first shrub rose to win an AARS award, and deservedly so. This 1987 introduction bears a profusion of small, full double, pastel pink flowers from early spring until frost. Tolerant of partial shade and disease resistant, it is an ideal candidate for massing in a mixed border or planting against a wall.

Rosa cv. "Meimodac" / Royal Bonica

HEIGHT: 1.25–1.5 M / 4–5 FT	SPREAD: 1.25–1.5 M / 4–5 FT	ZONE: 4
FLOWERING PERIOD: EARLY SUMMER–AUTUMN		

A newer cultivar (introduced in 1996) with fully double, deep pink blooms that do not fade in hot weather, Royal Bonica flowers continuously from early summer to autumn and is a good choice for mass plantings. The medium green foliage is also very disease resistant.

Rosa cv. "Meikrotal" / Scarlet Meidiland

HEIGHT: 1.2 M / 4 FT	SPREAD: 1.5–1.8 M / 5–6 FT	ZONE: 4
FLOWERING PERIOD: EARLY SUMMER–FROST		

One of the more vigorous Meidiland roses — making it a good choice for growing down slopes, spilling over walls or as a tall ground cover — "Meikrotal" features very double, vivid scarlet blooms held in clusters. It flowers heavily for four weeks in early summer and then blooms sporadically until frost.

Rosa cv. "Meiplatin" / Pearl Meidiland

HEIGHT: 60–75 CM / 2–2½ FT	SPREAD: 1.5–2 M / 4½–6½ FT	ZONE: 4
FLOWERING PERIOD: SPRING–FROST		

This cultivar produces very unusual pastel ochre flowers that are borne continuously during summer. Pearl

Meidiland is a good rose for massing as a foreground display or for growing down slopes. It also features dense, dark green foliage that serves as a good foil for the pale blossoms.

Rosa cv. "Meigekanu" / Sevillana

HEIGHT: 1–1.5 M / 3½–5 FT	SPREAD: 90 CM / 3 FT	ZONE: 6
FLOWERING PERIOD: JUNE–OCT		

An excellent hedge rose that looks good late into the season, as the foliage is retained until early winter and contrasts well with the abundant red **hips**, Sevillana bears deep scarlet blooms in clusters of up to five, from June until October. This landscape rose also features bronzed new growth that matures to an attractive glossy, dark green.

Rosa cv. "Meigeroka" / Pink Sevillana

HEIGHT: 1–1.5 M / 3½–5 FT	SPREAD: 90 CM / 3 FT	ZONE: 6
FLOWERING PERIOD: JUNE–OCT		

This landscape rose makes a superb hedge specimen with its eye-catching dark carmine pink flowers. It is very similar in growth habit to Sevillana but differs with its light green foliage. "Meigeroka" also produces an abundance of large red **hips** in autumn.

Rosa cv. "Meicoublan" / White Meidiland

HEIGHT: 45–60 CM / 1½–2 FT	SPREAD: 1.25–1.5 M / 4–5 FT	ZONE: 4
FLOWERING PERIOD: JUNE–FROST		

The low profile and horizontal growth habit of this vigorous rose make it an ideal ground cover. In fact, "Meicoublan" grows so densely that it is quite capable of smothering weeds with its large, deep green leaves. Add to this fully double, pure white blooms (up to 10 cm / 4 in across), and the White Meideland is a perfect lawn substitute, slope planting or wall accent.

Romantica Roses
Recently, Meilland has introduced a series of roses that display Old World charm in form and fragrance. Those who appreciate the David Austin or new "English roses" will certainly want to give the "Romantica" line a serious look.

Toulouse Lautrec / Rosa "Meirevolt"— Hybrid Tea / lemon yellow

Jean Giono / R. "Meirokoi" — Hybrid Tea / golden yellow-tangerine

Auguste Renoir / R. "Meitoifar" — Hybrid Tea / deep pink, fragrant

Traviata / R. "Meilavio" — Hybrid Tea / vibrant red, quartered

Johann Strauss / R. "Meioffic" — Floribunda / pink, sweetly fragrant

Abbaye de Cluny / R. "Meibrinpay" — Hybrid Tea / apricot, fragrant

Guy de Maupassant / R. "Meisocrat" — Floribunda / full pink bloom

Frederic Mistral / R. "Meitebros" — Hybrid Tea / soft pink, fragrant

Hardy Miniature Roses by Meilland
Available in a wide range of colours, these hardy miniature roses work equally well as low ground covers or as container specimens. The average height is 30–40 cm / 12–15 in tall.

Apricot Sunblaze / Rosa "Meifruije" — yellow-edged orange

Debut / R. "Meibarke" — cream-red, bicolour

Red Sunblaze / R. "Meirutral" — vivid red, vigorous

Royal Sunblaze / R. "Schobitet" — medium yellow

Amber Flash / R. "Wildak" — yellow-orange bicolour

Lady Sunblaze / R. "Meilarco" — soft pink, double

Candy Sunblaze / R. "Meidanclar" — hot pink, double

Rugosa, Species & Old Garden Roses

Roses have not always been one of my favourite plants. That changed when I came across a hedge of Pink Meidiland — its low maintenance requirements, abundant flowers and disease resistance finally convinced me that this was a rose worth planting. Since then, I have learned not to focus on the few troubled rose cultivars and have gone on to discover many varieties that thrive here in the Pacific Northwest. While I am certainly not an expert, I still thought it was important to include this chapter, so that these rose groups would be represented at least in part.

Mike Lascelle
Amsterdam Graden Centre
Pitt Meadows, B.C.

Rugosa, species and old garden roses have been with us for a long time — some have been cultivated for centuries. Most of the Rugosa varieties featured in this chapter are at least 90 years old, and it is only now that these durable plants are starting to gain widespread appeal. Species or wild roses can be every bit as beautiful as any **hybrid tea** or **floribunda**, but they are often difficult to find at the retail level and subsequently are rarely planted. "Old garden roses" is simply a catch phrase for a veritable family tree of rose groups that includes albas, gallicas, centifolias, hybrid perpetuals and bourbons, to name a few.

Rosa "Blanc Double du Coubert" (1892 — Rugosa)

HEIGHT: 1.5–1.8 M / 5–6 FT	SPREAD: 1.25–1.5 M / 4–5 FT	ZONE: 3

A clear white rugosa rose with blossoms reminiscent of camellia, "Blanc Double du Coubert" repeat blooms from late May right through the summer, into early fall, with very fragrant, double flowers. The disease-resistant foliage

Moss Roses

*Moss roses are actually attractive mutations, primarily of centifolia lineage, which feature, covering the **sepals**, moss-like glands that often emit a fresh, balsam fir scent. All are very hardy (Zone 4), attractive and quite fragrant — although the flowers may droop or hang a bit without support. Most have a limited flowering period (usually in mid summer), but a few are repeat bloomers. Despite the short blooming period, moss roses make a fascinating addition to the rose garden or the mixed border. They can be a little hard to find at retail nurseries, but here are a few of the most common varieties:*

Rosa *"Chapeau de Napoleon"* — fully double deep pink flowers / fragrant

R. *"Henri Martin"* — bright crimson semi-double blooms / lightly fragrant

R. *"Comtesse de Murinais"* — pink buds open to white blooms / fragrant

R. *"Laneii"* (Lane's Moss) — deep crimson blossoms, double / very fragrant

R. *"Alfred de Dalmas"* ("Mousseline") — pale pink, repeat bloomer / fragrant

R. *"William Lobb"* (Old Velvet Moss) — semi-double magenta blooms that fade / fragrant

R. *"Common Moss"* — double pink blossoms / highly fragrant

turns a beautiful yellow-gold in autumn and contrasts well against the large red **hips** (which are sometimes produced sparsely).

Rosa **"Fru Dagmar Hastrup"** (1914 — Rugosa)

HEIGHT: 90 CM–1.2 M / 3–4 FT	SPREAD: 90 CM–1.2 M / 3–4 FT	ZONE: 3

This is the perfect rose for those gardeners who absolutely love the iridescent silvery-pink flower colour of *Lavatera* "Silver Cup." The single blooms open slightly cupped, flatten with age and are accented with darker veins and golden stamens. Highly fragrant, "Fru Dagmar Hastrup" is also compact enough to use in small urban gardens. This rugosa rose repeat blooms all summer and bears absolutely huge red **hips**.

Rosa **"Roseraie de l'Hay"** (1901 — Rugosa)

HEIGHT: 2 M / 6½ FT	SPREAD: 1.8 M / 6 FT	ZONE: 3

One of the most regarded rugosa roses, "Roseraie de l'Hay" has been around for a century now. The semi-double, wine-purple blooms emit a heavy perfume and are borne repeatedly from June until frost. As with most rugosas, the deep apple-green foliage is quite disease resistant.

Rosa **"Hansa"** (1905 — Rugosa)

HEIGHT: 1.2 M / 4 FT	SPREAD: 1.2 M / 4 FT	ZONE: 3

"Hansa" is a great choice as a hedge rose, as it is a nice balance of beauty and durability. The double blooms of dark reddish-purple are deeply scented with a hint of clove fragrance. It also features attractive red **hips** in fall and good autumn colour.

Rosa glauca / *Rosa rubrifolia* (Species)

HEIGHT: 1.8–2.5 M / 6–8 FT	SPREAD: 1.5 M / 5 FT	ZONE: 4

Even if this rose never produced a single bloom, I would still have it in my garden. The spectacular mature foliage of grey-green is well highlighted with tints of copper-purple. The single cerise-pink flowers are small and short-lived, but adequately contrasted with a white centre backing golden **stamens** — these mature to attractive deep red **hips**.

Rosa moyesii (Species)

HEIGHT: 2.75 M / 9 FT	SPREAD: 2.5 M / 8 FT*	ZONE: 6
	*cultivars more compact	

This native of western China is primarily grown for its huge, flagon-shaped orange-red **hips** that are held in **pendulous** clusters. The single, pink to blood-red blossoms have no fragrance but are nicely highlighted with bright yellow **anthers**. Several cultivars are available, including "Geranium" (very large **hips**), "Regalia" (compact) and "Highdownensis" (red blooms).

Rosa "Fantin-Latour" (circa 1900 / Centifolia)

HEIGHT: 1.8 M / 6 FT	SPREAD: 1.5 M / 5 FT	ZONE: 4

This centifolia rose was named after the French artist, who was renowned for his realistic painting of flowers. "Fantin-Latour" features large, beautifully formed cup-shaped blooms that open flat and are less prone to being blemished by the rain. The blush-pink flowers are also sweetly scented.

An "Old Garden Rose" Sampler

Alba Rose / Rosa "Maiden's Blush" — *fragrant pale pink blooms / fragrant*

Damask Rose / R. "Madame Hardy" — *pure white / highly fragrant*

Hybrid Musk Rose / R. "Ballerina" — *single pink with white centres*

China Rose / R. "Cecile Brunner" — *tiny, well formed double pink blooms*

Bourbon Rose / R. "Madame Isaac Pereire" — *deep pink flowers / very fragrant*

Gallica Rose / R. "Alain Blanchard" — *semi-double crimson blooms / fragrant*

Noisette Rose / R. "Madame Alfred Carriere" — *climber, white flushed pink*

Hybrid Perpetual Rose / R. "Ferdinand Pichard" — *attractive pink with red stripes*

Portland Rose / R. "Jacques Cartier" — *clear light pink / fragrant*

Centifolia Rose (Cabbage Rose) / R. "Pompom de Bourgogne" — *pink "pompom" flowers / dwarf*

Roses that Produce Large or Showy Hips

Rosa woodsii *"Kimberley"*
— *bright red hips*

R. glauca — *oval dark red hips*

R. *"Kiftsgate" (Rambler)*
— *small red hips*

R. moyesii *"Geranium"*
— *very large orange-red hips*

R. acicularis
— *pure red hips, pear-shaped*

R. rugosa
— *bright red, round hips*

R. *"Meipoque" (Pink Meidiland)*
— *orange-red hips*

R. *"Fruhlingsmorgen" (Scotch Rose)* — *dark maroon hips*

Rosa "Mutabilis" (introduced to Europe 1896 / China Rose)

HEIGHT: 2–2.5 M / 7–8 FT	SPREAD: 1.5–1.8 M / 5–6 FT	ZONE: 7

A truly spectacular specimen if set in a sheltered site out of cold winds, "Mutabilis" is also known as the "Butterfly Rose," since the heavy display of single blooms is often mistaken for a profusion of butterflies. The flowers are copper in bud, opening to pale yellow and fading in succession to pink and crimson. This China rose is quite disease resistant and features bronzed new growth.

Rosa "Reine de Violettes" (1860 / Hybrid Perpetual)

HEIGHT: 1.2 M / 4 FT	SPREAD: 60–90 CM / 2–3 FT	ZONE: 5

"Queen of the Violets" lives up to its name with sweetly scented blooms of deep cerise that pick up shades of lavender-blue as they age. This hybrid perpetual rose repeat blooms for most of the summer, although the petals tend to drop quickly. It also features nearly thornless stems and moderate disease resistance.

Rosa mundi / Rosa gallica versicolor (Gallica)

HEIGHT: 90 CM–1.2 M / 3–4 FT	SPREAD: 90 CM–1.2 M / 3–4 FT	ZONE: 4

Rosa mundi is one of the oldest cultivated striped roses, with large semi-double blooms up to 9 cm / 3½ in wide. The ever-changing variegation of white, crimson and pink means the grower will be hard pressed to find any two flowers that are alike. Reversion is common with this **sport** of *Rosa gallica* "Officinalis" (Apothecary's Rose) and is best handled by cutting that particular stem back to the ground.

Conifers

Conifers usually receive attention from gardeners who have had time to develop a palette beyond the brightly coloured flowers and begun to appreciate foliage and texture as foils for colour. Conifers are the perfect medium for this use in landscape design — providing a wide range of needles, cones and variegation patterns, most of which are present year-round.

While a sampling of conifers can be found in most gardens, they are usually seen in the form of hedging cedars on the property line or as a poor specimen of last year's live Christmas tree, tucked in the back corner of the yard. Unfortunately, these examples fail to reflect the immense diversity of plant form and foliage colour that can even be found within a single species. Conifers are also capable of providing seasonal interest, with many cultivars exhibiting winter colour with the onset of cooler temperatures and a handful shedding their needles in an unusual show of autumn glory. Regardless of what time of year the gardener is out enjoying the landscape, there is a conifer for every season.

Dwarf Conifers

**Hans
van der Pouw Kraan**
*Erica Enterprises Ltd.
Pitt Meadows, B.C.*

Dwarf conifers are just starting to gain widespread popularity in Canada, in large part due to long-term interest in Europe, and in particular, the individual efforts of Adrian Bloom. They offer an unending variety of plant form, foliage texture, colour and seasonal interest that no landscape should be without. These versatile ornamentals can be the perfect ground cover, container planting, border specimen or hedge ... what more could one ask for from any group of plants?

Erica Enterprises has become well known for their high quality plant stock, and the nursery is constantly expanding to keep up with demand. This wholesale operation, situated in Pitt Meadows, is run by Hans van der Pouw Kraan and his wife Marianne. Hans' keen interest in unusual conifers is well represented in the cultivars they offer — along with their many varieties of heather and rhododendrons.

Chamaecyparis obtusa "Fernspray Gold"

HEIGHT: 2 M / 6½ FT	SPREAD: 1-2 M / 3¼–7 FT	ZONE: 4

"Fernspray Gold" is a recent introduction from New Zealand with branches held in flat sprays resembling a fern. The golden-yellow, upward-facing foliage does not burn in the sun, although some afternoon shade can be beneficial. This conifer requires annual pruning to maintain its dense form and to keep it from becoming leggy.

Abies balsamea "Nana"

HEIGHT: 60 CM / 2 FT	SPREAD: 1 M+ / 3¼ FT+ (in 10 years)	ZONE: 3

Dwarf balsam fir is an extremely slow-growing shrub that may only reach its maximum height in approximately 10 years. The deep green foliage is held on short branches, varying in colour only in spring when it emerges a bright lime green. This is a compact, globe-shaped plant that tolerates full sun or partial shade.

Chamaecyparis pisifera "Filifera Aurea"

HEIGHT: 1 M / 3 FT+   SPREAD: 1.2 M / 4 FT+ (in 10 years)   ZONE: 5

Golden threadleaf cypress is a moderate grower that forms a mop-like mound of branches that weep gracefully at the tips. The branchlets are very thin, making this an effective choice in the rockery, where it can cascade downward. Dwarf forms are also available, including "Nana" and "Sungold."

Juniperus squamata "Blue Star"

HEIGHT: 60 CM / 2 FT   SPREAD: 1–1.25 M / 3 –4 FT   ZONE: 4

Unusual steel-blue foliage combined with a tightly crested, almost star-like growth habit makes this a very distinct juniper. An excellent choice for smaller gardens or rockeries where standard junipers might prove too invasive, this particular conifer has fared very well in our Pacific Northwest climate.

Chamaecyparis obtusa "Nana Gracilis"

HEIGHT: 1.2 M / 4 FT+   SPREAD: 1 M+ / 3 FT+ (in 10 years)   ZONE: 5

A classic choice for the Japanese garden, dwarf Hinoki cypress will enhance almost any landscape design. The lustrous, dark green foliage is somewhat crested and held in twisted sprays on the branches. It is considered one of the larger "dwarf" conifers.

Tsuga canadensis "Jeddeloh"

HEIGHT: 30–60 CM / 1–2 FT   SPREAD: 60 CM / 2 FT   ZONE: 5

An excellent conifer for partial shade or filtered light, young specimens have a distinct "birdnest" hollow or depression in the centre of the plant. The soft green

---

*Dwarf Conifers
for the Rock Garden*
Many dwarf conifers make fine specimens in the rock garden, providing year-round interest. The use of other plants such as perennials, heather, low shrubs and broadleaf evergreens allows for a nice contrast of flowers or variegation against the coniferous foliage. Here is a short list of dwarf conifers suited for rockeries, each with a companion plant suggestion.
Thuja occidentalis *"Rheingold"* / Erica carnea *"Springwood Pink" (Gold Cedar / Heather)*
Juniperus squamata *"Blue Star"* / Caryopteris clandonensis *(Juniper / Blue Spiraea)*
Picea abies *"Ohlendorfii"* / Genista pilosa *"Vancouver Gold" (Dwarf Spruce / Creeping Broom)*
Chamaecyparis obtusa *"Confucious"* / Lavandula angustifolia *"Munstead" (False Cypress / Lavender)*
Pinus mugo *"Pumilo"* / Euonymus fortunei *"Emerald Gaiety" (Pine / Variegated Euonymus)*
Thuja occidentalis *"Hetz Midget"* / Lithodora diffusa *"Grace Ward" (Globe Cedar / Lithodora)*
Taxus baccata *"Fastigiata"* / Ilex crenata *"Golden Gem" (Yew / Golden Japanese Holly)*
Chamaecyparis obtusa *"Kosteri"* / Rhododendron *"Purple Gem" (False Cypress / Rhododendron)*

Choosing the Right Form
Dwarf conifers come in a variety of shapes and sizes. One of the most common mistakes gardeners make is to try to shear a plant in a form contrary to the natural growth pattern or to place a cultivar where it will eventually outgrow its allotted space. Here are a few of the most common shapes to choose from at your local garden centre.

conical: *tapers sharply from a broad base to the pointed tip / e.g., Alberta Spruce*

columnar: *very upright branching with a thin profile / e.g., Irish Yew*

rounded: *forms a somewhat rounded crown without pruning / e.g., Globe Cedar*

pendulous: *a weeping habit that will cascade over walls / e.g., Weeping Hemlock*

standard: *trained or grafted on a straight stem of various heights / e.g., Standard Hinoki Cypress*

prostrate: *a creeping, spreading habit — stays close to the ground / e.g., Blue Carpet Juniper*

shrubby: *includes irregular vase-shaped and crested plants / e.g., Hollywood Juniper*

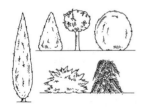

foliage gently drips at the ends of the branches and requires no pruning to keep its form.

Chamaecyparis pisifera minima aurea

HEIGHT: 15 CM / 6 IN	SPREAD: 25 CM / 10 IN (in 10 years)	ZONE: 5

This tiny ball-shaped plant is best suited to a small rockery or patio planter where it will not get lost. The finely textured, golden foliage on this compact conifer requires no maintenance. Several cultivars are available, including "Gold Dust" (golden specks) and "Silver Load" (white specks).

Podocarpus alpinus "Blue Gem"

HEIGHT: 50 CM / 20 IN	SPREAD: 1 M / 3¼ FT (in 10 years)	ZONE: 6

This alpine is a new introduction to British Columbia, with attractive blue needles that densely cover the branches. *Podocarpus nivalis* has much the same form as a spreading English yew (*Taxus baccata repandens*) and is just as versatile — tolerating full sun to partial shade. Its disease resistance and growth habit make it an excellent substitute for junipers as a ground cover.

Chamaecyparis obtusa "Verdonii"

HEIGHT: 1 M / 3¼ FT	SPREAD: 70 CM / 28 IN	ZONE: 5

This false cypress is an upright, dwarf conifer that grows approximately 10–15 cm annually. The golden foliage generally does not suffer any sunburn, but allowing for some afternoon shade will promote healthy-looking sprays.

Tsuga canadensis "Pendula"

HEIGHT: VARIABLE	SPREAD: 1–2 M+ / 3¼–6½ FT+	ZONE: 5

Weeping hemlock is quite literally a shrub that expands with your garden as it grows only as tall as you are willing to stake it. When left on its own, it forms a low, spreading mound with overlapping, **pendulous** branches. This conifer is probably best displayed as a staked specimen, planted on top of a large rock feature or wall, where its cascading branches can spill down. Weeping hemlock tolerates full sun to partial shade.

Conifers for Containers

Chamaecyparis obtusa *"Mariesii" / Variegated False Cypress*

Picea omorika *"Nana" / Dwarf Serbian Spruce*

Taxus baccata *"Fastigiata Aurea" / Golden Irish Yew*

Chamaecyparis thyoides *"Heatherbun" / Heatherbun False Cypress*

Juniperus virginiana *"Skyrocket" / Skyrocket Juniper*

Picea glauca *"Albertiana Conica" / Alberta Spruce*

Chamaecyparis obtusa *"Torulosa" / Contorted False Cypress*

Pinus strobus *"Nana" / Dwarf White Pine*

Abies balsamea *"Nana" / Dwarf Balsam Fir*

Juniperus chinensis *"Kaizuka" / Hollywood Juniper*

Pruning Conifers the Right Way

Always use sharp tools for pruning, as a dull blade damages with every cut.

Never prune a conifer until you know its general growth pattern or form.

Avoid a late season pruning as this exposes tender foliage to winter damage.

*Prune pines, spruce and fir just as the buds or **candles** shoot out in spring.*

Fine-textured conifers such as yews and hemlock can be pruned any time during the growing season until late summer.

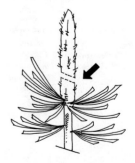

Specimen Conifers

Gerhard Gerke
Green Thumb Nurseries
Nanaimo, B.C.

It seems more time is spent cutting down large conifers than planting them, these days. The problem is not with the trees themselves, but with lack of foresight and planning when designing the gardens. There is a specimen conifer to suit every landscape — whether it is a large hillside property with a view or a newly built urban residence that needs some greening.

Green Thumb Nurseries specializes in containerized, grafted conifers as well as rhododendrons and many other broafleaf evergreens grown on their 19-hectare / 45-acre site in Nanaimo. They supply both retail and wholesale nurseries throughout the Pacific Northwest with everything from potted **liners** to huge **balled and burlapped** specimens. Owner Gerhard Gerke has chosen 10 favourites that demonstrate a nice balance of specialty varieties for their interesting form or colour, with a few larger species.

Using Specimen Trees in the Landscape
Whenever you decide to plant a large coniferous tree, it is always a good idea to assess the planting area in advance. Quite often, people plant trees that quickly outgrow their allotted space or require drastic pruning (which ruins the form) to keep it within bounds. Also, not every form or foliage colour will suit a particular landscape — so to help choose the right specimen conifer, here are a few descriptions of the basic groups along with a few examples.

Narrow Conifers
*Columnar or **pendulous** conifers with a narrow profile are useful for planting near tall buildings to add some scale or as specimens in large entrance beds.*
Chamaecyparis nootkatensis *"Jubilee" / Weeping Yellow Cedar — graceful, arching branches*
Sequoiadendron giganteum *"Pendulum" / Weeping Giant Sequoia — irregular form unless staked*
Juniperus virginiana *"Skyrocket" / Skyrocket Juniper — silvery-blue needles*
Pinus sylvestris *"Fastigiata" / Columnar Scots Pine — very hardy plant*
Taxus baccata *"Fastigiata" / Irish Yew — narrow, dark green column*

Pinus koraiensis "Glauca" / Blue Korean Pine

HEIGHT: 3 M+ / 10 FT+
HARDY TO: -23° C / -10° F

This slow-growing pine, native to Japan and Korea, really should be planted more often in urban gardens. *Pinus koraiensis* "Glauca" features long blue needles in bundles of five, which twist slightly to reveal silver highlights. The growth form is generally pyramidal and mature specimens bear large, resinous cones.

Picea pungens "Glauca Procumbens" / Spreading Blue Spruce

HEIGHT: 60–90 CM / 2–3 FT	SPREAD: 1.5–1.8 M / 5–6 FT
HARDY TO: -37° C / -35° F	

This rare cultivar of blue spruce looks spectacular when grafted on a 1.2–m / 4–ft standard stem. Otherwise, this slow-growing variety forms graceful mounds of arching branches. Spreading blue spruce prefers full sun.

Pinus thunbergii "Yatsubusa" / Yatsubusa Pine

HEIGHT: 1.5–2 M / 5–7 FT	SPREAD: 90 CM–1.5 M / 3–4 FT
HARDY TO: -23° C / -10° F	

Yatsubusa pine is a perfect conifer for seaside planting, as it is hardy and quite tolerant of salt spray. This slow-growing, upright tree with dense foliage may be sheared in bonsai forms. The attractive, bright green needles emerge from beautiful white **candles** each year.

Cedrus brevifolia / *Cedrus libani var. brevifolia* / Cyprus Cedar

HEIGHT: 7.5–9 M / 25–30 FT
HARDY TO: -20° C / -5° F

This native of Cyprus somewhat resembles the Cedar of Lebanon (*Cedrus libani*) but is smaller in stature. It has the shortest needles of all true cedars (.5–1 cm / ¼–½ in long), which are borne on small, horizontal branches. The dark green foliage is also available on several dwarf cultivars, including "Epstein" (extreme dwarf) and "Trevoron" (open form).

Golden Conifers
Golden conifers are a good choice on the edge of a greenbelt where one or two well-placed specimens will help to brighten the landscape and provide a focal point.

Cedrus deodara aurea / Golden Himalayan Cedar — *golden spring foliage*

Chamaecyparis lawsoniana *"Lanei"* / Golden Lawson False Cypress — *bright golden tips*

Cupressocyparis leylandii *"Castlewellan"* / Golden Leyland Cypress — *new growth yellow*

Thuja plicata *"Zebrina"* / Golden Red Cedar — *yellow banded foliage*

Chamaecyparis obtusa *"Crippsii"* / Cripp's Golden Hinoki False Cypress — *golden-yellow sprays*

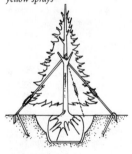

Pendulous Conifers
Pendulous conifers are excellent specimens for rockeries or wall plantings, where their cascading foliage can spill down gracefully.

Tsuga canadensis *"Pendula"* / Weeping Hemlock — *good rockery specimen*

Picea abies *"Pendula"* / Weeping Norway Spruce — *dark green foliage*

Cedrus atlantica *"Glauca Pendula"* / Weeping Blue Atlas Cedar — *irregular form*

Pinus strobus *"Pendula"* / Weeping White Pine — *pendulous blue-green foliage*

Cedrus libani *"Sargentii"* / Weeping Lebanon Cedar — *should be partially staked*

Pinus flexilis
"Vanderwolf's Pyramid" / Vanderwolf's Limber Pine

HEIGHT: 4.5–7.5 M / 15–25 FT	SPREAD: 1.5–3 M / 8–10 FT
HARDY TO: -40° C / -40° F	

Columnar when young to narrow pyramidal, this pine's upright branching habit is ideal for use in small, confined areas. Extremely hardy, Vanderwolf's limber pine features attractive bluish-green, twisted needles and a very symmetrical mature form.

Picea omorika "Brun's" / Brun's Serbian Spruce

HEIGHT: 6–7.5 M / 20–25 FT	SPREAD:3–4.5 M / 10–15 FT
HARDY TO: -37° C / -35° F	

This form of Serbian spruce was introduced to North America by Green Thumb Nurseries. The beautiful blue-green foliage of "Bruns" should enable it to eventually replace seedling forms of *Picea omorika*. It features an extremely narrow upright form, pendulous arching branches and perfect symmetry — making it ideal for formal landscape designs.

Pinus parviflora
"Brevifolia" / Dwarf Japanese White Pine

HEIGHT: 2.5–2.75 M / 8–9 FT	SPREAD: 60–90 CM / 2–3 FT
HARDY TO: -26° C / -15° F	

This slow-growing form of Japanese white pine is an excellent bonsai specimen. The short blue-green needles are held in clusters of five on sparse branches that twist irregularly as they grow, making for an interesting form. It also bears fascinating pale purple, male pollen cones in spring.

Metasequoia glyptostroboides / Dawn Redwood

HEIGHT: 24 M+ / 80 FT+	SPREAD: 7.5 M+ / 25 FT+
HARDY TO: -26° C / -15° F	

This **deciduous** conifer was thought to be extinct until the 1940s, when several specimens were discovered in an ancient Chinese temple. Dawn redwood is the only member of its **genus** and has very good seasonal appeal. The newly emerging needles are a bright green, maturing to a deep green by mid summer and changing to a beautiful bronze in autumn, just before they drop. It features a nice structural form even in winter and prefers moist, organic soils.

Pinus densiflora
"Umbraculifera" / Tanyosho Pine or Table Top Pine

HEIGHT: 1.5–3 M / 5–10 FT	SPREAD:1.5–3 M / 5–10 FT
HARDY TO: -32° C / -25° F	

This dense-growing form features a distinct flat-topped or umbrella-shaped crown. Sheared specimens of this cultivar of Japanese red pine make excellent conifers for an Oriental garden. Mature specimens are usually wider than tall and bear small brown cones. It is often sold as a grafted standard.

Picea omorika "Nana" / Dwarf Serbian Spruce

HEIGHT: 3–3.5 M / 10–12 FT*	SPREAD:60 CM+ / 2 FT+
HARDY TO: -37° C / -35° F	* without pruning

This very popular dwarf cultivar of Serbian spruce produces a very dense pyramidal mound of bluish-green needles with silver undersides. Although "Nana" is extremely slow-growing (averages 5–10 cm / 2–4 in a year), it can get fairly large unless it is pruned annually. A sheared specimen can be maintained at 1–1.5 m / 3¼–5 ft tall on average.

Conifers Native to the Pacific Northwest

This group of conifers is well adapted to our local conditions and many have good ornamental value as well.

Pinus contorta *var.* contorta / Shore Pine — *irregular, bonsai-like form*

Pseudotsuga menziesii / Douglas Fir — *quite conical when young*

Picea sitchensis / Sitka Spruce — *attractive mature bark*

Tsuga mertensiana / Mountain Hemlock — *very slow-growing, dense*

Abies lasiocarpa / Alpine Fir — *narrow profile, very hardy*

Conifers with Unusual Features

The unusual needles, foliage colour or form of these conifers add whimsy and interest to any garden design.

Thujopsis dolobrata / Deerhorn Cedar — *thick, coarse foliage*

Sciadopitys verticillata / Japanese Umbrella Pine — *whorls of dark green foliage*

Cryptomeria japonica *"Elegans"* / Plume Cedar — *purple-bronze winter foliage*

Cunnighamia lanceolata / Chinese Fir — *sharp needles, similar to monkey puzzle tree*

Larix decidua / European Larch — *deciduous conifer, yellow in autumn*

Perennials

Perennials are perhaps some of the most adventurous plants we have in our gardens and quite generously reward the small investment in a tiny plant or root division. In most cases only a few dollars will purchase an attractive species from halfway across the globe. That is not to say that every perennial can be bought so inexpensively — new introductions can be quite costly — but considering factors such as the many years it can take to create a new hybrid and the wait from seed to flower, it is money well spent.

Many perennials such as irises, peonies and hemerocallis are still field grown the old-fashioned way — where they are nurtured in fertile soil and harvested in season for use in residential landscapes. Others are either container grown from divisions or tissue-cultured in a sterile laboratory. Regardless of the propagation technique, perennials find their way to our local garden centres and manage to find a home in our gardens in innumerable ways. The plant and garden design chapters in this section will be a valuable resource when planning a garden.

Hostas

Elke and Ken Knechtel
The Perennial Gardens Inc.
Maple Ridge, B.C.

Hostas are shade lovers, although in their natural habitat they are mostly found in wet meadows in full sun. They prefer good soils, rich in **humus** and nutrients, but are capable of surviving in most conditions, even dry shade. Many gardeners purchase hostas for their diversity of foliage colour and texture — but the flowers are just as important, as many are fragrant and quite beautiful in their own right.

The Perennial Gardens started as a small specialty nursery in the early 1980s and has grown to one of the largest mail-order perennial nurseries in Canada. Hostas were one of the nursery's first specialities because, at its original location in the wooded mountainside of Anmore, shade was the garden situation. Now the collection of available hostas has grown to several hundred varieties, each hand-picked for their reliability or incredible foliage and flowers.

Hosta "Abiqua Hallucination"

HEIGHT: 30 CM / 1 FT	SPREAD: 45 CM / 18 IN	ZONE: 2
FLOWERING PERIOD: MID SUMMER		

A bizarre twist on the *tokudama* type hosta, featuring blue-green foliage overlaid with an irregular gold centre, this slow-growing cultivar has intensely puckered leaves that are round and cupped. The attractive variegation coupled with mauve flowers in mid summer makes this an excellent container specimen.

Hosta "Blue Angel"

HEIGHT: 90 CM / 3 FT	SPREAD: 1.5 CM / 5 FT	ZONE: 2
FLOWERING PERIOD: EARLY SUMMER		

"Blue Angel" is probably one of the best large blue hostas with its smooth leaves that are deeply veined. The broadly spade-shaped foliage grows in a lovely cascading mound that covers a large area, making it an ideal ground cover. Light lavender flowers are produced in early summer.

Hosta "Sagae"

HEIGHT: 80 CM / 32 IN	SPREAD: 60 CM / 2 FT	ZONE: 2
FLOWERING PERIOD: MID SUMMER		

This is a classic plant that has always been in the top 10 of North American hostas collectors. The foliage is held in a vase-like arrangement, making "Sagae" a good choice for an ornamental pot or as a focal point in the garden. The pale violet flowers and slow growth rate also make this a desirable hostas.

Hosta "Gold Standard"

HEIGHT: 60 CM / 2 FT	SPREAD: 1 M / 3¼ FT	ZONE: 2
FLOWERING PERIOD: MID SUMMER		

"Gold Standard" is the "standard" for ground cover hosta, with gold foliage edged in a rich green. When this plant receives more sun, the centre will turn almost a parchment white by late summer. This is a reliable variety that forms a dense mound of slightly puckered foliage.

Hosta "Canadian Shield"

HEIGHT: 30 CM / 1 FT	SPREAD: 60 CM / 2 FT	ZONE: 2
FLOWERING PERIOD: LATE SUMMER		

"Canadian Shield" is a tough hosta that tolerates dry shade or even a sunnier location. The deep forest green leaves are so intensely glossy that the foliage looks almost plastic. This is the ultimate ground cover hosta for smaller gardens, as it is fairly compact in its growth habit. The late summer blooms are pale violet in colour.

Maintaining a Hostas

Hostas are easy-care perennials that prefer a semi-shade exposure with rich, fertile soil. Annually amending the soil with manure (mushroom manure is best) will greatly increase the health and vigour of the plants. Gardeners need only remove flower stalks and control the slugs during the summer — hostas will continue producing leaves throughout this season, as long as nutrients and moisture are available. The foliage collapses into the soil after a severe frost, making fall clean-up almost non-existent. Hostas in containers should be fed weekly with a balanced soluble fertilizer and, although they are fully hardy in coastal regions of the Pacific Northwest, in colder climates the pot may have to be heeled into the ground for winter. Remember that these plants do change as they mature, with puckered-leaf varieties often taking two to four years before they show this attribute. The best season to divide is in the fall but, in general, hostas look best if they are left alone over a long period of time.

Companion Plants

Contrasting foliage and flower shapes are ideal companions to hostas. Early spring ephemerals also work well, as they come up and bloom before the hosta foliage emerges — after which the hostas mature to cover their dying leaves.*

Sanguinaria canadensis
/ *Bloodroot**

Rodgersia aesculifolia
/ *Fingerleaf Rodgersia*

Geranium versicolor
/ *Woodland Cranesbill*

Anemone nemerosa
/ *Wood Anemone**

Corydalis lutea
/ *Golden Corydalis*

Primula sieboldii
/ *Japanese Star Primula*

Fritillaria meleagris
/ *Snakeshead Lily**

Cryptotaenia japonica
f. atropurpurea
/ *Purple-Leaved Mitsuba*

Polygonatum odoratum
/ *Fragrant Solomon's Seal*

Dicentra eximia
/ *Eastern Bleeding Heart*

Hosta "Fragrant Bouquet"

HEIGHT: 45 CM / 18 IN	SPREAD: 90 CM / 3 FT	ZONE: 2
FLOWERING PERIOD: LATE SUMMER		

This plant features smooth, apple-green foliage with pronounced creamy-yellow to white margins. The enormous white flowers borne in late summer have a fragrance reminiscent of gardenia. Good as a ground cover or container specimen — the *Plantaginea* lineage of this hosta also makes it quite drought and sun tolerant.

Hosta "Night Before Christmas"

HEIGHT: 50 CM / 20 IN	SPREAD: 90 CM / 3 FT	ZONE: 2
FLOWERING PERIOD: EARLY SUMMER		

An **undulata** type hostas, "Night Before Christmas" catches everyone's eye with its green foliage accented in the centre with pure white, all season long. The lance-shaped leaves are slightly wavy at the edges, adding to the foliage interest. A good, bright ground cover or specimen feature in a dark corner, this hosta produces violet flowers in early summer.

Hosta "September Sun"

HEIGHT: 50 CM / 20 IN	SPREAD: 75 CM / 30 IN	ZONE: 2
FLOWERING PERIOD: LATE SUMMER		

This **sport** of hosta "August Moon" features heavily textured, puckered leaves. The chartreuse foliage is edged in bright green, making it a very attractive groundcover. Gardeners with smaller spaces will appreciate this plant's modest growth rate.

Hosta "Anne Arett"

HEIGHT: 10 CM / 4 IN	SPREAD: 30 CM / 1 FT	ZONE: 2
FLOWERING PERIOD: EARLY SUMMER		

A tidy-looking dwarf hostas, "Anne Arett" is ideal for container use or for a shady spot in the garden. It features smooth, lance-shaped leaves that are gold in colour and edged in white. An abundance of violet flowers is produced in early summer.

Hosta "Sum and Substance"

HEIGHT: 1M / 3¼ IN	SPREAD: 2 M / 6½ FT	ZONE: 2
FLOWERING PERIOD: AUG		

This is the ultimate large hosta, with leather-like chartreuse foliage that is heavily puckered. Gardeners will need a lot of space for the platter-sized leaves to develop — but even at that it makes an excellent specimen or large-scale groundcover. Expect this one to live up to its name.

Ferns and Ornamental Grasses
Despite their obvious lack of showy flowers, ferns and ornamental grasses contrast well against hostas, with their finely cut foliage, complementing variegation patterns, or both.

Dryopteris filix-mas "Linearis polydactyla" / *Ruffled Male Fern*

Athyrium otophorum / *Auriculate Lady Fern*

Dryopteris aff. ssp. affinis / *Golden-Scaled Male Fern*

Adiantum pedatum / *Maidenhair Fern*

Luzula sylvatica / *Greater Woodrush*

Carex siderostica "Variegata" / *Variegated Broad-Leaved Sedge*

Milium effusum "Aureum" / *Bowle's Golden Grass*

Carex morrowii "Aureo-variegata" / *Variegated Japanese Sedge*

Woodland Perennials

Dyann Goodfellow
Made in the Shade Nursery
Langley, B.C.

Woodland perennials can be described as herbaceous or evergreen plants that thrive in shady, humus-rich conditions. Most prefer an overhead canopy of both deciduous and coniferous trees, as this allows some light to penetrate from fall through to late spring. All of these plants can be adapted to garden situations with some attention to recreating woodland conditions.

Made in the Shade Nursery is a small cottage business that specializes in shade plants, including ferns, hostas, shrubs and ground covers. Located in a wooded area of Langley, the nursery borders a salmon river that runs through a mostly undisturbed forest, full of native woodland plants. One of the nursery's goals is to help gardeners appreciate foliage as the primary focus of the shade garden and to treat flowers as a bonus.

Kirengishoma palmata

HEIGHT: 1.2–1.5 M / 4–5 FT	SPREAD: 1.2–1.5 M / 4–5 FT	ZONE: 5

"Temple Bells" is a large structural plant that is in prime form from August until frost. The **pendulous** clusters of lemon-yellow bell flowers are held high above the unusual **palmate** leaves on this multi-stemmed perennial. Kirengishoma is herbaceous in nature and will form wide clumps in only a couple of years, when planted in the proper environment.

Euphorbia amygdaloides "Robbiae"

HEIGHT: 60–70 CM / 2–2¼ FT	SPREAD: 60 CM / 2 FT	ZONE: 6

This spreading euphorbia is almost a colour study in green. Chartreuse flowers are borne from May through July on shiny, dark green foliage, which is outstanding for the balance of the year. "Robbiae" is an evergreen perennial that thrives in dry shade once it is established.

Pulmonaria longifolia "Roy Davidson"

HEIGHT: 40–50 CM / 16–20 IN	SPREAD: 60–70 CM / 2–2¼ FT	ZONE: 3

"Roy Davidson" is an excellent form of lungwort with masses of baby blue flowers accented with strap-like foliage, which is heavily spotted in silver. This particular variety is not prone to mildew and self-seeds very little. As with any semi-evergreen perennial, trim off any spoiled foliage in early spring.

Polygonatum multiflorum

HEIGHT: 60–90 CM / 2–3 FT	SPREAD: 90 CM–1.2 M / 2–4 FT	ZONE: 3

Solomon's seal is a staple planting in the woodland garden or shade border. An abundance of white, bell-shaped flowers appear up the length of the arching stems in April and May. This herbaceous perennial is a great companion plant for hostas and ferns — or use it to soften the base of a tree.

Epimedium x *perralchicum* "Frohnleiten"

HEIGHT: 30–40 CM / 16 IN	SPREAD: 1.2–1.5 M / 4–5 FT	ZONE: 5

Dyann rates this plant as the most reliably evergreen barrenwort. The bright yellow spring flowers are followed by a fresh flush of leathery leaves, the foliage is generally a marbled bronze-green colour. The plant is quite a fast grower and can easily cover a square metre in three to four years.

Asarum europaeum

HEIGHT: 10–15 CM / 4–6 IN	SPREAD: 30 CM / 1 FT	ZONE: 4

European wild ginger makes a wonderful woodland carpet. This particular species has very shiny, rounded leaves with rather unusual brown flowers that appear under the

The Mulch Factor
Woodland plants are generally not very demanding, requiring very little fuss or feeding and, although their maintenance needs are quite simple, regular care is very necessary to preserve health and vigour. Those requirements can be summed up in just one word — mulch — and the most beneficial mulch is leaf mould. The lushest woodlands have a primarily deciduous or half deciduous/half coniferous forest canopy — so when trying to grow shade plants under evergreens, the gardener will have to be even more diligent with mulch. Leaf mould applied year after year will give the humusy, woodland soil that shade plants need, even if grown under conifers. The key is to apply it annually — just as the deciduous trees in the forest supply their cover every year. One proviso would be that the leaves must be chopped or shredded before being applied as a mulch. This helps them decompose rapidly and does not provide as welcome a cover for slugs and their eggs as would freshly fallen leaves. If a chipper is not available, the lawnmower works well — as does a weed trimmer placed in a garbage can full of leaves (a homemade leaf blender).

Woodland Ground Covers
Some of the following ground covers are fairly invasive in nature — but that is what makes them so useful for erosion control or covering utility areas. Some of them may be used as small accents to underplant shrubs or encircle taller perennials.

Maianthemum dilatatum / *False Lily–of–the–Valley*

Gaultheria procumbens / *Wintergreen*

Cornus canadensis
/ *Bunchberry*

Brunnera macrophylla
/ *Siberian Bugloss*

Waldsteinia ternata
/ *Barren Strawberry*

Tolmiea menziesii
/ *Piggyback Plant*

Gymnocarpium dryopteris
/ *Oak Fern*

Galium odoratum
/ *Sweet Woodruff*

Lysimachia nummularia
"Aurea" / Golden Creeping Jenny

Viola sempervirens
/ *Trailing Yellow Violet*

Planting a Fallen Log
Many gardens in forested areas come complete with half-rotten, fallen logs that make ideal natural planters. Use a chainsaw or axe to hollow out the centre portion of the log and fill the cavity with a blended, organic soil. If the wood still feels solid, be sure to cut or drill a few drainage holes in the bottom. The planting material is the gardener's choice, but ferns, low perennials and small shrubs (i.e., Mahonia nervosa) will all work well. It might be nice to soften the base or ends of the log with a few evergreen plants, such as deer fern or salal (Gaultheria shallon).

foliage. The reference to ginger comes from the distinct odour that is released when the leaves and stems are crushed. It is a semi-evergreen plant, which can be a little slow to establish.

Tiarella cordifolia "Mint Chocolate"

HEIGHT: 20–30 CM / 8 IN–1 FT   SPREAD: 30–50 CM / 1–1½ FT   ZONE: 4

The many hybrids of tiarellas native to eastern Canada, and the closely related heucheras, are quickly gaining popularity. This variety has a distinctive cross-shaped leaf overlaid in chocolate brown. The delicate sprays of light pink, bottlebrush flowers appear in late spring through to summer. Foamflower has evergreen foliage that becomes more colourful (bronze) as the season progresses.

Hacquetia epipactis

HEIGHT: 10–15 CM / 4–6 IN   SPREAD: 40–50 CM / 16–18 IN   ZONE: 5

A unique little woodlander that flowers very early — usually February to April — it features tiny, clustered yellow flowers surrounded by green **bracts** on a small plant that slowly spreads into a small mat. This herbaceous perennial is a native of the eastern Alps in Europe.

Sanguinaria canadensis "Flore Pleno"

HEIGHT: 15 CM+ / 6 IN+   SPREAD: 30 CM / 1 FT   ZONE: 3

Bloodroot is a native of eastern Canada, and this particular cultivar is the longer flowering, double form of this plant. Even at that, gardeners may find the display of pure white flowers quite fleeting. The leaves emerge from the ground folded vertically and open to reveal variably lobed, blue-grey foliage that turns to a beautiful gold colour before dormancy. As the common name implies, a red sap exudes from the fleshy roots.

Dicentra formosa "Luxuriant"

HEIGHT: 20–30 CM / 8 IN–1 FT   SPREAD: 30–40 CM / 16 IN   ZONE: 2

This low-growing bleeding heart is superior to our native species for its long blooming period and durable foliage. "Luxuriant" features cherry-red, heart-shaped flowers from spring through to early fall, and finely cut blue-green leaves — reminiscent of fern. Combine this herbaceous perennial with bold-leaved perennials, such as hostas.

Woodland Perennials Native to the Pacific Northwest
All of the following perennials are available as cultivated stock from retail nurseries. Never remove native plants from the wild.

Erythronium revolutum / *Pink Fawn Lily*

Achlys triphylla / *Vanilla-Leaf*

Smilacina racemosa / *False Solomon's Seal*

Adiantum pedatum / *Maidenhair Fern*

Trillium ovatum / *Western Trillium*

Linnaea borealis / *Twinflower*

Aruncus sylvester / *Goat's Beard*

Tiarella trifoliata / *Foamflower*

Goodyera oblongifolia / *Rattlesnake Plantain*

Disporum hookeri / *Hooker's Fairybells*

Ferns

Richard Fraser
Fraser's Thimble Farm
Salt Spring Island, B.C.

Ferns are one of the most overlooked and underutilized groups of perennials and until recently, very few were available. This diverse group of plants can be most satisfying to grow and are among the easiest perennials to culture, thriving even on neglected sites. From the glossy, strap-shaped leaves of the hart's tongue fern to the pinkish new **fronds** of *Blechnum penna-marina* to the palm-like *Dicksonia* (tree fern), there is a fern to suit every gardener.

All of these exciting plants can be found at Fraser's Thimble Farm, along with an impressive array of Pacific Northwest natives, woodland perennials and other rarities — all naturally displayed in a forested nursery on the northern tip of Salt Spring Island. For gardeners unable to visit, Richard offers much of his stock through mail order, and his catalogue is a wealth of helpful plant information. Like many seasoned gardeners, he had a difficult time choosing only 10 ferns to recommend — especially when his favourites seem to change every time a new introduction comes along. So, for the benefit of this place in time, here are Richard's "current" top 10 ferns.

Polystichum polyblepharum / **Japanese Tassel Fern**

HEIGHT: 60–70 CM / 2–2¼ FT	ZONE: 5

This is a fantastic evergreen fern with lustrous, dark green mature foliage and slightly lighter green younger fronds. It features fuzzy brown **croziers** that unfurl into perfectly arching fronds. Quite tall, it is a great specimen or background plant. This very shiny, attractive fern will thrive in shade to part sun with average soil.

Osmunda cinnamomea / Cinnamon Fern

HEIGHT: 90 CM–1.5 M / 3–5 FT   ZONE: 4

Imagine a perfect fern with arching fronds and a cluster of cinnamon-coloured feather dusters in the centre. The sterile, mid-green fronds are deeply lobed and held in vase-shaped clusters — while the **fertile fronds** are erect and held centrally, lack leaves and have terminal **panicles**, which turn from green to a cinnamon colour. It is hard to beat this species once it is established. Tolerant of shade to part sun with drier soil, it will thrive in full sun in moist sites. Deciduous.

Adiantum aleuticum / Maidenhair Fern

HEIGHT: 40 CM / 16 IN   ZONE: 3

A **deciduous** fern, maidenhair fern bears delicate, fan-shaped fronds with lacy green leaves set atop shiny black stems. This plant will form impressive clumps over time, provided it is planted in moist, humus-rich soil. Maidenhair fern will also do well in full sun if enough moisture is present.

Blechnum penna-marina solidus / Falkland Islands Fern

HEIGHT: 10–20 CM / 4–8 IN   ZONE: 5

This fern comes to us from the islands off South America and its new frond colouration is a unique pinkish-bronze, which ages to a rich dark green. The **fertile fronds** are quite erect, while the sterile fronds lie more or less flat. A small, spreading fern useful in the rock garden or for use as a low ground cover, this fern is evergreen.

Fertile Fronds

*While it is true that ferns do not bear flowers, many have fertile fronds that are just as showy. The average fern carries its reproductive structure (*spores*) on the underside of the fronds, but a few have separate reproductive fronds or distinct clusters. These are "blooming ferns" and are highly recommended for the shade border. Osmunda cinnamomea (*cinnamon fern*) is a favourite — with pale green, feather duster-like fertile fronds that turn a rich cinnamon colour and persist for quite some time, thus enhancing the show. The closely related Osmunda claytonia (*interrupted fern*) has a jet black fertile structure in the middle of the fronds, interrupting the green* **pinnae** *and providing a striking contrast to the vivid green foliage. The fertile fronds of Blechnum spicant (*deer fern*) are held erect, while the broader sterile fronds lie quite horizontal, giving a distinct two-tiered effect. A few other ferns that exhibit these fertile fronds are Osmunda regalis (*royal fern*), Onoclea sensibilis (*sensitive fern*), Blechnum penna-marina (*alpine water fern*), Woodwardia areolata (*narrow chain fern*) and Matteuccia struthiopteris (*ostrich fern*).*

Sun-tolerant Ferns

Most of the following sun-tolerant ferns require even soil moisture.

Polystichum munitum / *Sword Fern*
Blechnum spicant / *Deer Fern*
Cheilanthes lanosa / *Hairy Lip Fern*
Polystichum braunii / *Braun's Holly Fern*
Polypodium glycyrrhiza / *Licorice Fern*

Polystichum neolobatum / Long-Eared Holly Fern

HEIGHT: 30–60 CM / 1–2 FT	ZONE: 5

This is another Asian beauty with stiff textured, glossy green fronds. Long-eared holly fern is an excellent com-panion for *P. polyblepharum* and thrives in shade to part sun. A good plant to use when one wants shiny foliage — as the narrow fronds are held somewhat upright and are evergreen. This is one of our favourites, a real looker.

Phyllitis scolopendrium / Hart's Tongue Fern

HEIGHT: 40 CM / 16 IN	ZONE: 5

An easy plant to identify, the medium green fronds of hart's tongue fern are strap or tongue-shaped with no division at all. Hart's tongue fern is reliably evergreen and needs the addition of lime from time to time to raise the pH. It is also known as *Asplenium scolopendrium*.

Dryopteris affinis "Cristata the King"

HEIGHT: 70 CM–1 M / 2¼–3¼ FT	ZONE: 4

The new frond stalks of this evergreen fern are densely covered in beautiful golden-brown scales. Mature foliage has a glossy, dark green texture and is well crested. This is a robust fern for shade to part sun.

Polypodium vulgare "Bifidum Multifidum" / Crested Polypody Fern

HEIGHT: 25–35 CM / 10–14 IN	ZONE: 5

This is a small, showy fern for rock walls and rockeries, as it slowly spreads along the cracks. The **pinnae** tips on this particular **cultivar** are forked and, like many polypodi-ums, it can withstand extreme drought in summer. It tol-erates these extremes by going dormant during droughts and then leafing out again when moisture permits. It is easily grown, but rare.

Dryopteris dilatata "Jimmy Dyce"

HEIGHT: 50–60 CM / 20 IN–2 FT   ZONE: 4

An unusual, stiffly erect fern, this dryopteris bears very nice dark bluish-green foliage. This evergreen plant was originally collected by Jimmy Dyce from the Isle of Arran. It is easy to grow in shade to part sun.

Polystichum setiferum
"Divisilobum"/ Divided Soft Shield Fern

HEIGHT: 25–50 CM / 10–20 IN   ZONE: 5

A beautiful medium-sized fern, the fronds of divided soft shield fern are four times divided, with finely cut segments. This lends a very lacy appearance to this plant and, with age, it can develop almost a three-dimensional look. This evergreen fern is suitable in shade to part sun.

Colour and Texture
It should not be too surprising that ferns can be used either in mass or as specimens to add colour or to lighten a shady spot. The light apple-green fronds of Dryopteris carthusiana *(Golden Shield Fern) contrast nicely with the dark green foliage of* Dryopteris affinis *"Cristata the King." For a little colour in the shade border, try the silver hue of* Athyrium niponicum *"Pictum" (Japanese Painted Fern) or the pinkish-red new fronds of* Dryopteris erythrosora *(Autumn Fern). Lovely green foliage is not all that ferns have to offer — they also provide an amazing range of textures, from the delicate* Gymnocarpium dryopteris *(Oak Fern) to the harsh fronds of (Scott's Wood Fern) to the soft texture of* Polystichum setiferum. *Many ferns look more like other plants than ferns —* Cyrtomium caryotideum *bears a close resemblance to Oregon Grape (*Mahonia aquifolium*) while a crested form of Hart's Tongue Fern (*Asplenium scolopendrium *"Kaye's Laceratum") has fronds that look almost like a leaf of lettuce.*

Companion Plants for Ferns
Oxalis oregana / *Redwood Sorrel*
Dicentra formosa / *Western Bleeding Heart*
Trillium species / *Wake Robin*
Anemone nemerosa / *Wood Anemone*
Linnaea borealis / *Twinflower*
Helleborus cultivars / *Hellebores*
Jeffersonia diphylla / *American Twinleaf*
Hostas cultivars / *Plantain Lily*
Dodecatheon dentatum / *Shooting Star*
Anemonella thalictroides / *Rue Anemone*

Specimen Perennials

John Valleau
Valleybrook Gardens
Heritage Perennials
Abbotsford, B.C.

Bold, large-leaved perennials seem to frighten a lot of gardeners — it could be some genetic instinct from our Jurassic beginnings or perhaps emotional scars from those scary "man-eating plant" movies of childhood. In any case, when hearing about an interesting plant, many people cringe at the thought of unleashing a perennial in the garden that will get bigger than themselves. Fortunately, most of these bold specimens are just big pussycats, with little tendency to invade the rest of the landscape. The scale of foliage and flower is certainly larger than many gardeners are used to, but these are focal points, not blending plants — the very thing we sometimes need to lend an air of the exotic.

Valleybrook Gardens was started by John and Kelly Schroeder in 1980 — initially as a grower of shrub **liners**, heaths and heathers. They began to produce container perennials shortly after, just when this group of plants was gaining widespread popularity once again. John Valleau joined the company in 1987, taking over the job of producing the wholesale catalogue, which eventually became a self-published book entitled the *Heritage Perennial Gardening Guide*, now in its third edition. He moved to the Niagara area in 1988 to start a sister nursery supplying eastern Canada, and now functions as corporate horticulturist.

Eupatorium maculatum

HEIGHT: 2–3 M / 7–10 FT	SPREAD: 90 CM / 3 FT	ZONE: 7
FLOWERING PERIOD: AUG–OCT		

Often described as an architectural plant, "Joe-Pye Weed" forms a very large clump of coarse, medium-green leaves that are arranged around the stems in whorls — much like the spokes of a wheel. Big umbrella-like heads of rosy-purple flowers appear in late summer and fall, attracting much attention from both people and butterflies. This plant suits a prime spot toward the back or middle of the border, preferring a sunny site with rich, moist soil. The selection "Gateway" is a little shorter than the rest of the species.

Acanthus mollis / Bear's Breeches

HEIGHT: 90 CM–1.5 M / 3–5 FT	SPREAD: 90 CM / 3 FT	ZONE: 7
FLOWERING PERIOD: JULY–AUG		

This bold specimen plant is very popular with landscape designers for use in both the perennial border and tubs and containers. The foliage is quite large and vaguely rounded in outline, with deep lobes and a smooth, polished finish on top. Bear's Breeches can get quite enormous over time and produces tall spikes of mauve-pink flowers in mid-summer, which are excellent for cutting. Gardeners in coastal regions of the Pacific Northwest are fortunate because they can easily succeed with this species, which is difficult to winter in other parts of North America.

Angelica gigas / Red-Flowered Angelica

HEIGHT: 90 CM–1.25 M / 3–4 FT	SPREAD: 75 CM / 30 IN	ZONE: 4
FLOWERING PERIOD: JULY–AUG		

A cousin to common parsley and dill, Red-Flowered Angelica was all the rage among elite gardeners a few years back. Plants can only be described as stout in nature, producing (in the second year from seed) a tall, upright stem that branches several times along the way to bearing huge **umbels** of crimson-red flowers — which are quite nice for cutting, if you can bring yourself to do it. Since this is a short-lived perennial or **biennial**, allow some of the fallen seeds to germinate for future generations to appear.

Giving Them Room

Many of these bold specimen perennials will take up a fair bit of space and for the most part require a rich, moist soil — because of the large amount of foliage transpiring during summer. These plants will show when they need water, usually appearing a little wilted toward the end of the afternoon but perking up quickly after a deep watering. For the shade-lovers, avoid sites where they would be competing with the roots of large trees, particularly conifers and maples. Since these plants form sizeable clumps and may take a few years to reach mature height and spread, they are not likely to need dividing for awhile. When they become thin in the middle, simply lift the entire plant in spring, choose the strongest outside pieces for division and replant. The larger the remaining root, the sooner the plant will mature and, with these selections, size matters!

Cimicifuga simplex "Brunette" / Bugbane

HEIGHT: 1.5–2 M / 5–6½ FT	SPREAD: 75 CM / 30 IN	ZONE: 4
FLOWERING PERIOD: AUG–SEPT		

This bugbane features very exotic foliage, forming a medium-sized clump of dark purple, lacy leaves reminiscent of astilbe. The rich black-purple foliage tones come out best when the plant is grown in some direct sun, with a morning exposure being particularly good. In late summer or early fall, tall stems are formed, bearing nodding wands of the palest pink bottlebrush flowers, which are sweetly fragrant over quite a distance. "Brunette" was virtually impossible to obtain until recently, with large numbers of plants being produced through the modern miracle of tissue culture cloning.

Gunnera manicata

HEIGHT: 1.8–3 M / 6–10 FT	SPREAD: 1.8 M+ / 6 FT+	ZONE: 7
FLOWERING PERIOD: JULY–AUG		

The gunnera is probably the first plant that most gardeners in the Pacific Northwest think of when asked to name a bold perennial, to the point that the plant has nearly become a cliche. The huge prehistoric-looking stands of this species in places like VanDusen Gardens and Queen Elizabeth Park are a true spectacle to behold. Those enormous, rough leaves demand a constant supply of moisture, so a waterside planting is the perfect location. For those of you looking for something along the lines of a miniature gunnera, try *Darmera peltata*, which matures at around 90 cm–1.25 m / 3–4 ft tall.

Macleaya cordata / Plume Poppy

HEIGHT: 1.8–2.5 M / 6–8 FT	SPREAD: 90 CM–1.25 M+ / 3–4 FT+	ZONE: 2
FLOWERING PERIOD: JULY–AUG		

I could not resist including just one "thug" on the list. This plant will certainly romp and spread throughout the sunny border, sometimes growing not at all where desired. That being said, the Plume Poppy is a classic perennial with very tall stems that produce some of the finest leaf texture and colour, with a display of creamy plumes overhead in mid summer. The large leaves are deeply lobed and covered in a striking, powdery blue finish. This is a favourite plant for cutting, and the gardener will learn to live with its spreading nature, as the shoots that pop up in odd places are easy enough to pull out.

Podophyllum pleianthum

HEIGHT: 60–70 CM / 24–30 IN	SPREAD: 60–70 CM / 24–30 IN	ZONE: 6
FLOWERING PERIOD: MAY		

An exotic relative of our native mayapple, this charming woodland perennial comes to us from Taiwan and China. These plants bear huge, glossy leaves held in pairs on medium-tall stems — similar in size and shape to the common fatsia. The clusters of oxblood-red flowers are produced close to the main stem and later mature to silvery, then finally yellow pods. Where this plant truly shines is near shaded entranceways, with contrasting fine-textured ferns as companions.

Rudbeckia nitida "Herbstsonne"

HEIGHT: 1.5–2.5 M / 5–8 FT	SPREAD: 90 CM–1.25 M / 3–4 FT	ZONE: 2
FLOWERING PERIOD: JULY–AUG		

Another monstrous grower, suited to the back of a small or large border, this coneflower performs admirably when given enough moisture through the summer. It offers a long display of huge, lemon-yellow flowers with brownish cones encircled by the graceful drooping petals. The rigid stems mean that this perennial seldom needs staking unless it is grown on soil that is too rich. Our friend Geoff Lewis often describes it as the "Godzilla of coneflowers."

Maintenance Tricks

Some of the taller perennials will require staking, but see what they do in the garden for the first season. If they fall over or get too floppy, try and remember to use a few stout bamboo stakes early in the season the following year — so the plants can be securely tied in. The idea is to make the stakes and strings as unobtrusive as possible. Some of these perennials will have good winter interest, others not — so leave them the first couple of years and then decide. If they give the wrong effect, simply cut them back to the ground in late fall.

Miscanthus sinensis Cultivars

HEIGHT: 90 CM–2.75 M / 3–9 FT	SPREAD: 90 CM / 3 FT	ZONE: 4–6
FLOWERING PERIOD: AUG–OCT		

From coast to coast, this group of ornamental grasses has taken gardens by storm. Among the tallest of ornamental grasses, these have the added feature of being very well behaved and not spreading throughout the garden. Many selections of Japanese silver grass are now available in a variety of foliage textures, heights and flower colours. All produce upright clumps of long, grassy leaves followed by showy plumes in fall and winter. Some of the better cultivars include "Variegatus" (striped lengthwise in white), "Zebrinus" (gold horizontal bands) and "Gracillimus" (narrow, thread-like leaves).

Rodgersia Species

HEIGHT: 90 CM–1.25 M / 3–4 FT	SPREAD: 75 CM / 30 IN	ZONE: 4–9
FLOWERING PERIOD: JULY–AUG		

This group of plants is deserving of much wider use in our gardens and is well suited to the climate of the Pacific Northwest. They produce a long-lived clump of coarse foliage — reminiscent of horse chestnut or elderberry leaves in size and texture. Above them, upright spikes of fluffy flowers appear in summer, similar to the plumes of astilbe, in shades of white, ivory or pink. A moist woodland setting in partial shade is ideal, but these plants will tolerate full sun if the soil is constantly wet. Several selections are available, including *R. aesculifolia* (white), *R. henrici* (rose-pink) or *R. pinnata* "Elegans" (creamy-white).

Daylilies

Daylilies (*Hemerocallis*) are herbaceous perennials and probably one of the easiest plants to grow no matter where you live. While part of the *Lilium* family, they are not to be confused with the Asiatic, Oriental or trumpet bulb lilies. Each flower does indeed last for one day as the name implies, but the profusion of buds on the flower **scape** allows the plant to bloom for a long time — so that discerning gardeners can have continual flowering from May to October!

Erikson's Daylily Gardens has the largest display of *Hemerocallis* in Canada, with more than 1,600 varieties planted in a natural setting among other perennials and specimen trees. The garden itself is an official American Hemerocallis Society display site and is open to the public for viewing during peak bloom time in July. Pam Erikson also offers retail and mail-order sales, and is currently concentrating on breeding new varieties for the colder Canadian climate.

There are currently more than 40,000 registered varieties of daylilies, with 1,000 new **cultivars** being added each year. While all are beautiful, certain varieties will always stand out for either aesthetic (i.e., form and colour) or practical (hardiness and blooming period) reasons. All plants from Erikson's are tested in diverse weather conditions, with the following being Pam's most recent recommendations.

Pam Erikson
Erikson's Daylily Gardens
Langley, B.C.

Hemerocallis "Janice Brown"

HEIGHT: 50 CM / 20 IN	SPREAD: 60 CM / 2 FT	ZONE: 2
FLOWERING PERIOD: JULY–SEPT		

An award-winning, light pink daylily with a deep rose **eyezone**, "Janice Brown" produces 10-cm / 4-in wide flowers that open by 7 AM, no matter how cool the weather. The beauty of this variety is that it starts blooming in early July and continues easily through to September.

Hemerocallis "Banquet at Versailles"

HEIGHT: 60 CM / 2 FT	SPREAD: 60 CM / 2 FT	ZONE: 4
FLOWERING PERIOD: JULY–AUG, SEPT–OCT		

A new variety out of Florida, this one may be hard to get right now, but in a few years it is expected to be a highly popular **cultivar**. It features large, 15-cm / 6-in wide soft purple blossoms with an outstanding heavy gold, braided edge. "Banquet at Versailles" is a good rebloomer, meaning that it will take a short rest in late summer and continue flowering through September and October.

Hemerocallis "Satisfaction in Syracuse"

HEIGHT: 55 CM / 22 IN	SPREAD: 60 CM / 2 FT	ZONE: 2
FLOWERING PERIOD: JULY–AUG		

This is a brand new **cultivar** that was created at Erikson's. The 10-cm / 4-in wide flowers display a dark maroon-purple **eyezone**, which is a fabulous contrast to the soft orchid pink petals. "Satisfaction in Syracuse" is also slightly fragrant, which is an unusual trait when considering that most scented daylilies are yellow in colour.

Hemerocallis "Stella de Oro"

HEIGHT: 35 CM / 14 IN	SPREAD: 35 CM / 14 IN	ZONE: 2
FLOWERING PERIOD: MAY–NOV		

Still one of the world's best selling, *Hemerocallis* "Stella de Oro" is a miniature, with 7-cm / 3-in wide ruffled blooms of soft gold. This is not just a reblooming daylily, it is a continual bloomer — sending up **scapes** constantly from May to November. Only a very hard frost will eventually knock this plant down for a rest.

Hemerocallis "Tuscawilla Tigress"

HEIGHT: 75 CM / 30 IN	SPREAD: 90 CM / 3 FT	ZONE: 4
FLOWERING PERIOD: JULY–OCT		

Hot orange! Not many people want to work with this colour in their gardens, but this plant is worth a try simply because it will amaze. "Tuscawilla Tigress" stands a little taller than most daylilies and makes a wonderful backdrop or centrepiece feature. It blooms heavily from summer right into fall, with the last flowers appearing in my southern B.C. garden in mid-November.

Hemerocallis "Puddin"

HEIGHT: 60 CM / 2 FT	SPREAD: 60 CM / 2 FT	ZONE: 2
FLOWERING PERIOD: JULY–AUG		

An older variety and fairly easy to find, this soft lemon-yellow cultivar produces such masses of flower **scapes**, that it is a display all on its own! Despite its smaller blooms measuring just 7 cm / 3 in across, "Puddin" is an extremely heavy bloomer during the months of July and August.

Hemerocallis "Canadian Border Patrol"

HEIGHT: 65 CM / 26 IN	SPREAD: 75 CM / 30 IN	ZONE: 4
FLOWERING PERIOD: JULY–SEPT		

This newer variety may be hard to find, but is worth the search. It features huge 15-cm / 6-in wide blooms that sit atop a tall plant. The flowers are of a soft cream with a big maroon **eyezone** and delicate **picotee** edge of the same colour.

Planting Tip
Try planting daffodil and tulip bulbs around daylilies — the bulbs will come up early in the spring and bloom just as your Hemerocallis *are emerging. As the foliage of the spring bulbs starts to look messy (leave it intact to replenish the bulb for the following year), the daylily foliage will grow up and gracefully arc over the decaying tulip or daffodil leaves.*

Hemerocallis "All in the Attitude"

HEIGHT: 50 CM / 20 IN	SPREAD: 60 CM / 2 FT	ZONE: 2
FLOWERING PERIOD: JULY–SEPT		

Another new introduction from Erikson's, this smaller plant attracted the attention of many visitors to the nursery last year. One of our breeding lines is geared toward the gardener who works in small spaces or patio areas, and this variety makes a wonderful container plant. The 9-cm / 3½-in wide blooms are a soft lavender-pink with an outstanding broad purple eyezone.

Hemerocallis "Wine Me Dine Me"

HEIGHT: 50 CM / 20 IN	SPREAD: 45 CM / 18 IN	ZONE: 2
FLOWERING PERIOD: JULY–SEPT		

A relatively new miniature, this daylily is also well suited for containers and borders. This **cultivar** features 7-cm / 3-in wide blossoms of a soft ivory cream-yellow, contrasted with a wide maroon eye. The most loveable thing about this flower is the echo effect in the eye pattern with a halo of soft pink in between the maroon eye and the intense lime-green throat.

Border Perennials

Perennials are a beautiful component of any landscape, providing colour and interest throughout the year. Gardeners in the Pacific Northwest are particularly fortunate with the large selection available — and the many possible combinations of height, spread, flowering periods and foliage textures. Perennial borders provide a living canvas for these plants — with surprise bursts and shifts of colour as spring moves to summer, and summer wanes into autumn.

Clare Philips
Phoenix Perennials Nursery
Vancouver, B.C.

Clare Philips developed Phoenix Perennials Nursery to provide a wide range of hardy plants for the gardens she designs in Vancouver and outlying regions. Both the perennials (**herbaceous** and evergreen) and the flowering shrubs she grows are selected for their reliability, ease of care, long flowering periods, interesting foliage and broad spectrum of colour. The stock seems to change constantly as Clare finds new and more interesting plants to add to her designs.

Geranium macrorrhizum "Bigroot Cranesbill"

HEIGHT: 30 CM / 1 FT	SPREAD: 60 CM / 2 FT	ZONE: 2
FLOWERING PERIOD: MAY–JULY		

This geranium features fragrant leaves that form a dense ground cover for the front of the border. This particular species tolerates dry shade quite well, making it an excellent choice for planting below cedars. The magenta-pink flowers are borne in early summer, followed by attractive autumn foliage. Several **cultivars** are available, including "Bevan's Variety" (deep magenta-pink) and "Ingwersen's Variety" (pale pink).

Penstemon glaber

HEIGHT: 30 CM / 1 FT	SPREAD: 30–40 CM / 16 IN	ZONE: 5
FLOWERING PERIOD: SUMMER		

A long-flowering perennial, this penstemon bears unusual tubular, blue-pink flowers emerging from a mound of attractive evergreen foliage. While some **deadheading** may be required, the plant provides a long succession of cut flowers and is best suited for the mid–front of the border. This beardtongue is native to the central United States.

Anthriscus sylvestris "Raven's Wing"

HEIGHT: 90 CM / 3 FT	SPREAD: 60 CM / 2 FT	ZONE: 7
FLOWERING PERIOD: SPRING		

One of the popular "black-leaved" plants, "Raven's Wing's" masses of lacy plum foliage contrast well with the early lime-green growth of many perennials. The **umbels** of tiny pale pink flowers much resemble a spray of baby's breath (*Gypsophila*). This is a short-lived perennial with a tendency to self-sow, so be sure to **deadhead** before the seeds set, but leave a few to provide for the next generation.

Geranium phaeum "Lily Lovell"

HEIGHT: 60 CM+ / 2 FT+	SPREAD: 60 CM+ / 2 FT+	ZONE: 5
FLOWERING PERIOD: LATE SPRING–SUMMER		

One of the earliest perennial geraniums to come into flower (May), it forms mounds of light green foliage. The perfectly formed violet-mauve blooms are a good foil for peach-coloured poppies (i.e., *Papaver orientale* "Carneum") or *Geum rivale* "Leonard's Variety." Place this plant in the mid-border and be sure to deadhead to get a late summer repeat flowering.

Veronica whitleyi

HEIGHT: 5–10 CM / 2–4 IN	SPREAD: 30–40 CM+ / 16 IN	ZONE: 3
FLOWERING PERIOD: SPRING–EARLY SUMMER		

An impressive low edger with tiny grey-green leaves, this veronica forms a dense mat or ground cover. The foliage is shrouded for months in a mass of sky-blue flowers contrasted with white centres. Pair this semi-evergreen perennial with plum-leaved *heucheras* (i.e., "Emperor's Cloak" or "Pewter Veil") or *Geranium sessiliflorum* "Nigricans."

Agastache foeniculum "Alba"

HEIGHT: 60–80 CM / 24–32 IN	SPREAD: 60 CM / 2 FT	ZONE: 2
FLOWERING PERIOD: SUMMER–FALL		

Anise hyssop is a bold prairie native with wands of creamy-green flowers held very erectly. The August blooms help to revive the waning perennial border and they look spectacular in late summer sunsets. A herbal tea can be made from the deliciously scented foliage, which is reminiscent of anise.

Salvia verticillata "Purple Rain"

HEIGHT: 50 CM+ / 20 IN+	SPREAD: 60 CM / 2 FT	ZONE: 6
FLOWERING PERIOD: JUNE–OCT		

This ornamental sage bears masses of violet-purple flowers on arching stems over mounded foliage. This herbaceous perennial will continue to bloom from June to October if it is sheared back or **deadheaded**. A lovely alternative to nepeta (catmint) in combination with roses.

Geranium wallichianum "Buxton's Variety"

HEIGHT: 30–50 CM / 1–1½ FT	SPREAD: 30 CM+ / 1 FT+	ZONE: 5
FLOWERING PERIOD: SUMMER–FALL		

Also known as "Buxton's Blue," this attractive cranesbill is fairly low in its growth habit but will gladly sprawl into obliging neighbours, such as *Penstemon* "Garnet" and

Designing a Perennial Border

Planning the Beds
When designing a bed, be sure to leave enough room for flowering perennials so that there is enough space for a number of drifts between the front of the border and its backdrop (usually a fence or shrubbery) — as it is extremely difficult to get lush, cross-seasonal effects without adequate bed width. Consider 1.2–1.5 m / 4–5 ft as a minimal depth, with areas 3.5–4.5 m / 12–15 ft wide creating exceptional borders.

Using Colour
Consider limiting the colour palette initially, expanding it as the border matures. Too many colours may result in a tense, unrestful space that can appear overcrowded. Try starting with just two or three colours and then add sparingly when a section needs a bit of brightening. The perennial garden can and should evolve, changing with age and the gardener's interests.

Plant Texture
When choosing plants, consider the many foliage textures available. Some examples would be spiky (Iris sibirica), rounded (Phlox paniculata), architectural (Euphorbia c. wulfenii) and wandering (Verbena bonariensis). These different textures can be very useful additions to the garden's design and are often used to emphasize focal points in the landscape. Plan the garden's plant material with as much attention as you have given your home, and you will not be disappointed with your garden.

Knautia macedonica. The nearly pure blue flowers are quite large and accented with a white centre and slightly mottled foliage.

Euphorbia characias wulfenii

HEIGHT: 1.2–1.8 M / 4–6 FT	SPREAD: 60–90 CM / 2–3 FT	ZONE: 7
FLOWERING PERIOD: SPRING		

This bold architectural plant lends a powerful blue-green focus to the landscape — accenting a sunny doorway or punctuating the back of the border. As well, this evergreen spurge bears stunningly huge clusters of greenish-yellow flowers. Be sure to give it enough space and cut back the flower stem after it blooms to encourage new growth for next year's display.

Irises & Peonies

Peonies are some of the most beloved perennials, giving magnificent blossoms that range from the purest white to deep reds, verging on black. Irises also hold a prominent place in spring and early summer's glorious celebration — with the many "tall bearded" varieties often providing the most spectacular show of the season. Together, these perennials form the backbone of many remarkable formal borders or old-fashioned cottage gardens.

David Jack and his wife, Sheila, have owned and operated Ferncliff Gardens for more than 25 years. This specialty mail-order nursery had its beginnings with his grandfather back in 1920 and David would, quite literally, grow up with the family business. Situated on a fertile bench overlooking the Fraser River in Mission, this field growing operation is presently a major supplier of irises, peonies and dahlias — all of which can be viewed on site in full bloom.

David Jack
Ferncliff Gardens
Mission, B.C.

Paeonia "Age of Gold" (Hybrid Tree Peony)

HEIGHT: 1.2 M / 4 FT	SPREAD: 75 CM / 30 IN	ZONE: 4
FLOWERING PERIOD: EARLY JUNE	APS GOLD MEDAL WINNER 1973	

This semi-double hybrid features creamy-yellow flowers that deepen to gold and are accented with small red flares at the base of each petal. The medium-sized blooms are produced well above the attractive foliage on this hardy plant.

Paeonia "America" (Herbaceous Single)

HEIGHT: 75 CM / 30 IN	SPREAD: 50 CM / 20 IN	ZONE: 2
FLOWERING PERIOD: LATE MAY	APS GOLD MEDAL WINNER 1992	

This peony is a large single hybrid of brilliant scarlet, a hue with great carrying power in any landscape. The stems are quite straight and rigid, displaying the vibrant blooms perfectly.

Paeonia "Festiva Maxima" (Herbaceous Double)

HEIGHT: 90 CM / 3 FT	SPREAD: 60 CM / 2 FT	ZONE: 2
FLOWERING PERIOD: LATE MAY–EARLY JUNE		

The most popular old white, this peony was first introduced in 1851 by Miellez. It features large, double blooms that are fragrant and quite unusual for their contrasting crimson flecks and globular form. This peony is also quite floriferous.

Paeonia "Gay Paree" (Herbaceous Japanese)

HEIGHT: 80 CM / 32 IN	SPREAD: 45 CM / 18 IN	ZONE: 2
FLOWERING PERIOD: EARLY JUNE		

This novelty peony is very bright and extraordinarily beautiful. The bicolour blooms have creamy-white centres encircled with cerise-pink petals. It is a good choice for those gardeners with a taste for the unusual.

Paeonia "Red Charm" (Herbaceous Double)

HEIGHT: 80 CM / 32 IN	SPREAD: 60 CM / 2 FT	ZONE: 2
FLOWERING PERIOD: MID–LATE MAY	APS GOLD MEDAL WINNER 1956	

Jack has been known to say that if he could have only one peony in the garden, this would be it. The waxy, dark red flowers develop into a high rounded mound, surrounded with a skirt of broad collar petals. The plant exhibits a beautiful balance of vibrant colour and attractive form.

Iris "Vanity"

HEIGHT: 90 CM / 3 FT	SPREAD: 30 CM / 1 FT	ZONE: 4
FLOWERING PERIOD: MID–LATE MAY		

This very reliable iris was first introduced back in 1928. "Vanity" features well-formed blooms of a medium pink, with lighter **falls** and contrasting red **beards**. This particular **cultivar** is very hardy.

Iris "Ask Alma"

HEIGHT: 45 CM / 18 IN	SPREAD: 30 CM / 1 FT	ZONE: 3
FLOWERING PERIOD: MID MAY		

This intermediate iris fills the gap in the flowering period, blooming just after the dwarfs but before the tall bearded. It features rich, shrimp-pink blossoms with good form. This vigorous plant deserves a place at the front of a mixed perennial border.

Iris "Jazzed Up"

HEIGHT: 1 M / 40 IN	SPREAD: 30 CM / 1 FT	ZONE: 4
FLOWERING PERIOD: EARLY JUNE		

In a simple phrase, this iris is best described as a "huge ruffled beauty." The gently formed flowers are pleasantly accented with white **standards** and wide, rosy-lavender **falls**. This is a bold cultivar, growing quite tall.

Iris "Sun Doll"

HEIGHT: 25 CM / 10 IN	SPREAD: 20 CM / 8 IN	ZONE: 3
FLOWERING PERIOD: LATE APRIL		

"Sun Doll" is a dwarf bearded iris with remarkable bright yellow blooms. The flower petals are wide and ruffled, often overpowering the diminutive plant below. This iris is absolutely stunning when contrasted with red tulips.

Planting Iris

For the best results, iris should be planted from July to September in a full sun exposure with good drainage. Iris will grow in any good garden soil but, for the best growth and blooms, incorporate some 4–10–10 fertilizer into the soil along with a generous application of bonemeal. If the pH is acidic, amend the soil with some ground limestone. Dig a wide, shallow planting hole with a small raised mound in the middle — place the **rhizome** *on the mound and spread the roots out around it. Be sure to set the rhizomes with the fans facing the outer edge of the bed, so that future growth will not result in crowding. Fill the hole with soil, making sure that the rhizome is just at the surface and barely exposed. Water it in with a good transplant fertilizer (i.e., 10–52–10) but be sure to provide even moisture when the weather is dry. A spacing of 30–45 cm / 12–18 in between plants is usually sufficient.*

Planting Peonies

It is best to plant peonies in the fall — this also applies to dividing established clumps, which should be divided in the fall and not in spring. Start by choosing a site in full sun with well-drained soil. The original planting should allow plenty of room for growth, with a spacing of 60 cm–1.2 m / 2–4 ft between crowns. When properly planted, peonies can be left undisturbed for up to 15 years or more. Dig a hole large enough to accommodate the root system (30 cm / 12 in wide and deep) and improve the existing soil by adding bonemeal, compost, alfalfa pellets and about 250 ml / 1 cup of ground limestone. The depth of the planting is very important, and care should be taken to avoid placing the eye too deeply. In all circumstances, the buds should not be more than 7 cm / 2 in below the soil surface, with only the root ends going deeper. Once the division is oriented, simply fill the hole with soil and gently firm down. Newly planted peonies should be mulched to help them through their first winter.

Iris "Dusky Challenger"

HEIGHT: 1 M / 40 IN	SPREAD: 30 CM / 1 FT	ZONE: 5
FLOWERING PERIOD: EARLY JUNE		

Gardeners looking for a deep purple foil for the whites in the garden will find it in "Dusky Challenger." This award-winning plant features gigantic blooms of a silky black-violet. It is well ruffled and beautifully branched.

Specialty Perennials from Seed

Growing perennials from seed is an easy way to share your favourite plants with friends, or to acquire rare specimens from across the world. With seed catalogues offering more exotic selections each year and the proliferation of seed-exchange groups on the Internet, many gardeners have succumbed to the allure of growing their own ornamentals.

Hansi Pitzer is one of those gardeners, and her love of rare perennials has brought her to the place of creating a truly unique nursery. I'll have to admit that I was a little sceptical when I heard her claim that the majority of the plants she offers are not available locally — but after an extensive tour, I found that this was not an exaggeration but simply a modest truth. Hansi's passion for the perennials she grows is evident in the diversity of her collection and the time she spends guiding her customers to yet another "gem" for their garden.

Hansi Pitzer
Hansi's Nursery
Whonnock, B.C.

Anemone nemorosa

HEIGHT: 10–12.5 CM / 4–5 IN	ZONE: 4
FLOWERING PERIOD: APRIL–MAY	

This is one group of woodland plants that Hansi has fallen in love with — not only for their beautiful flowers but also for their ease of care. European wood anemone prefers shade to filtered light and goes dormant in summer. Here are a few of Hansi's favourites:

"Allenii" / blue star-shaped flowers with white centres

"Robinsoniana" / large lilac blooms (to 2.5 cm / 1 in across), also slightly taller (to 15 cm / 6 in)

"Vestal" / a slow-growing cultivar with pure white, camellia-like blooms

"Wilk's Giant" / a robust anemone with white flowers

Cardiocrinum giganteum

HEIGHT: 1.8–3.5 M / 6–12 FT	ZONE: 7
FLOWERING PERIOD: JULY–AUG	

The giant Himalayan lily is one of those plants that none of your gardening friends will be able to ignore. This towering bulb forms enormous stems with up to 20 white (with maroon striping) trumpet-shaped flowers, which are heavily scented. The bulbs generally take two to three years before they bloom and require a winter mulch.

Codonopsis clematidea

HEIGHT: 45 CM / 18 IN	ZONE: 6
FLOWERING PERIOD: JUNE–AUG	

This unusual perennial bears bell-shaped, pastel blue flowers accented with striking orange, red and yellow highlights (with a black centre) on the inside. *Codonopsis* prefers partial shade with moist, well-drained soil and features a subtle fragrance when in bloom.

Androsace pyrenaica "Millstream"

HEIGHT: 1.25 CM / ½ IN	ZONE: 4
FLOWERING PERIOD: SPRING	

Another one of Hansi's favourite plants, "Millstream" is reminiscent of a tight pincushion with tiny pink flowers. This miniature alpine is evergreen and prefers full sun with well-drained soil.

Symphytum grandiflorum "Hidcote Blue"

HEIGHT: 45 CM / 18 IN	ZONE: 4
FLOWERING PERIOD: MAY–JULY	

This large-flowered comfrey has hairy leaves and pulmonaria-like flower clusters of blue, with red and white highlights. "Hidcote Blue" blooms in late spring to early summer and tolerates partial shade quite well.

Arisarum proboscideum

HEIGHT: 10 CM / 4 IN	ZONE: 5
FLOWERING PERIOD: MARCH–APRIL	

Hansi calls this her little mouse plant and, while it may not be considered very beautiful, it certainly has one of the most interesting flowers of any perennial. The **spathe** is shaped much like a peanut with a white base and purplish-brown crown, capped with a long tail-like tip — hence the common name.

Chrysanthemum "Elsie Gilbert"

HEIGHT: 60–90 CM / 2–3 FT	ZONE: 4
FLOWERING PERIOD: JULY–SEPT	

So far, this chrysanthemum has been an almost exclusive plant for Hansi's Nursery but, judging by its immense beauty, it should prove to be very popular. It features hundreds of thin, feather-like white petals that are layered in thick rows (to 1 cm / ½ in deep), surrounding a brilliant yellow centre. Individual blooms are 5–8 cm / 2-3 in wide.

Anthyllis montana "Rubra"

HEIGHT: 10 CM / 4 IN	ZONE: 6
FLOWERING PERIOD: ALL SUMMER	

This alpine perennial bears unusual, reddish-orange flowers all summer. It is reputed to be short-lived but self-seeds rather generously.

Growing Perennials from Seed

Hansi has a slightly unorthodox seeding method but, judging from the results, it has proven very successful over the years. For the curious, here is a brief outline of her unique approach to seeding.

Always use fresh seed. Fresh seed will give 100% germination; old seed only about 20% to 50%.

Put the seed in a lightly moistened, folded paper towel and place it in a zip-lock bag. Leave the bag slightly open.

If the seeds need a cold period to break dormancy, place them in the fridge or freezer (Hansi uses the top part of her freezer, which is slightly warmer).

Afterward, hang the bags in a window with bright, indirect light (Hansi uses clothespins to make chains of bags).

The germinated seeds will show quite easily through the moistened paper towel.

If the seeds do not germinate in six weeks, return the seed bag to the freezer or fridge for another six weeks.

Once the seeds are germinated, plant the seedlings in regular soil (Hansi uses her soil blend, not a starter mix, because she feels that the seedlings go into shock when different soil types are used while they are being grown).

Seedlings can be grown on in a 10 cm / 4 in pot until they become crowded. At that time Hansi dips the root mass in water, allowing the seedlings to fall apart with no root damage. Individual plants are then planted one per 10 cm / 4 in pot and grown on until they are ready to be sold or planted in the garden.

Using Manure in the Garden
Well-rotted manure is Hansi's only source of fertilizer and a fall top dressing on the perennial border is one of her essential garden tasks. Hansi prefers a fall application of manure over one in the spring for the following reasons.
1. Feeds all winter as the rain leaches the nutrients.
2. Protects tender perennials from hard frost or freezing.
3. Improves soil structure by adding organic matter.
4. Leaves a healthy mulch by spring time

Hansi never works manure into the soil after planting, as the action disturbs the plant's hair roots.

Ornamental Edibles for the Garden
Hansi has a very large clump of rhubarb that attracts the attention of many of her customers looking for unusual perennials — the problem is that once they are told that it is just rhubarb, they no longer seem to be interested in it as an ornamental. Hansi feels that many attractive vegetables and herbs are often overlooked simply because they are edible plants — so, here are a few choices that will look right at home in the mixed perennial border:
Silver Thyme — silver edged, mid-green leaves
Tricolor Sage — bold variegation of purple and cream
Chives — beautiful pink flowers, edible
Nasturtium — spicy edible leaves and flowers
Artichoke — bold specimens with thistle-like blooms
Swiss Chard "Bright Lights" — multicoloured stems
Asparagus — beautiful fern-like foliage
Beets — very similar foliage to Rumex sanguineus / sorrel
Bronze Fennel — fine bronze foliage, licorice flavour
Angelica — huge clusters of greenish-white flowers

Dryas octopetala

HEIGHT: 7.5–10 CM / 3–4 IN · ZONE: 3

FLOWERING PERIOD: MAY–OCT

This semi-evergreen, creeping alpine has shiny, dark green foliage with drifts of large yellow-centred white cup-shaped flowers that turn with the sun. This *Dryas* blooms heavily from May to June, but every new shoot will also sprout another flower, right into October.

Gentiana

Gentians are probably Hansi's favourite genus of plants — so rather than making her pick just one, we have listed a few species:

Gentian acaulis / deep gentian-blue flowers up to 5 cm / 2 in long (ZONE: 5)

G. asclepiadea / the willow gentian is an arching perennial with blue flowers in each leaf axil (ZONE: 6)

G. asclepiadea "Alba" / a white-flowering willow gentian (ZONE: 6)

G. sino-ornata / a fall gentian, blue flowers with white and dark blue stripes (ZONE: 5)

G. straminea / a Himalayan native with purple-tipped, ivory-coloured blooms (HARDY TO -20°C)(ZONE: 6)

Ornamental Grasses & Bamboos

Some people are under the impression that the only good place for an ornamental grass is beneath the blades of their lawnmower, once a week. The middle ground of opinion seems to be solidly occupied by gardeners who admire the ornamental grasses but are unsure as to how to incorporate these plants into the landscape. For the few who have ventured into grasses these past few years, the rewards of elegant plumes, bold structural lines and graceful movement with the slightest breeze are self-evident.

Bamboo is also a member of this family, but unfortunately most people's first impression is in the form of a neglected *Phyllostachys* that is sprouting throughout their newly purchased property. This bad reputation is gradually changing with the advent of professional root barriers, newly introduced "clumping" varieties and the promotion of container culture. Actually, we have many good years of exciting new introductions ahead of us, as North American gardeners are only now starting to appreciate this versatile group of plants.

Together, ornamental grasses and bamboo are poised to make a big impact at local garden centres — gardeners have only to recognize their landscape potential and forget past prejudices in order to take full advantage of them.

Ornamental Grasses

George and Lea Feddes
Pepindale Nursery
Aldergrove, B.C.

Ornamental grasses have been an important component of European gardens for years and are only now catching on in North America. Many gardeners have become aware of their role in softening the landscape and giving it a more natural look. Unlike most perennials, chosen for their bold colours, the appeal of grasses has more to do with the form, texture, movement and the sound they provide. Their grace, beauty and subtle interplay with light make them worthy additions to our plant borders.

George and Lea Feddes own and operate Pepindale Nursery, a wholesale operation specializing in ornamental grasses, sedges and reeds. They are located south of Aldergrove, along the U.S. border, where they enjoy a Zone 7 climate that allows them to grow a wide assortment of grasses, ranging from the highly ornamental to more naturalistic varieties. They have decided to share some of the major grass **genera**, as well as a few specific **cultivars**.

Pennisetum / Fountain Grass

The *Pennisetums* include some of the showiest grasses. Their flowers are typically soft bottlebrush foxtails. They are easy to grow, thriving in moist well-drained soil in full sun. The plants form mounds of varying size depending on the species, with flowers held above the foliage.

Pennisetum alopecuroides "Hameln"

HEIGHT: 75 CM / 2½ FT	SPREAD: 75 CM / 2½ FT	ZONE: 6
FLOWERING PERIOD: JULY–AUG		

The "Hameln" fountain grass is an excellent cultivar, useful for its compact size. The creamy-white flowers emerge mid-July, continue into August, dry to a buff colour and hold well into the fall. The plant forms a 75 cm / 2½ ft mound, with the flowers borne 30 cm / 12 in above the foliage.

Styrax japonicum / Japanese snowbell (flowering trees)

Manglietia insignis / Red Lotus Tree (magnolias)

Acer shirasawanum "*Aureum*" / Golden Fullmoon Maple (japanese maples)

Daboecia cantabrica "Atropurpurea" (heaths & heathers)

Symphoricarpos x *doorenbosii* "Marleen"
(ornamental shrubs) PHOTO: PRIDE OF PLACE PLANTS

Hydrangea macrophylla "Blaumeise" / Teller's Blue (hydrangeas)

"Blue Boy" (rhododendron) PHOTO: LES CLAY

"Gibraltar" (deciduous azaleas) PHOTO: LES CLAY

Rosa "Albertine" (climbers & ramblers) PHOTO: CAROL QUIN

Rosa "Tournament of Roses" (hybrid teas & floribunda)

Rosa "Abraham Darby" (David Austin's English roses)

Rosa "Green Ice" (miniature roses)

Rosa "Bonica" (meidiland roses)

Chamaecyparis pisifera "Filifera Aurea" / Golden Threadleaf Cypress
w/ *Pinus sylvestris* / Scots Pine (dwarf conifers)

Tsuga canadensis "Pendula" / Weeping Hemlock (specimen conifers / dwarf conifers)

Hosta "Canadian Shield" (hosta) PHOTO: PERENNIAL GARDENS

Trillium ovatum / western trillium (woodland perennials)

Dryopteris erythrosora / autumn fern (ferns)

Miscanthus sinensis (specimen perennials)

Hemerocallis "Tuscawilla Tigress" (daylilies)
PHOTO: PAM ERIKSON

Salvia verticillata "Purple Rain"
w/ Geranium "Bressingham Flair" (border perennials)

Paeonia "Paula Fay" (irises and peonies) PHOTO: DAVID JACK

Arisarum proboscideum / mouse plant
(specialty perennials from seed)

Pennisetum alopecuroides "Hameln" (ornamental grasses)

Sasa veitchii (bamboo)

Pelargonium "Frank Headley" (summer flowers)

Clematis "Multi Blue" (clematis)

Hydrangea anomala petiolaris / climbing hydrangeas (climbing vines)

Nymphaea "Attraction" (hardy waterlilies)

Colocasia "Black Magic" /
Black Magic Taro (aquatic plants)

Dactylorhiza elata / Marsh Orchid (bog perennials)   PHOTO: GERALD GIBBENS

Eucomis bicolor / pineapple lily (specialty bulbs)

variety of herbs (herbs)

Cynara cardunculus / cardoon (vegetables)

Vaccinium vitis-idaea / lingonberry (exotic fruits & nuts)

Raspberry "Fall Gold" (cane fruits)

Blueberry "Duke" (blueberries)

Malus "Scarlet & Golden Sentinal" (apples & pears)
PHOTO: MISTY MEADOW NURSERY

Aronia melanocarpa
"Autumn Magic" (UBC plant introductions)

Potentilla fruticosa "Pink Beauty"(zone 4 hardy plants)

Acer circinatum / vine maple (native plants)

Hedychium gardnerianum
"Tara" / Kahili Ginger (exotic plants)

R. Obtusum var Amoenum (bonsai / evergreen azaleas)
PHOTO: WRENHAVEN NURSERY

Catananche caerulea
Cupid's Dart (drought tolerant plants)

Syringa vulgaris "Krasavitsa Moskvy" (fragrant plants)

Betula jacquemontii / Himalayan birch (winter garden)

Pennisetum setaceum
"Rubrum" / Purple-leaved Fountain Grass

HEIGHT: 1.5 M / 5 FT	SPREAD: 1.5 M / 5 FT	ZONE: 9
FLOWERING PERIOD: JULY–FROST		

The glossy burgundy foliage grows in upright arching clumps and is topped with red purple plumes. Extremely showy, it is an excellent planter specimen and, despite its tenderness, is worth growing as an annual.

Carex / Sedge

The sedge family includes plants from widely diverse habitats, ranging from sandy beaches to alpine **scree**. They are commonly associated with moist ecologies and some can grow in water. Others are able to adapt to drought and heat. Their foliage may be red, orange, copper, silver, brown and all shades of green.

Carex comans
"Frosty Curls" / "Frosty Curls" New Zealand Sedge

HEIGHT: 30 CM / 1 FT	SPREAD: 30 CM / 1 FT	ZONE: 7
FLOWERS INSIGNIFICANT		

A finely textured, clumping evergreen, this sedge features hair-like leaves of an iridescent green. It can be grown in sun or light shade, but prefers moist, well-drained soil.

Carex flagellifera / Weeping Brown New Zealand Sedge

HEIGHT: 50 CM / 20 IN	SPREAD: 90 CM / 3 FT	ZONE: 7
FLOWERS INSIGNIFICANT		

Another finely textured sedge that is more upright than *C. comans*, Weeping Brown New Zealand sedge features coppery-brown foliage. It does best in light shade with moist, well-drained soil.

Basic Grass Groups:

Warm-season Grasses: *Warm-season grasses grow vigorously from spring to summer, flower, then begin dormancy in the fall. Most change foliage colour in autumn, eventually bleaching to a shade of tan late in the season. The dormant foliage persists throughout the winter, providing attractive silhouettes and shelter for wildlife. Before the arrival of spring, it is necessary to cut back last year's growth. We find a small sickle-shaped tool particularly helpful for this task. Miscanthus and Pennisetum are two examples of warm-season grasses.*

Cool-season Grasses: *Cool-season grasses begin growth in the late fall and are some of the earliest plants to flower. They are usually evergreen and generally do not need cutting back each year, but rather benefit from a light grooming. Often, just pulling out the old foliage by hand is sufficient.*

Propagation

Grasses are propagated by seed or division. Most seed-grown grasses are reasonably true to type, but the only way to ensure uniformity is by division. Generally speaking, warm-season grasses should be divided in late winter to early spring — and cool-season grasses from fall to early spring.

Companion Planting

*Shade-loving grasses fit beautifully into mixed beds of hosta, heuchera, ferns and hellebores. The lively chartreuse foliage of golden wood millet (*Milium effusum *"Aureum"*) will help to brighten a shady bed, while the delicate spring flowers of hairgrass (*Deschampsia caespitosa*) will glisten and sway in the slightest breeze. Fall-blooming grasses such as *Pennisetum, Cortaderia *and* Miscanthus *are wonderful when teamed with showy autumn perennials, including *Eupatorium, Rudbeckia *and Border Sedums.*

Carex morrowii
"Ice Dance" / Variegated Japanese Sedge

HEIGHT: 30 CM / 1 FT	SPREAD: 30 CM+ / 1 FT+	ZONE: 6
FLOWERS INSIGNIFICANT		

Variegated Japanese sedge is evergreen with strap-like leaves (2 cm / ¾ in wide) and bold white variegation. The plant is **rhizomatous** but spreads slowly and is not invasive. Its fresh appearance, even in the middle of winter, makes it a good container plant in milder climates.

Molinia / Moor Grass

Mostly warm-season grasses, moor grasses range in size from miniatures to huge specimens. They have showy flowers and brilliant yellow to orange fall colours that glow in the autumn sunlight.

Molinia caerulea "Variegata" / Variegated Moor Grass

HEIGHT: 60 CM / 2 FT	SPREAD: 30 CM / 1 FT	ZONE: 4
FLOWERING PERIOD: JUNE–JULY		

Variegated moor grass is a compact *Molinia* noted for its creamy-yellow, linear striped variegation. The flowers are a rich burgundy that fade to brown and the autumn colour is exceptional. Its compact size makes it suitable for small urban gardens.

Deschampsia / Tufted Hair Grass

Tufted hair grass is a cool-season, mostly evergreen grass that forms dense tufts of dark green foliage. The silky green flowers emerge in spring and gradually change colour as they mature — ranging from yellow to bronze and purple.

Deschampsia caespitosa "Northern Lights"

HEIGHT: 15 CM / 6 IN	SPREAD: 15 CM / 6 IN	ZONE: 4

Unlike most *Deschampsia*, "Northern Lights" is a variegated **cultivar** with tones of yellow, white and pink. The highly ornamental foliage keeps its beautiful colour throughout the winter in mild areas. This particular variety has not been observed to flower.

Panicum virgatum / Switch Grass

Switch grass is a clumping, warm season grass. It features an upright form, showy flowers, beautiful foliage and an interesting winter silhouette.

Panicum virgatum "Prairie Sky"

HEIGHT: 1.2 M / 4 FT	SPREAD: 30 CM / 1 FT	ZONE: 5
FLOWERING PERIOD: JULY		

"Prairie Sky" is a little shorter and a brighter blue (almost turquoise) than the other well-known *Panicum* cultivar, "Heavy Metal." The airy flower **panicles** emerge in July — eventually turning yellow in the fall and remaining strongly upright throughout the winter.

Miscanthus sinensis / Japanese Silver Grass

Japanese silver grass and its many cultivars comprise some of the most desirable ornamental grasses available. It is a clumping, warm-season grass, with whisk-like plumes that emerge from July through September, depending on the cultivar. The smaller varieties reach only 90 cm–1.2 m / 3–4 feet high, while *Miscanthus giganteus* can grow to heights of 4 m / 13 ft.

Growth Habit:

Running Grasses: *Running grasses spread by means of above-ground stems called stolons or underground stems called* **rhizomes***. They can be invasive — so it is important to know their growth habits and locate them appropriately.* Carex morrowii *"Ice Dance" is an example of a running grass that spreads slowly, while ribbon grass* (Phalaris arundinacea) *is potentially invasive.*

Clumping Grasses: *Clumping grasses grow in tufts, slowly increasing in girth over time.* Most Miscanthus and Pennisetums *are clumping grasses.*

Miscanthus sinensis "Sarabande"

HEIGHT: 2 M / 6½ FT	SPREAD: 1.5 M / 5 FT	ZONE: 5
FLOWERING PERIOD: AUG		

Like many varieties, it features a showy silver midrib on the leaves. "Sarabande" has a particularly graceful form, with rich copper-tinted flowers that emerge in August.

Miscanthus sinensis "Strictus" / Porcupine Grass

HEIGHT: 2 M / 6½ FT	SPREAD: 1 M / 3¼ FT	ZONE: 5
FLOWERING PERIOD: SEPT		

This cultivar gets its name from its narrow, upright form, which is accented by stiff, upward-pointing leaves. Porcupine grass is further distinguished by horizontal bands of bright yellow variegation and copper-coloured plumes

Bamboos

Bamboos are unique in their place in Asian history — no family of plants has so intertwined itself into the fabric of a culture as has this group of species. Even the red cedar (*Thuja plicata*), a staple of construction and artistic endeavours for native peoples of the Pacific Northwest, pales in comparison. In Asia, the cultural significance of bamboo continues today with its extensive use for housing, boats, scaffolding and tools and as a food source (as bamboo shoots).

More than 150 varieties of bamboo can be planted in the Pacific Northwest — with more than a dozen of these hardy in Quebec, the Maritimes and southern Ontario. Jeff Savin grows an extensive selection of bamboos (more than 60 cultivars and species) at his Salt Spring Island nursery, which he offers by mail order to gardeners across the country. The Plant Farm is a family-run nursery, with Jeff and his wife Morgan propagating a fascinating array of shrubs and perennials. Their 1.5 hectares / 4 acres of display gardens actually feature more than 100 varieties of bamboo — so you are sure to appreciate his unusual choices.

Jeff Savin
The Plant Farm
Salt Spring Island, B.C.

Fargesia nitida

HEIGHT: 2.5–3 M / 7–10 IN	SPREAD: 90 CM–1.2 M / 3–4 IN	ZONE: 5

This graceful, clumping bamboo grows to its maximum height and then stays put — you don't need to worry about fountain bamboo spreading throughout the garden. It features delicate purple stems and correspondingly fine foliage, but it can be a little slow to establish. Like most *Fargesia*, it tolerates partial shade quite well.

Containing Running Bamboos
Some of bamboo's reputation as a horticultural Genghis Khan is well deserved — but along with rampant spreaders there are also well-behaved clumping plants such as Chusqueas, Fargesias *and* Drepanostachyums. *Unfortunately, only the Fargesias are reliably hardy in many regions of Canada. The spreading types (i.e.,* Phyllostachys bambusoides*) can and will grow under sidewalks, crack septic tanks or take over perennial beds. These bamboos should only be used on large lots or contained within concrete, rigid plastic or rubber barriers at least 90 cm–1.2 m / 3–4 ft deep. The barrier material should be thick enough to withstand pressure from the new growth and angled slightly outward, so the new* culms *can be deflected up. Keep in mind when placing bamboos that none of them thrive in strong winds, as they tend to dry out quickly.*

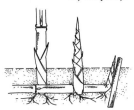

Phyllostachys viridis "Robert Young"

HEIGHT: 7.5 M+ / 25 FT+	SPREAD: 1.8–2.5 M / 6–8 FT	ZONE: 7

This well-behaved spreader grows quite tall in the Pacific Northwest, but is much more vigorous in warmer climates. "Robert Young" bears bright yellow **culms** up to 5 cm / 2 in in diameter, with thin green stripes running down the **internodes**. It forms a fairly tight clump and prefers a warm, sheltered site.

Yushania anceps

HEIGHT: 3.5 M / 12 FT	SPREAD: RUNNING	ZONE: 7

Indian Mountain Bamboo is a frost-hardy species native to the Himalayas. It forms tall, arching stems and bears thin, pendulous foliage. This is an excellent hedging or large-scale ground cover bamboo, as it is quite invasive. For those with limited space, consider using it as a container specimen.

Pleioblastus shibuyanus "Tsuboi"

HEIGHT: 60 CM / 2 FT	SPREAD: RUNNING	ZONE: 7

Probably the most elegant of all the dwarf bamboos, this particular cultivar is popular in Japan, where it is used in the garden or in containers. "Tsuboi" is an evergreen plant and features tightly packed, dark green leaves with a thin white centre. Tolerates sun or partial shade.

Otatea acuminata aztecorum

HEIGHT: 4.5 M / 15 FT*	SPREAD: 60 CM+ / 2 FT+	ZONE: 9–10
* when grown outside		

This is a true tropical plant that is hardy only to -7°C / 19°F at best — so the landscape applications are probably limited to oceanside gardens in the southern-most parts of the Pacific Northwest. The rest of us can enjoy it as the superb greenhouse plant it really is. It features thousands of thin, elegant leaves borne on weeping **culms**, which thrive in sun or partial shade.

Phyllostachys bissetii

HEIGHT: 6 M+ / 20 FT+	SPREAD: RUNNING	ZONE: 5

This fast-growing bamboo with 2.5-cm / 1-in wide **culms** often reaches heights of more than 6 m / 20 ft tall. This spreading species should be contained in smaller gardens but can be trained to form a superb hedge. It is extremely hardy, having survived temperatures as low as -26°C, and is an attractive dark green colour.

Chusquea breviglumis

HEIGHT: 6 M / 20 FT	SPREAD: 90 CM–1.5 M / 3–5 FT	ZONE: 7

This is an extremely rare South American native that is hardy to -16°C / 3°F. This bamboo is relatively well-behaved, forming a clump of multi-stemmed branches that are enveloped in a cloud of deep green leaves. The new **culms** are red and reach a maximum size of about 4 cm / 1½ in wide.

Fargesia utilis

HEIGHT: 4.5–6 M / 15–20 FT	SPREAD: 90 CM–1.5 M / 3–5 FT	ZONE: 7

The largest of the clumping *Fargesia*, this plant is fully hardy on the Pacific Northwest coast. Blue mountain bamboo is native to the mountains of Yunnan province in China and features thin (2-cm / ¾-in) **culms** with delicate, pale green foliage.

Hibanobambusa tranquillans "Shiroshima"

HEIGHT: 4.5 M / 15 FT	SPREAD: RUNNING	ZONE: 7

Spectacular variegation that is held all year-round on large leaves make this is a good choice to brighten dull corners of the garden. This fast-spreading bamboo should be contained in smaller landscapes but will not do well in pots smaller than 45 L / 12 US gal in size. This bamboo is hardy only in Zone 7 or higher.

Ground Cover Bamboos

Be forewarned that all these ground cover choices form dense, invasive masses ranging anywhere from 60 cm–1.5m / 2–5 ft tall. However, few ground covers can offer such a multiplicity of foliage colour, partial shade tolerance and low maintenance needs. Many of these plants also make fine container specimens in warmer parts of the Pacific Northwest(Zone 7+).

Pleioblastus fortunei — *white striped foliage*

Sasa veitchii — *palmate leaves / white margins*

Sasaella masamuniana albostriata — *cream striping*

Pleioblastus viridi-striatus — *yellow with green striping*

Sasaella masamuniana aureostriata — *gold stripes*

Sasa pygmaea — *green / very fast spreading*

Edible Bamboo Shoots

All of these edible bamboos are modest to rampant spreaders — so once they are established it might be nice to enjoy the occasional new shoot, be it raw in a salad (try P. dulcis) or cooked in a stir-fry. Harvest bamboo shoots in early spring as they emerge — the thinner ones can be lopped off at soil level while the larger shoots should be cut below ground with a sharp knife, taking care not to damage the remaining rhizome.

Phyllostachys aurea / *Golden Bamboo*

Phyllostachys dulcis / *Sweet Shoot Bamboo*

Phyllostachys bambusoides / *Timber Bamboo*

Phyllostachys aureosulcata / *Yellow Groove Bamboo*

Phyllostachys viridis / *Green Sulphur Bamboo*

Fertilizing Bamboo

As members of the grass family, bamboo requires adequate moisture and regular feeding with high nitrogen during the growing season — most lawn fertilizers (except Weed and Feed™ types) provide an ideal formulation. Well-rotted mushroom manure used as a mulch in fall will provide some nutrients and protect the rhizomes from frost. Bamboo also uses a lot of silica, and the best way for you to supply this micronutrient is to recycle it, by allowing the fallen leaves to rot at the base of the plant.

Arundinaria angustissima / Temple Bamboo

HEIGHT: 3.5 M / 12 FT	SPREAD: 60–90 CM / 2–3 FT	ZONE: 7

This recently discovered species was found in a Japanese temple in the 1980s, hence the common name, Temple Bamboo. An extremely rare plant that has so far exhibited a clumping habit with tiny 2-cm / ¾-in long leaves and dark, upright **culms**, it should be considered a slow growing specimen and may yet be reclassified as a *Fargesia*.

Annuals

You may be asking yourself how it is that a single chapter merits an entire section in this book. The simple answer would be that annuals or summer flowers are such a diverse group of plants that it is difficult to place them entirely into any of the other chapters — even those that could be classified as vines, shade plants, ornamental vegetables or even tender bulbs. The only common denominator is that all will finish their life cycle by summer's end or perish with the heavy frosts of autumn, unless they are given some protection.

The diversity of annual plants is well reflected in the New Westminster parks that Claude Ledoux manages. One in particular, Queen's Park, is a showcase of massive hanging baskets, elaborate carpet bedding, robust fuchsia trees and intricate mixed borders surrounding a formal rose garden. While flowers are certainly one of the highlights of these displays, the focus has shifted somewhat to foliage colour and texture, and this is quite evident in Claude's work. So regardless of your personal preferences, I am sure that you are bound to find something of interest in this short but significant section.

Summer Flowers

Claude Ledoux
*New Westminster
Parks and Recreation
New Westminster, B.C.*

Summer flowers or annuals are a diverse group of plants that encompass many varied forms, textures and flower colours. They are defined by their ability to produce flowers within one season, after which time they die — although many other types of plants (biennial and tender perennials) are also employed in summer bedding. Annuals can be used in mass plantings, containers or as colour accents in the perennial border and, with the number of species available, the possibilities are endless.

Claude Ledoux has been the Parks Manager for New Westminster since 1991. His background includes a major in horticulture from the University of Louisiana at Lafayette. Since 1975, he has worked in retail and wholesale nurseries, lectured for gardening organizations and taught his well-known hanging basket class. Claude's experience while working at Bota Gardens (now Fantasy Gardens World) cultivated his interest in the use of annuals, which continues today as he introduces new or overlooked plant material into the New Westminster parks system.

Onopordum acanthium

HEIGHT: 2 M / 6½ FT	SPREAD: 1.5 M / 5 FT

"Scot's Thistle" is a bold architectural specimen equally at home in alpine or desert-like settings. It features large, deeply lobed foliage that is prickly and covered in a soft silvery-white **pubescence**. The thistle-like flowers are pale purple in colour and are borne from July into early fall. This **biennial** flower does exceptionally well in poor soils with limited moisture, but requires full sun and sharp drainage.

Nicotiana sylvestris

HEIGHT: 1.2–1.5 M / 4–5 FT	SPREAD: 1 M / 3¼ FT

This old-fashioned flowering tobacco delights everyone with its early evening fragrance. The species bears pure white flowers, but several varieties are also available, including "Aztec Jasmine" (pink fading to white) and "Only the Lonely" with intensely fragrant white tubular blooms. This bold plant will tolerate full sun to partial shade.

Abutilon "Bella Mix"

HEIGHT: 50 CM / 20 IN	SPREAD: 30 CM / 1 FT

This is a new, exciting series of compact "Flowering Maples," which produce large single flowers, reminiscent of hibiscus. The blooming period continues from mid summer until frost and features a colour range of eight pastel shades. These bush-like plants are good candidates to train as a standard, and they are superb patio or container specimens as well.

Pelargonium "Frank Headley"

HEIGHT: 50 CM / 20 IN	SPREAD: 50 CM / 20 IN

Deep green leaves that are heavily edged in clear white make this zonal geranium a useful plant for brightening up the garden. The variegated foliage is complemented with single, salmon-pink blossoms from summer until late fall. This compact grower is an ideal container or bedding specimen.

Sanvitalia procumbens

HEIGHT: 10–20 CM / 4–8 IN	SPREAD: 40–60 CM / 16 IN–2 FT

Creeping zinnia is a good choice for hot, dry sites in full sun. This dwarf, spreading plant has self-cleaning flowers that persist from June until frost. While they are best used in mass plantings or borders, they perform equally well in

---

Developing a Fuchsia Standard

Few specimens look so impressive as a fuchsia standard, by itself in a large container or planted as an accent in the background of an annual border. Unfortunately, the cost of purchasing a ready-made fuchsia tree is quite high — so, for gardeners with a little patience, here are a few simple steps for training a fuchsia standard.

Choose any upright variety, as they are the easiest types to train into a standard.

Select a single, strong growing stem and pinch out any side shoots.

Secure the stem to a stake and allow the shoot to grow to desired height (usually 90 cm– 1.2 m / 3–4 feet).

Once the desired height is reached, pinch out the growing tip to develop side shoots.

Pinch back several times to encourage the development of a full, bushy head.

Allow only the top three sets of shoots to grow; remove all lower shoots.

A small standard can be created within one season.

Overwintering Fuchsia Standards

Almost all fuchsia standards are not winter hardy and in order to enjoy them from year to year, use one of the following techniques. Both methods require the plant crown to be pruned back by half at the time of winterizing.

1. The entire plant can be unpotted and buried 40 cm / 15 in under the ground, covered with sand and mounded with mulch. In March, the buried plants should be dug up, repotted and placed in a greenhouse where they can begin to grow.

2. Potted plants can be brought into a cool greenhouse or conservatory, but be sure to keep the soil moist.

hanging baskets and containers. Several varieties are available, including "Gold Braid" (golden-yellow flowers) and "Mandarin Orange" (intense orange with black centres).

Asarina barclaiana

HEIGHT: 3 M / 10 FT	SPREAD: 1 M / 3¼ FT

This vigorous vine bears soft triangular leaves that support a profusion of flowers resembling snapdragons. Although several other species are also available (*A. purpusii* and *A. scandens*), the better varieties include "Snow White," "Joan Lorraine" (deep violet blue) and "Mystic Rose" (bright rose). Chickabiddy vine tolerates most soil types but prefers evenly moist conditions in full sun to light shade. It will climb up through a trellis but can also easily be used as a trailing plant in hanging baskets.

Begonia semperflorens

HEIGHT: 20–50 CM / 8–20 IN	SPREAD: 20 CM / 8 IN

Wax begonias are probably one of the most reliable and versatile plants for mass bedding. The foliage colour ranges from green (including variegated) and bronze to chocolate — complementing a dazzling array of white, carmine, pink, rose and bicolour flowers. The single or double blooms average 2.5 cm / 1 in, but larger flowers are available from both the "Party Series" and "Lotto" varieties. These annuals perform well in sun or shade and thrive in ordinary, well-drained garden soil.

Manettia bicolor

HEIGHT: 2 M / 6½ FT	SPREAD: 1 M / 3¼ FT

Firecracker vine bears waxy, bright scarlet flowers tipped in yellow that strongly resemble candy corn from a distance. The non-invasive, twining habit of this tender evergreen makes it a good candidate for hanging baskets, trellis and rambling through shrubbery and fencing. It will tolerate full sun to partial shade without affecting blooming but grows best in rich, well-drained soil.

Pelargonium "Evka"

HEIGHT: 15 CM / 6 IN	SPREAD: 40–50 CM / 16–20 IN

This mini cascade geranium is a fine specimen for window boxes, hanging baskets and containers. These plants feature a compact growth habit with variegated, dark green foliage (edged in cream) smothered in clouds of single scarlet blossoms.

Zinnia "Profusion Series"

HEIGHT: 30 CM / 1 FT	SPREAD: 25 CM / 10 IN

A new series of this popular flower combines many of the vibrant colour selections, including "Profusion Cherry" and "Profusion Orange." Compact plants produce large, single blossoms with bright yellow stamens. This annual is best suited to mass planting or patio containers in full sun.

Fuchia's Care

Allow the new growth to develop and begin pinching back to three sets of leaves — pinching can occur two or three times before the plants begin to set flower buds. Fuchsias should be fertilized with a high phosphorous fertilizer (i.e., soluble 15–30–15) to encourage flowering. Fertilize every two or three weeks from the time new shoots appear until early fall.

Companion Foliage Plants

1. Rhoeo spathacea "Variegata"
2. Perilla frutescens / *Beefsteak Plant*
3. Phormium tenax / *New Zealand Flax*
4. Euphorbia heterophylla *"Yokoi's White"*
5. Coleus blumei / *Flame Nettle*
6. Helichrysum petiolatum
7. Pilea cadierei / *Aluminum Plant*
8. Plectranthus argentea
9. Ipomoea batatus / *Sweet Potato*
10. Halorages erecta *"Melton's Bronze"*

Vines

Gardeners are often so preoccupied with shrubs and perennials when landscaping the yard that the vertical element of the garden is neglected. It is only after the lawn has been laid and the beds fleshed in with plants that gardeners look up to see the bare house walls and fence panels staring back.

The first reaction is usually a quick trip to the local garden centre to purchase the fastest-growing vines available. One to two years later, the gardener is busy pruning the wisteria that is crushing the fencing lathe or the English ivy that is working its way into the vinyl siding of the house. It is not that wisteria and English ivy cannot be well behaved when planted in the proper location, it is just that many gardeners are under the false impression that all vines will suit every planting site.

If, on the other hand, gardeners take the time to assess the sun exposure, soil structure and type of support the vines are intended to grow on, then they can look forward to many years of enjoyment from clematis, honeysuckles and other vines. Fortunately, there are also many cultivars to choose from as far as blooming season and flower colour is concerned — so that a spring-to-fall display is easily within grasp.

Clematis

Fred Wein
Clearview Horticultural
Products Inc.
Aldergrove, B.C.

Clematis are the aristocrats of climbers. Their rich hues and varied blooming periods allow the gardener to have masses of colour from late winter into autumn. Be it large or small, there is a variety to suit any landscape, including plants that will wander 9 m / 30 ft or more and hybrids that mature at only 1.8–2.5 m / 6–8 ft tall. With several hundred species worldwide, ranging from flowering ground cover to evergreen, even the most discerning of plant collectors is bound to find something of interest.

Clearview Horticultural Products started as a family business on their current Aldergrove site back in 1970. With the later addition of his sons, Fred and Rob, Fred Wein Sr. has transformed his family enterprise into one of the major clematis propagators in North America.

Clematis "Comtesse de Bouchaud"

HEIGHT: 2.5–3.5 M / 8–12 FT	PRUNING GROUP: C	ZONE: 4

An old cultivar that was introduced in 1903, this clematis is probably still one of the most popular ever grown. The flowers are a unique clear pink, slightly tinged with mauve, and borne from June to September.

Clematis "The President"

HEIGHT: 2.5–3.5 M / 8–12 FT	PRUNING GROUP: B	ZONE: 4

The intense colouring of this variety has few rivals after 125 years of cultivation. The large (15–20 cm / 6–8 in wide), deep purple-blue flowers are contrasted with striking red-tipped stamens. This clematis blooms quite heavily in June and continues to flower through to September.

Clematis montana

HEIGHT: 9 M+ / 30 FT+	PRUNING GROUP: A	ZONE: 6

This species does so well in temperate coastal regions that to pick a specific variety would do a great injustice to the rest. The *montanas* are vigorous vines that can easily reach great heights and, although the blooms are smaller (5 cm / 2 in) than most, they are produced in huge masses in May and June. The colour range of the flowers varies from white to dark pink and most are fragrant.

Clematis macropetala "Blue Bird"

HEIGHT: 2.5–3.5 M / 8–12 FT	PRUNING GROUP: A	ZONE: 3–4

A Canadian introduction bred by Dr. F. L. Skinner of the Morden Research Centre in Manitoba, this variety combines extreme hardiness with unusual lavender-blue, bell-shaped blooms on a very robust plant. The flowers are borne in abundance in early spring, usually April to May.

Clematis "Hagley Hybrid"

HEIGHT: 1.8–2.5 M / 6–8 FT	PRUNING GROUP: C	ZONE: 4

Also known as "Pink Chiffon," this compact cultivar does extremely well in both small and large gardens. The shell-pink flowers (10–15 cm / 4–6 in) attract a lot of attention and are produced from June to September on the current year's growth.

Clematis "Blue Ravine"

HEIGHT: 1.8–2.75 M / 6–9 FT	PRUNING GROUP: B	ZONE: 4

"Blue Ravine" is a University of British Columbia introduction with very large (20–25 cm / 8–10 in) blooms that are soft violet, with slightly darker veins. This clematis flowers in May or June on last year's wood and again in late summer on the current season's growth. You will have to exercise some patience when growing "Blue Ravine," as it has a tendency to want to bloom all the time. Some

---

Pruning Categories

The first February or March after planting, all *clematis* varieties should be cut back to two strong sets of buds for each stem (increases vigour), after which they should be pruned according to category.

Group A — *Flowers on growth produced the previous year. Restrict pruning to cutting out weak or dead stems as soon as they finish blooming in May or June. Some examples include C. montana, C. alpina and C. macropetala.*

Group B — *Includes plants that bloom on the previous season's growth as well as those that flower on old and current wood. Both prefer a light pruning in late February or March with some variation in the length of the stems. Some examples include the double flowering "Duchess of Edinburgh," "Countess of Lovelace" and "Proteus."*

Group C — *Blooms on the current year's growth. Cut back in late February or March to two strong sets of buds on each stem. Some examples include C. "Jackmanii," "Hagley Hybrid" and "Ernest Markham."*

Pests and Diseases:

Clematis Wilt — *Refers to various fungi that cause the stems to wilt just as the flowers begin to open. Remove and destroy damaged stems (2.5 cm / 1 in into healthy wood) and use a systemic fungicide such as benomyl for serious outbreaks. The disease rarely affects species clematis or viticella hybrids.*

Powdery Mildew — *This fungus is not a problem with good air circulation and can be controlled in its early stages with various fungicides.*

Earwigs — *Earwigs cause damage in midsummer, making holes in both foliage and flowers. Use an earwig bait at the first sign of damage.*

Slugs — *Slugs generally attack young, tender shoots. Use a slug bait containing metaldehyde in early spring.*

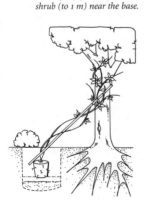

other good choices in this colour range include "H. F. Young," "General Sikorski," "Ramona" and "Horn of Plenty."

Clematis "Dr. Ruppel"

HEIGHT: 2–3 M / 6½–10 FT	PRUNING GROUP: B	ZONE: 4

A relatively new introduction from Argentina (1975), "Dr. Ruppel" has already established itself as one of the most popular modern varieties. The attractively formed rose-red flowers are highlighted with a central carmine bar on each petal. As with "Nelly Moser," the flower colour will be more intense if the plant is grown in partial shade.

Clematis "Jackmanii"

HEIGHT: 3–5.5 M / 10–18 FT	PRUNING GROUP: C	ZONE: 3–4

The best known of all clematis and one of the easiest varieties to grow, "Jackmanii" has been flowering in gardens since 1863. The reliable display of deep purple blooms is evident throughout the summer and is particularly impressive on larger, more mature vines. "Etoile Violet" and "Polish Spirit" are good alternate cultivars in the same colour range.

Clematis "Nelly Moser"

HEIGHT: 3 M / 10 FT	PRUNING GROUP: B	ZONE: 4

This *Clematis patens* hybrid has proven to be the people's favourite for well over 100 years. The pale mauve-pink blooms, accented with deep pink bars, will fade somewhat if the plant is grown in full sun.

Clematis "Ville de Lyon"

HEIGHT: 2–3.3 M / 6½–11 FT	PRUNING GROUP: B OR C	ZONE: 3–4

A standard clematis since its introduction at the turn of the 20th century, "Ville de Lyon" has unique crimson-red blooms edged in dark carmine. These spectacular flowers are borne continuously from June through September and are contrasted with large yellow stamens. The bloom size varies from 10–15 cm / 4–6 in when hard pruned, and to 12–18 cm / 5–7 in across when pruned lightly. "Niobe," "General Wyszynski" and "Rouge Cardinal" are good substitutes in this colour range.

Clematis in Containers
Many clematis make fine container specimens, but there are a few limitations — with the first being the container itself. The pot should be a minimum of 45 cm / 18 in deep by 45 cm / 18 in wide and be thick enough to provide some insulation for the roots. This means thin plastic or metal pots should be avoided in preference to half-barrels, heavy terra cotta or custom wooden containers. These pots should have adequate drain holes and several inches of gravel on the bottom, with the balance filled with a peat-based container mixture. Choose one of the many compact clematis (see list below), plant the root ball deep and be sure to have a permanent support structure in place — mini-obelisks, trellis or sturdy stakes tied in teepee fashion will work quite well. Grow annuals or low perennials on the soil surface to help shade the roots, and try mixing several Clematis varieties in larger containers.

Clematis *"Multi Blue" — double purple-blue flowers*

C. *"Miss Bateman" — white with dark red stamens*

C. *"Pink Champagne" — purple-pink blossoms*

C. *"Hagley Hybrid" — large, shell-pink blooms*

C. *"Niobe" — almost black, ruby-red flowers*

C. *"Bees Jubilee" — mauve-pink with carmine bars*

C. *"Daniel Deronda" — deep purple-blue / semi-double*

C. *"Rouge Cardinal" — deep crimson with brown stamens*

C. *"Asao" — pale rosy carmine blossoms*

C. *"Silver Moon" — mother-of-pearl with yellow stamens*

Climbing Vines

Todd Major
Park & Tilford Gardens
North Vancouver, B.C.

In small urban gardens, the use of vertical planting provides the opportunity to "grow up" where there is no room to "grow out." At Park & Tilford Gardens, they make use of all the perpendicular space available — with each of their nine theme gardens featuring a different vine to help adorn existing architecture or trees. By training plants vertically, they have been able to grow in a defined space, many more vines than can be found in the average residential landscape.

Todd Major currently serves as the director of Park & Tilford Gardens in North Vancouver. Aside from his regular duties maintaining this showpiece enclosure, he gives lectures to garden clubs, helps to train horticulture students from Capilano College and always seems to find a few minutes to talk plants with anyone who drops by. The volume and diversity of plant material thriving within the walls of Park & Tilford is a testament to Todd's passion for his trade.

Akebia quinata / Chocolate Vine

HEIGHT: 9 M / 30 FT	ZONE: 5
FLOWERING PERIOD: APRIL	

The chocolate vine is a twining Asian vine with good vigour and deliciously fragrant, pendulous purple flowers. Contrary to some garden books, our akebia thrives in an open north-facing position. Plant in full sun or light open shade in any reasonable, well-drained soil. As far as hardiness is concerned, our chocolate vine has endured low temperatures of -25°C / -13°F at Park & Tilford Gardens. The leaves are semi-evergreen.

Parthenocissus henryana / Silvervein Creeper

HEIGHT: 7.5 M / 25 FT	ZONE: 7
PRIMARILY A FOLIAGE VINE	

This deciduous vine has compound foliage very similar to Virginia creeper except for the attractive silvery-white veins and contrasting purple undersides. The variegation is more prominent when it is grown in partial shade, preferably with a north- or east-facing exposure. Like all *Parthenocissus*, silvervein creeper attaches itself by means of small adhesive pads that can damage wood siding, so some care should be taken when placing this vine. It features excellent scarlet to reddish-purple fall colour.

Tropaeolum speciosum / Flame Creeper

HEIGHT: 3 M / 10 FT	ZONE: 8
FLOWERING PERIOD: JUNE–SEPT	

This perennial nasturtium is rather rare and the subject of conflicting cultural advice, as it can be quite difficult to establish. The bright scarlet blooms (2.5 cm / 1 in wide) are borne from mid-June to September and are followed by dull red capsules, which open to stunning, metallic blue seeds. Support for the delicate apple-green foliage is best provided by training it to the face of a fine textured hedge, such as yew. It will proliferate if planted in a deep, organic soil with good drainage and, although it dies back to the ground in winter, it can be hardy to -20°C / -4°F once established.

Hedera colchica "Dentata Variegata" / Variegated Persian Ivy

HEIGHT: 6 M / 20 FT	ZONE: 7
PRIMARILY A FOLIAGE VINE	

A beautiful evergreen vine, variegated Persian ivy can be quite difficult to place simply because of the large-scale foliage. The rich green leaves (to 15 cm / 6 in across) are

---

Vines for Shade

Most shade-tolerant vines will seek out light if it is too dark or oppressive. Open shade (i.e., north- or east-facing), filtered woodland light and intermittent sunlight provide better growing exposures than deep shade. Here are a few vines that will tolerate these conditions.

Clematis macropetala — *flowers better with more light*

Hedera colchica "Dentata Variegata" / *Variegated Persian ivy*

Actinidia kolomitka / *Variegated kiwi — pink, white, green*

Lonicera henryi — *many honeysuckles thrive in light shade*

Hydrangea anomala petiolaris / *Climbing hydrangea*

Akebia quinata / *Chocolate Vine — small purple flowers*

Schizophragma hydrangeoides — *similar to climbing hydrangea*

Parthenocissus henryana — *fabulous in open or light shade*

Companion Plants
There are an infinite number of
combinations when using vines
as companion plants. Quite
often, flowering vines such as
clematis are used to brighten
lacklustre summer foliage or bare
lower stems. In other applications, the blooms are meant to
either complement or contrast
those of its host. Here are just a
few examples of companion
planting.

Eccremocarpus scaber *on red-
and white-flowered fuchsia
standards*

Clematis *"Ramona"*
(lavender-blue) on Rosa
"Constance Spry" (climber)

Cobaea scandens
(Cup and Saucer Vine) on wisteria floribunda

Hydrangea anomala. petiolaris
*on large tree trunks (provide
adequate moisture)*

Dicentra torulosa *on* Taxus
x media *"Hicksii" hedge
(Hick's yew)*

Tropaeolum speciosum *on*
Lonicera nitida
"Baggesen's Gold"

Clematis *"Perle D'Azur"*
(sky blue) on Hamamelis mollis
(Witch hazel)

generously enhanced with irregular splashes of pale yellow to gold variegation. Like most ivies, it is not fussy about soil types and will tolerate full sun or partial shade. With training, it will adorn a fence or bare wall with a solid sheet of variegated foliage.

Actinidia kolomitka / Variegated Kiwi

HEIGHT: 6 M / 20 FT	ZONE: 5
PRIMARILY A FOLIAGE VINE	

In April and May as the new growth appears, gardeners will see the green leaves develop spectacular white and pink variegation on the tips. Once established, this clambering vine can grow quite high, but responds well to selective pruning. Variegated kiwi matures with an attractive brown peeling bark and is best placed in an east-facing position. The male plants have the best colour display.

Trachelospermum asiaticum / Yellow Star Jasmine

HEIGHT: 4.5 M+ / 15 FT+	ZONE: 7–8
FLOWERING PERIOD: MAY–EARLY JULY	

This evergreen twining vine is actually hardier than the more commonly found Chinese star jasmine (*T. jasminoides*). It will need a south- or west-facing position to produce the deliciously fragrant yellowish-white flowers. The small leaves are glossy and attractive all year long, but it can suffer dieback in hard winters.

Vitis vinifera "Purpurea" / Ornamental Grape Vine

HEIGHT: 3.5–5.5 M / 12–18 FT	ZONE: 5
PRIMARILY A FOLIAGE VINE	

From the species that has produced some of the finest wine grapes comes an outstanding ornamental variety. The new growth has a silvery down coating and later matures to a purplish-green colour. Autumn finds the foliage changing to an eye-catching claret red to deep purple. Grow in full sun for the best fall display.

Hydrangea anomala petiolaris / Climbing Hydrangea

HEIGHT: 9 M+ / 30 FT+	ZONE: 5
FLOWERING PERIOD: JUNE	

Although this climbing shrub is commonly found at retail nurseries, climbing hydrangea is still not widely planted. This could be due to its self-clinging **aerial roots** (on the new growth), which should only be allowed to cling to stone, brick or other such impervious surfaces. The shiny heart-shaped leaves, shaggy bark and white **lacecap** flowers have a distinctive "Old World" flavour. This plant grows well in open shade or full sun with shaded roots.

Mina lobata / Spanish Flag

HEIGHT: 6 M / 20 FT+
FLOWERING PERIOD: MID JUNE–FROST

This native of Mexico is a perennial down south, but is often treated as an annual vine in northern climes. We like to train this unusual climber to the face of hedges, where the **racemes** of boat-shaped flowers can best be appreciated. The blossoms open scarlet, fading progressively to orange, yellow and creamy-white. The plant is usually available from seed.

Lonicera henryi / Evergreen Honeysuckle

HEIGHT: 6 M+ / 20 FT+	ZONE: 5
FLOWERING PERIOD: JUNE–JULY	

Evergreen honeysuckle is a good hardy substitute for evergreen clematis (*C. armandii*) and has similar deep green, elongated leaves. The light purplish-red fragrant blooms appear in June and July but are often obscured by the vigorous foliage. These are followed by handsome black fruit. Although it is hardy to Zone 5, it is only reliably evergreen to about Zone 6 or 7.

Annual Climbers
A short list of tender or annual vines that you can use to create a temporary summer screen.

Rhodochiton atrosanguineum / *Purple Bell Vine*

Eccremocarpus scaber / *Chilean Glory Vine*

Cobaea scandens / *Cup and Saucer Vine*

Thunbergia alata / *Black-Eyed Susan Vine*

Ipomoea alba / *Moonflower*

Convolvulus *"Star of Yelta"* / *Blue Morning Glory*

Tropaeolum peregrinum / *Canary Creeper*

Solanum jasminoides *"Album"* / *White Potato Vine*

Water Plants

Water plants probably represent one of the fastest-growing sectors of retail nursery sales in recent years. It seems that we have only just now discovered what has been common knowledge in Europe for quite some time — that water gardens make great additions to any landscape, regardless of size.

Aquatics also bring a whole new set of rules to landscape design — instead of considering a plant's ultimate size, the greater factor with submerged and marginal plants is the water depth in which they will be standing. A pond or bog feature can also be the perfect solution for a chronic wet spot in the garden, and installation costs are certainly offset by avoiding the expense of a proper drainage system.

Lastly and most importantly, water features bring life to a landscape and, besides the fish we may choose to put in them, it is only a matter of time before an established pond will invite the likes of frogs, dragonflies, raccoons and blue herons — so rather than just adding another facet to the landscape, we end up creating a whole new habitat.

Hardy Water Lilies

Merv Zakus
Unique Koi
and Water Gardens
Whonnock, B.C.

Water lilies have been a part of popular culture ever since Claude Monet decided to build a garden in Giverny, France, and spend the rest of his days painting them. These enticing plants give us spectacular blooms in exchange for relatively calm water, full sun and a little mud to grow in. There is a *Nymphaea* for every gardener, be it the diminutive "Helvola" in a small tub or the robust "Attraction" sprawling over a large pond.

Merv Zakus has been impressing the public with his whimsical water gardens at the VanDusen and B.C. Home shows for the past few years now. Quite often, his displays are a themed composite of sculpture, music, water and plants. Merv also develops large-scale natural or lined ponds and frequently consults with homeowners who are looking to plant water features.

The flowering period indicated for each variety may vary with water temperature, sun exposure and fertilization. To remain hardy in the zones indicated, the rhizome must remain below ice level.

Nymphaea pygmaea "Helvola"

SPREAD: 30–60 CM / 1–2 FT	ZONE: 4
FLOWERING PERIOD: JUNE–SEPT	

"Helvola" is perhaps the most popular of all the pygmy varieties and deservedly so. The pale yellow blooms are star-shaped and borne just above the surface of the water — providing a perfect foil for the green mottled brown foliage. A mature plant will bear flowers that are only 5 cm / 2 in across, making it an ideal choice for small-scale water features such as half-barrels.

Nymphaea "Paul Hariot"

SPREAD: 30–60 CM / 1–2 FT	ZONE: 4
FLOWERING PERIOD: JUNE–SEPT	

This dwarf *Nymphaea* bears rather large (10–12 cm / 4–5 in) flowers that open a vibrant yellow, change to a bronze-pink and then fade to deep red. Also known as a change-able water lily, "Paul Hariot" has a reputation for its free-flowering nature and beautifully mottled foliage.

Nymphaea "James Brydon"

SPREAD: 90 CM–1.25 M / 3–4 FT	ZONE: 4
FLOWERING PERIOD: JUNE–SEPT	

This is a popular water lily among aquatic enthusiasts — mostly in part to its fragrant peony-shaped blossoms, which are crimson red accented with orange **stamens**. The rounded foliage is a rich bronze-green, and this particular plant will tolerate partial shade, flowering in as little as three or four hours of sunlight. "James Brydon" is a small water lily, worth considering for miniature ponds or the shallows of a larger feature.

Nymphaea "Attraction"

SPREAD: 1.2–1.8 M / 4–6 FT	ZONE: 4
FLOWERING PERIOD: JUNE–SEPT	

A Marliac variety which was introduced back in 1910 but is still a popular choice for those with deep natural ponds, "Attraction" is considered a vigorous plant. Mature specimens bear ruby-red flowers flecked in white, which darken with age, while younger plants (such as those at the local nursery) often have rose-pink blossoms.

Deep-water Nymphaea

Many people with deep, natural ponds are often faced with the problem of finding a water lily that will tolerate planting depths of 4' or more. The following species and cultivars will thrive under these conditions (once they are adapted), but a few like Nymphaea alba *are considered very vigorous and may take over.*

"Attraction" — *red*	
"Charles de Meurville" — *plum*	
Nymphaea alba — *white*	
"Gladstone" — *white*	
"Colossea" — *pink*	
"Col. A.J. Welch" — *yellow*	

Planting a Water Lily

Quite often a water lily will out-grow the container in which it was purchased, or you may decide to mail order a rhizome — which will arrive bareroot and wrapped in shredded wet paper. Proper planting of either the new or overgrown water lily will ensure large plants (depending on cultivar) and bountiful flowers. Here are a few simple steps for potting Nymphaea.
1. Choose a plastic container such as a black nursery pot (10–25 L / 2–5 gal size), available at most garden centres.
2. Fill the pot half full with an aquatic soil mix or clay based soil (not a peat-based planter mix).

3. Place the water lily on the soil surface and carefully spread the roots. Position the rhizome horizontally and angle it upward so that the growing tip will protrude from the final soil surface by about 2.5 cm / 1 in.

4. Fill the rest of the pot with soil and water to allow settling.

5. Remove all dead or damaged foliage. Remove any mature leaves or buds from mail-order rhizome.

6. Push in one compressed fertilizer tablet (i.e., Pondtab 10–14–8) for every 2 L / ½ gal of soil used.

7. Top dress with 1 cm / ½ in of pea gravel and water again.

8. Slowly place the pot or basket into the pond to a depth of 30 cm / 12 in (except dwarf types). Lower it again later on as the leaves surface, adjusting the height with bricks.

Nymphaea "Texas Dawn"

SPREAD: 90 CM–1.5 M / 3–5 FT	ZONE: 5
FLOWERING PERIOD: JUNE–SEPT	best in zones 7–9

The abundant, bright yellow flowers of "Texas Dawn" sit well above the water, almost giving the appearance of a tropical water lily. They are both large and fragrant, a perfect contrast for the richly mottled foliage below. This cultivar is best grown in Zones 7 to 9, as it seems to resent colder climes.

Nymphaea "Comanche"

SPREAD: 1.25–1.5 M / 4–5 FT	ZONE: 4
FLOWERING PERIOD: JUNE–SEPT	

This is another of the changeable water lilies with a robust growing habit suitable for medium-sized ponds. The flowers open an apricot-orange and gradually change to a pink (flushed yellow) and copper-red over the course of a few days. This unusual trait is particularly attractive on mature specimens, when different coloured blooms are featured on the same plant.

Nymphaea "Pink Sensation"

SPREAD: 1.2 M / 4 FT	ZONE: 4
FLOWERING PERIOD: JUNE–SEPT	

This free-flowering water lily has silvery-pink petals that form fragrant, star-like blooms. The plant itself has a medium to large spread with dark green, oval foliage that is reddish underneath. Occasionally, the flowers remain open into the early evening hours.

Nymphaea "Chromatella"

SPREAD: 90 CM–1.25 M / 3–4 FT	ZONE: 4
FLOWERING PERIOD: JUNE–SEPT	

Perhaps one of the oldest and most reliable of all water lilies, "Chromatella" tolerates a wide range of exposures and will even bloom in partial shade. The canary yellow flowers generally float on the surface amid deep green foliage mottled with patches of reddish-brown. Its free-flowering nature and medium spread make it a good choice for gardeners unsure of their pond conditions.

Nymphaea "Arc-en-Ciel"

SPREAD: 1.25–1.5 M / 4–5 FT	ZONE: 4
FLOWERING PERIOD: JUNE–SEPT	

Merv's favourite water lily has spectacular deep green foliage variegated with splashes of yellow, cream, pink, purple and red — with no two leaves ever looking alike. This very old cultivar was once thought to be extinct until it was rediscovered in Japan. The blush pink blossoms highlighted with golden **stamens** are borne on a fairly robust plant — suitable for medium to large ponds.

Nymphaea "Gloire de Temple sur Lot"

SPREAD: 1.25–1.5 M / 4–5 FT	ZONE: 4
FLOWERING PERIOD: JUNE–SEPT	

This gorgeous water lily has extremely double blooms, each composed of well over 100 incurved petals. The buds open a soft pink and gently fade to white as they enlarge to an almost spherical flower (accented with bright yellow stamens), which sits just above the surface of the water. Some consider this slow-to-establish cultivar the most beautiful of all the hardy water lilies — so expect to pay a premium for this plant.

The Latour-Marliac Hall of Fame

A Frenchman named Joseph Bory Latour-Marliac was one of the first to successfully crossbreed Nymphaea and, from the late 1800s until his death in 1911, he introduced many of the water lily cultivars that we know today. Unfortunately, his techniques died with him, and it is only recently that newer hybrids are beginning to dominate the market. Here are just a few of Latour-Marliac's many introductions.

9. *"Virginalis" — 1910 / semi-double, pure white flowers*
10. *"Morning Glory" — 1887 / scented shell pink blossoms*
11. *"Attraction" — 1910 / changeable garnet red blooms*
12. *"Gloriosa" — 1896 / brilliant red semi-double flowers*
13. *"Comanche" — 1908 / changeable apricot to copper-red*
14. *"Helvola" — late 1800's / pygmy with yellow blooms*
15. *"Marliac Albida" — 1880 / fragrant white blossoms*
16. *"Splendida" — 1909 / medium-sized dark red flowers*
17. *"Chromatella" — 1887 / yellow blooms, mottled foliage*
18. *"Chrysantha" — 1905 / small reddish-yellow flowers*
19. *"Gonnere" — late 1800s / globular pure white blossoms*

Aquatic Plants

Jack and Jeanie Wootton
Hawaiian Botanicals and Water Gardens
Richmond, B.C.

Aquatic gardening was once the hobby of a few dedicated enthusiasts, but of late many gardeners have come to appreciate the beauty that even a small pond can bring to their landscapes. In response to this surge of interest, many retail nurseries are providing an ever-increasing variety of aquatic plant material. This phenomenon has also given rise to a few specialty aquatic nurseries — many of which offer a complete line of water garden supplies and "in-house" expert advice.

Hawaiian Botanicals was created in 1991, with the objective of offering Canadian tropical plant enthusiasts a mail-order source, without the "red tape" of import certificates and border inspections. Since then, Jack and Jeanie Wootton have expanded their operation by adding an extensive line of aquatic plants and fish, which are available at their retail outlet in Richmond. They have chosen a well-rounded selection of **marginals, oxygenators,** water lilies and tropicals in order to give you a balanced insight into the world of aquatic plants and their care.

Myosotis scorpioides / Water Forget-Me-Not

HEIGHT: 15–23 CM / 6–9 IN	WATER DEPTH: 2.5 CM / 1 IN	ZONE: 3
FLOWERING PERIOD: MAY–JULY		

An ideal edging plant for the shallow margin of any pond, *Myosotis scorpioides* is a reliable perennial that is quite easy to grow and a great plant for newcomers to aquatic gardening. It features yellow-eyed, sky blue flowers which bloom just above the surface of the water from May until July.

Ceratophyllum demersum / Hornwort

SUBMERGED OXYGENATOR	ZONE: 3

This **oxygenator** is not much to look at, but it performs the invaluable task of removing excess nutrients, which turn pond water green. Hornwort is very easy to introduce — simply drop the bundled cuttings into the pond, where they will act as a submerged plant. This plant will quietly do the work of keeping the water clear and can overwinter as dormant stems on the pond bottom.

Nymphaea "Sioux" / Changeable Water Lily

SPREAD: 90 CM–1.25 M / 3–4 FT	WATER DEPTH: 15–45 CM / 6–18 IN	ZONE: 3
FLOWERING PERIOD: JUNE–SEPT		

This Marliac hybrid is still one of the best orange changeables available, even though it was introduced back in 1908. "Sioux" is a prolific bloomer, with a flower colour that deepens from a yellowish-orange to an orange-red over the space of three days. The deep green foliage is mottled with attractive purplish-brown spotting.

Typha minima / Dwarf Cattail

HEIGHT: 30–45 CM / 12–18 IN	WATER DEPTH: 2.5–10 CM / 1–4 IN	ZONE: 3

The perfect marginal plant for small water features, *Typha minima* bears tiny oval catkins of velvet brown (about 2.5 cm / 1 in long). They contrast quite well against the very narrow, upright foliage of this hardy aquatic plant.

Nymphoides germinata / Yellow Snowflake

SUBMERGED AQUATIC	WATER DEPTH: 30–60 CM / 1–2 FT	ZONE: 5
FLOWERING PERIOD: JULY–SEPT		

This submerged aquatic has unusual fringed yellow blossoms, which account for the common name, yellow snowflake. *Nymphoides* features small water-lily-like foliage with interesting brown mottling. It is a good choice for providing surface coverage.

Introduction to Aquatic Lotus
The lotus genus, Nelumbo, consists of only two species: Nelumbo lutea and Nelumbo nucifera. Nelumbo lutea, the yellow lotus, is native to eastern and central North America. Nelumbo nucifera, the sacred lotus, is indigenous to many parts of Asia. Numerous varieties of N. nucifera exist, produced by both natural and deliberate crosses. Both lotus species and most cultivars are hardy in Zone 8 areas of the Pacific Northwest.

Lotus Culture in the Pacific Northwest

1. March–Early April — When the danger of any significant icing is past, the lotus can be raised from its winter resting depth to a sunny, shallow location. To compensate for our cool, temperate spring and summer, the lotus should be placed to a water depth of only 2.5–5 cm / 1–2 in.

2. April–June — An application of aquatic plant fertilizer should be added to ensure that the lotus receives adequate nutrients as it begins to grow. The fertilizer tablets (usually one or two per 5 L / 1 gal of soil) are pushed a finger's depth into the soil. This must be done carefully, as the lotus' brittle growing tips buried in the soil that can be easily broken. The lotus will produce small floating leaves, followed by larger leaves held high above the water on thick stems. As the growth rate increases, it is important to maintain a monthly application of aquatic plant fertilizer.

3. July–September — Lotus grown outside in the southern coastal parts of the Pacific Northwest generally begin blooming in mid-July if the plant was placed in an appropriate location. The monthly application of aquatic plant fertilizer should continue for July and August to ensure that there are adequate nutrients for flowering. The lotus will begin to show signs of approaching dormancy in mid-September.

4. October–November — As cooler temperatures set in, the lotus foliage will begin browning. The lotus should remain in shallow water until all the leaves have become brown and dry. In late October or early November, the dead leaves can be removed — but the leaf stem should not be cut too short (leave approximately 15 cm / 6 in or more of stem above the soil). The lotus should now be placed in deeper water with at least six inches of water over the soil in the pot. Lotus can also be overwintered in a frost-free greenhouse, but in this environment the plants must be kept cool to avoid rotting.

5. December–February — The lotus will be fully dormant in its winter resting spot.

Division and Repotting
Lotus are usually divided in February or March when the plant is totally dormant. Long runners and old shriveled tubers are trimmed off during division. Only one good tuber is placed in a pot filled with a heavy topsoil and clay mix. The pot should be at least 40 cm / 15 in in diameter.

Lotus in Water-Tight Containers
Many garden ponds are sited in partial shade or contain deep circulating water, which has the effect of lowering the temperature. This situation can inhibit lotus blooms. A lotus planted in a self-contained pot can be

Eichornia crassipes / Water Hyacinth

FLOATING PLANT	TENDER TROPICAL
FLOWERING PERIOD: FLOWERING SPORADIC WITHOUT A HOT SUMMER	

This floating plant is widely used to help prevent algae blooms by shading the water and removing excess nutrients with its thick root mass. Water hyacinth features shiny, deep green foliage and very attractive lilac-coloured flowers that usually last only one day. *Eichornia* is tropical and will not overwinter outdoors.

Iris laevigata
"Variegata" / Variegated Japanese Water Iris

HEIGHT: 60 CM / 2 FT	WATER DEPTH: 10 CM / 4 IN	ZONE: 4
FLOWERING PERIOD: JUNE–JULY		

One of the most beautiful aquatic iris, this *Iris laevigata* blooms pale lavender-blue flowers contrasted with lovely cream- and white-striped foliage. This native of Japan and eastern Siberia thrives in a water depth of up to 10 cm / 4 in above its container.

Pontederia cordata / Pickerel Weed

HEIGHT: 60 CM / 2 FT	WATER DEPTH: 7.5–15 CM / 3–6 IN	ZONE: 3
FLOWERING PERIOD: JULY–SEPT		

The glossy, deep green leaves of this marginal plant much resemble "Bird of Paradise" foliage. Pickerel weed features attractive spikes of soft blue flowers from July to September. This plant is full hardy, provided it is covered with several inches of water during the winter.

Colocasia "Black Magic" / Black Magic Taro

HEIGHT: 1.5 M / 5 FT	WATER DEPTH: 5–15 CM / 2–6 IN	ZONE: 10
PRIMARILY A FOLIAGE PLANT		

A tropical plant that makes a fine shallow water marginal, this cultivar features spectacular charcoal black leaves, with tints of purple. "Black Magic" taro rarely flowers but always attracts attention with its large, heart-shaped foliage towering over the water's surface. *Colocasia* can be overwintered as a houseplant.

Myriophyllum aquaticum / Parrot's Feather

HEIGHT: 15 CM / 6 IN	WATER DEPTH: 10–15 CM / 4–6 IN	ZONE: 4

This much-underused aquatic acts as both a marginal and an oxygenating plant. The feathery foliage of potted specimens will emerge to about 15 cm / 6 in above the water's surface and help to disguise the pond perimeter. All of the foliage left exposed to the air will die back from frost, but the submerged portions will grow again the following spring.

placed in the warmest and sunniest spot available. A tub-grown specimen will enjoy the higher temperature produced by the sun warming the outside of the container as well as the water surface. Also, a cold frame fashioned from plastic sheeting can be placed over the tub in March and April to stimulate growth of the lotus. The container should have rounded contours and be at least 90 cm / 3 ft in diameter in order to provide winter protection for the **tubers**. Be aware that a container this size will be very difficult to move after the soil has been added.

Helpful Hints

Two common mistakes can lead to disappointing results with lotus culture in the Pacific Northwest:

1. The lotus is placed is water that is too deep. Many aquatic books advise a depth of 15–20 cm / 6–8 in over the lotus pot. This is too deep for our climate — 2.5–1 cm / 1–2 in of water over the soil surface is adequate from late March to late October. The lotus should be placed in deeper water from November until March to protect the **tuber** from freezing.

2. Overwintering in an excessively warm location. We have found that lotus overwintered outside submerged in water produce larger **tubers**. Overwintering indoors at temperatures in excess of 5 °C (40 °F) will frequently cause the lotus to rot due to the lack of sunlight.

Bog Perennials

Gerald Gibbens
VanDusen
Botanical Garden
Vancouver, B.C.

Species of the Heath family (*Ericaceae*) seem to dominate most bog environments. Also present are members of the *Primula, Saxifraga,* Orchid and Lily families. Within these groups can be found literally hundreds of plants that will thrive in moist soils. Aside from plant selection, understanding the dynamic of bog conditions (i.e., soil pH, drainage) will enable gardeners to better design their pond edge or wetland feature.

As the horticulturist for VanDusen's Sino-Himalayan garden, Gerry Gibbens probably deals with more plant material than most of us will encounter in a lifetime of gardening. With the many wet spots (at the base of irrigated berms) and water features found here, bog perennials are an important component of this diverse landscape. A simple stroll through this garden would certainly provide many design ideas. For those of you unable to appreciate it in person, here are a few of Gerry's most successful bog plants.

Osmunda regalis / Royal Fern

HEIGHT: 90 CM–1.5 M / 3–5 FT	SPREAD: 90 CM / 3 FT	ZONE: 3

This fern thrives in moist, rich soil and has proven itself a magnificently large specimen when grown near water. Royal fern is quite adaptable, doing equally well in an open meadow as well as shaded woodland. Wonderful green **fronds** are produced from spring through summer. These turn a rich yellow and bronze toward autumn. The rust-coloured fertile tips also provide foliar interest late into the season.

Zantedeschia aethiopica / Calla Lily

HEIGHT: 90 CM / 3 FT	SPREAD: 30–60 CM / 1–2 FT	ZONE: 8
FLOWERING PERIOD: JUNE–JULY		

There is some question of hardiness when it comes down to newly planted specimens. That being said, once established, this striking plant forms a mass of arrow-shaped leaves with spectacular pure white flowers, standing well above the foliage. The root zone should be mulched during winter for frost protection.

Rheum palmatum / Ornamental Rhubarb

HEIGHT: 1.25 M / 4 FT	SPREAD: 1.5–2.5 M / 5–8 FT	ZONE: 4
FLOWERING PERIOD: MAY–JUNE		

This large, herbaceous perennial grows leaves almost 1. 5 m / 5 ft across. The flower stems are covered with red blooms, followed by attractive seed heads on stalks averaging 2.5 m / 8 ft tall. This relative of edible rhubarb is mostly used as a background plant with its large, textured, **palmate** foliage. A **cultivar** with deep red spring foliage (*"Atrosanguineum"*) is also available.

Primula japonica / Japanese Primula

HEIGHT: 30–60 CM / 1–2 FT	SPREAD: 30 CM / 1 FT	ZONE: 5
FLOWERING PERIOD: MAY–JULY		

This species, along with many other "candelabra type" primulas, is perhaps the most garden-worthy perennial for the bog garden, providing a wide colour range and the potential to crossbreed when planted together in mass. Long-flowering stalks bear up to eight rings of bloom clusters along the stem.

*Understanding
the Bog Environment*

*We must first understand bog conditions in order to choose plants that will thrive there. The soil of a bog consists mainly of partially decomposed vegetative matter, which breaks down slowly due to the high acidity of the peat as well as its ability to retain a large volume of water. This can be overcome with the addition of sand, which will allow for better drainage and encourage root growth. There are also **mycorrhiza** present in the soil and on the roots of many bog plants, helping them to convert nutrients to a useable form. Water levels in a bog can be stagnant or appear standing, but quite often there is still some percolation through the soil. Individual plant requirements are best understood by looking at local areas where moisture-loving plants grow. Here in the Pacific Northwest, we usually receive rainfall throughout the fall, winter and spring. Further investigation will reveal that these areas — although water-logged for most of the year — have a gravelly, porous soil. When the water level drops in mid to late summer, the subsequent drier conditions allow the plants a resting period and encourages the production of seed.*

Choosing a Mulch
*The regular addition of leaf
mulch will supply sufficient
nutrients for garden plants and
reduce competition from weeds.
Take care in the choice of leaf
used for mulching, as different
types of foliage decay at different
rates. Maple leaves will decompose within a year; however,
beech and oak can take quite a
bit longer, up to several years.
The presence of a light, airy
mulch will also ensure that the
soil temperature will remain cool
during the hottest weather,
reducing plant stress.*

Carex morrowii "Variegata" / Variegated Japanese Sedge

HEIGHT: 45 CM / 18 IN	SPREAD: 45 CM / 18 IN	ZONE: 6

An evergreen sedge featuring elegant arching blades with striking creamy-white variegation, variegated Japanese sedge forms an attractive clump and contrasts well against Japanese or Siberian Iris.

Dactylorhiza elata / Marsh Orchid

HEIGHT: 30–90 CM / 1–3 FT		ZONE: 6
FLOWERING PERIOD: JULY–AUG		

Probably the most outstanding species of the terrestrial orchids, these tuberous plants bulk up very quickly, sending 60-cm / 2-ft high flower stems with 20-cm / 8-in deep-purple bloom spikes emerging in early summer. *Orchis* (*latifolia / elata*) is synonymous with the genus *Dactylorhiza*.

Erythronium tuolumnense / Tuolumne Fawn Lily

HEIGHT: 23–30 CM / 9–12 IN	SPREAD: 15–30 CM / 6–12 IN	ZONE: 5
FLOWERING PERIOD: EARLY–MID SPRING		

This bulbous (**corm**) member of the lily family is well adapted to bog gardens. *Erythronium tuolumnense* is a robust species with bright green foliage and nodding golden-yellow flowers in early to mid spring. "Kondo" (pale yellow) and "Pagoda" (taller variety) are vigorous hybrids of this species and *Erythronium revolutum*. The Tuolumne fawn lily is native to California.

Iris laevigata / Water Iris

HEIGHT: 60 CM / 2 FT	SPREAD: 45 CM / 18 IN	ZONE: 4
FLOWERING PERIOD: JUNE–JULY		

This aquatic iris will thrive in rich, moist soils or under shallow water up to 15 cm / 6 in deep. It forms loose clumps with spiky, soft green leaves. The species generally flowers a deep purple-blue or white, although many cultivars are available in other colours or with leaf variegation.

Eomecon chionantha

HEIGHT: 30–40 CM / 12–16 IN	SPREAD: far-reaching underground stolons ZONE: 7
FLOWERING PERIOD: SPRING–EARLY SUMMER	

The natural habitat of this member of the poppy family is along stream banks. Although perennial by nature, its hardiness is questionable in colder regions. Flowering in June, the four petals are pure white contrasted by a mass of bright yellow **stamens**. The pale green basal leaves are deeply **cordate** and **glaucous** on the underside.

Fritillaria meleagris / Checkered Lily

HEIGHT: 30–45 CM / 12–18 IN	SPREAD: 25 CM / 10 IN	ZONE: 3
FLOWERING PERIOD: APRIL		

This European native has distinct purple-white checkered blossoms that name the plant. The nodding flowers are borne on long, thin stems in spring and are also available in white. This member of the lily family naturalizes easily in meadow areas and will tolerate occasional flooding.

Light Requirements

Most bog plants thrive in filtered light. Primulas, for example, are usually found at the edge of woodlands and along streams, where the forest canopy is deciduous. As the garden matures, this canopy should be thinned, or bog plants will diminish in the dense shade. This is a delicate balancing act that requires close observation and continual pruning. In addition to the filtered light they provide, deciduous trees create a continuous source of nutrients as their leaves fall and decompose. Some bog plants will thrive in a full sun exposure, provided there is sufficient soil moisture

Bulbs

Bulbs are a simple act of faith — gardeners just trust that those shriveled tubers and corms, once planted, will miraculously transform into the beautiful flowering plants pictured on the sales display. To be honest, few gardeners are disappointed with those handfuls of tulips and daffodils planted each fall, and perhaps that is why they keep coming back for more. Local garden centres are more than happy to cultivate an expanded interest in bulbs and each autumn oblige gardeners by stocking a dazzling array of these dormant gems, complete with full colour photographs of the expected results.

Even as the last of the tulips fade, late in the following spring, yet another planting season presents itself with the bulbs and corms of dahlias, canna lilies and gladiolas featuring prominently. Each year gardeners are faced with many new varieties of these old standards, as well as some relative newcomers such as pineapple lily and Chinese ground orchid (Bletilla). So wherever a gardener's tastes may lie — be it exotic or domestic, diminutive or imposing — there is at least one bulb to suit one's taste and garden.

Tulips

Bob Rogers
*Queen Elizabeth Park
Vancouver, B.C.*

Tulips have been a part of cultivated landscapes for hundreds of years now, with lily-flowered species finding particular favour in 16th-century Turkish gardens of the Ottoman empire. Later, in 17th-century Holland, "tulip fever" would reach such a frenzied state that a single rare bulb was sold for the equivalent of 20,000 dollars. While the price has settled down since then, many gardeners are still a little overwhelmed with the number of varieties of tulip bulbs available each fall.

Planting Tulips
Bob Rogers and the rest of the staff at Queen Elizabeth Park generally plant their tulip bulbs sometime in late October. They prepare the beds by pulling out any remaining summer flowers and weeding the beds thoroughly. The soil is then turned with a garden fork to a depth of 15–18 cm / 6–8 in. Since the tulip displays are changed annually, bone meal is only used every few years, as it breaks down rather slowly or, if needed, the soil is enriched by incorporating some of the parks board's own leaf mould (compost).

Queen Elizabeth Park had its origins as a rock quarry that provided much of the raw material for Vancouver's early roadways. The property languished for many years until the 1930s, when the B.C. Tulip Association suggested transforming the quarry into a sunken garden. Bob Rogers currently serves as the head gardener for the "large quarry" and has been responsible for many tulip displays at the park's two quarry gardens and at the Vancouver Parks Board office on Beach Avenue.

The flowering period in the plant descriptions that follow indicate which part of the season each tulip blooms. Tulips generally flower from early March until late May. Mid season would be about April and early would be in March in the Pacific Northwest.

Companion Plants for Tulips
Quite often, tulip displays are accented with companion plants, which are used for their complementing or contrasting flowers. They are generally planted at the same time as the bulbs and come into bloom with the tulips the following spring. Here are a few good choices to try in the garden:

Myosotis *(Forget-Me-Nots) — try "Blue Basket" or "Blue Ball." Pink and white varieties are also available*

Viola *Hybrids (Winter Pansies) — available in a rainbow of colours, many with bicolour blooms*

Erysimum *or* Cheiranthus *(Wallflowers) — generally come in orange, red, yellow, cream and mahogany*

Bellis perennis *(English Daisy) — small pompom blooms of pink, white and rose-red*

Tulipa "Negrita" (Triumph Tulip)

HEIGHT: 40 CM / 16 IN	FLOWERING PERIOD: MID SEASON

"Negrita" is probably one of the best dark-coloured tulips available — with deep purple-black petals. Excellent in combination with lighter tulips such as "Douglas Bader" (pale apricot to pink) and "Golden Melody" (bright yellow).

Tulipa "Queen of Sheba" (Lily-Flowered Tulip)

HEIGHT: 70 CM / 28 IN   FLOWERING PERIOD: LATE SEASON

Gardeners looking for an exotic touch in the garden should try a planting of "Queen of Sheba" with bright yellow wallflowers. Not only will they get an elegant lily-shaped bloom but also dazzling colours of vibrant red edged in gold.

Tulipa "Oxford" (Darwin Hybrid Tulip)

HEIGHT: 60 CM / 2 FT   FLOWERING PERIOD: MID TO LATE SEASON

This scarlet tulip has long been a standard planting in many parks and display gardens. Its reliable show is a welcome sight, and it also works well in combination with *T.* "Golden Oxford" (yellow) and "Oxford Elite" (red edged yellow).

Tulipa "Sweetheart" (Fosteriana Tulip)

HEIGHT: 45 CM / 18 IN   FLOWERING PERIOD: EARLY SEASON

"Sweetheart" brings spring to the garden with its cheery bright yellow blooms edged in white. All the larger-flowered Fosteriana tulips are good companions for daffodils, as they generally bloom at the same time.

Tulipa "Red Riding Hood" (Greigii Tulip)

HEIGHT: 20 CM / 8 IN   FLOWERING PERIOD: EARLY SEASON

This small gem features very large carmine-red blossoms and deep green leaves that are wonderfully variegated with dark purple highlights. "Red Riding Hood" will repeat bloom for many years in the garden.

Tulipa "Pink Impression" (Darwin Hybrid Tulip)

HEIGHT: 75 CM / 30 IN   FLOWERING PERIOD: MID TO LATE SEASON

A long-lasting tulip with huge blossoms of soft pink borne on very sturdy stems, "Pink Impression" makes a very bold statement but is best planted in mass in larger beds. It is excellent in combination with pale blue forget-me-nots.

Tulip Groups
Tulips are divided into several distinct groups — each with its own flowering characteristics, heights and blooming period.

Species Tulips
— generally smaller than their hybridized counterparts but good choices for naturalizing
Average Height: 15–25 cm / 6–10 in
Early to Mid-Season
e.g., T. pulchella — violet purple

Kaufmaniana *Tulips*
— short tulips that work well in rock gardens
Average Height: 15–25 cm / 6–10 in
Early Season
e.g., "Johann Strauss" — red with cream edges

Greigii *Tulips* *— large blooms on short plants, many with purple variegation on the foliage*
Average Height: 25–40 cm / 8–16 in
Early Season
e.g., "Colour Parade" — mixed colours

Fosteriana *Tulips* *— large flowers that last for a long time*
Average Height: 30–45 cm / 12–18 in
Early Season
e.g., "Red Emperor" — scarlet

Single Early Tulips
— very reliable tulips with cup-shaped blooms
Average Height: 30–40 cm / 12–16 in
Early Season
e.g., "Christmas Dream" — deep cherry pink

Double Early Tulips
— fully double blooms that are good for cutting
Average Height: 30–35 cm / 12–14 in
Early Season
e.g., "Schoonoord" — white

Triumph Tulips
— long-lasting blooms, slightly smaller than Darwins
Average Height: 40–50 cm / 16–20 in
Mid-Season
e.g., "New Design" — soft pink, variegated foliage

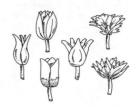

Tulipa "Marilyn" (Lily-Flowered Tulip)

HEIGHT: 55 CM / 22 IN   FLOWERING PERIOD: LATE SEASON

"Marilyn" features elegant blooms of creamy-white streaked with fuchsia-red. This bicolour lily-flowered tulip is also quite durable, with long-lasting flowers.

Tulipa "Princess Irene" (Single Early Tulip)

HEIGHT: 35 CM / 14 IN   FLOWERING PERIOD: EARLY–MID SEASON

This single early lives up to its royal namesake with salmon-orange blooms flamed in purple. "Princess Irene" is wonderful in combination with *T.* "Attila" (violet-purple), although the latter begins to bloom just slightly later.

Tulipa "Plaisir" (Greigii Tulip)

HEIGHT: 30 CM / 1 FT   FLOWERING PERIOD: EARLY SEASON

"Plaisir" features beautiful flowers of cherry-red edged in cream, which are quite conical before they begin to open. The large blooms are nestled on short stems just above broad leaves of deep green, striped with purple.

Tulipa "Douglas Bader" (Triumph Tulip)

HEIGHT: 40–45 CM / 16–18 IN   FLOWERING PERIOD: MID SEASON

A must for those who love pastel tones in the garden, "Douglas Bader" starts out the palest pink and later matures to a light apricot-pink. The intermediate height and constantly changing flower colour make this an interesting specimen.

Narcissus

Daffodils are known the world over as the forerunners of springtime. While *Narcissus* is the scientific or Latin name for these true bulbs, daffodil is the common alias and can be properly used for all the varieties in this family. Spring has much welcome beauty — including many delightful bulbs — yet no other group of flowers seems to bring us such joy and renewal, as they usher in the new growing season each year.

Matt Groves
formerly of
Bradner Bulb Gardens
Bradner, B.C

Matt and Cherry Groves have been growing bulbs for the past 20 years in the Bradner area of the Fraser Valley. Over that time they have participated in the cut flower and dry bulb industry as the operators of Bradner Bulb Gardens — a display garden and mail-order nursery that has since been transferred to Pick of the Crop, the business that currently distributes the bulbs. Matt is currently growing on the bulb collection of the late David Sheppard and hybridizing new varieties of daffodils for show and garden.

There are some 25 species of daffodils and in excess of 13,000 registered hybrids — so selecting a few favourites was a difficult task. In the end, Matt limited himself to choosing fairly common varieties that the gardener will be able to find at local garden centres in the fall.

The flowering period for daffodils generally runs from mid-February through to May. The classification system for daffodils is explained following the plant description.

General Care

All daffodils thrive in well-drained soil that is moist and not too rich in nitrogen. Avoid peat soils if possible, as they tend to hold too much water close to the bulb. Fresh compost and manure should also be avoided, as they encourage fungal diseases and rotting of the bulbs. Heavy clay soils should be broken up and mixed with sand or well-rotted compost to increase drainage. Most commercially grown daffodils are planted in "hilled" rows or raised beds to provide near perfect drainage. Home gardeners can easily mimic these conditions by planting bulbs (in groups) at a depth of 5–8 cm / 2–3 in and bringing the surrounding soil up over them to create a miniature raised bed. Always avoid locations where water sits on the soil surface at any time during the winter. Daffodils like as much sun as possible, although they can survive in partial shade. Gardeners who plant them directly under large trees must be prepared to replace the bulbs often, as the tree roots usually rob them of the moisture and nutrition they require to produce flowers the following year.

Narcissus "Unsurpassable"

HEIGHT: 45 CM / 18 IN   FLOWERING PERIOD: MID SEASON

One of the many fine successors to the well-known "King Alfred" daffodil, "Unsurpassable" features larger, brighter blooms on a slightly shorter, sturdy stem, which allows this flower to easily live up to its name.

Narcissus "Tahiti"

HEIGHT: 35 CM / 14 IN   FLOWERING PERIOD: MID-LATE SEASON

This narcissus looks as exotic as its namesake. "Tahiti" bears large, fully double golden-yellow blooms with interspersed dark orange **petaloids**. This daffodil has a good, solid stem but, like most doubles, it requires a sunny location that is protected from wind.

Narcissus "Bravoure"

HEIGHT: 45 CM / 18 IN   FLOWERING PERIOD: MID SEASON

"Bravoure" is best described as a gigantic, bright yellow **trumpet** set on a pristine white background. This stunning daffodil is not only tall but also quite sturdy.

Narcissus "Golden Ducat"

HEIGHT: 55 CM / 22 IN   FLOWERING PERIOD: EARLY–MID SEASON

Strong, tall stems support golden-yellow double blossoms of absolutely huge proportions. "Golden Ducat" is equally favoured as a cut flower or a dazzling background planting in the spring border.

Narcissus "Accent"

HEIGHT: 35 CM / 14 IN   FLOWERING PERIOD: MID–LATE SEASON

For the gardener looking for a "true" pink **cup** on a daffodil, this is the variety to find. The cup colour of this *Narcissus* just gets better as the flower matures and is well contrasted on a pure white background. "Accent" is also quite a vigorous grower.

Narcissus "Quail"

HEIGHT: 40–50 CM / 16–20 IN **FLOWERING PERIOD: MID–LATE SEASON**

"Quail" is the perfect balance of delightful fragrance and elegant plant form. This multiflowering *Narcissus* bears pure yellow blooms majestically displayed on tall, sturdy stems.

Narcissus "Papillon Blanc"

HEIGHT: 45 CM / 18 IN **FLOWERING PERIOD: MID–LATE SEASON**

This split-**corona** *Narcissus* resembles a "white butterfly" with its delightful white petals and partially split inner segment, which has just a hint of yellow and an attractive green eye. "Papillon Blanc" is an unusually strong grower for its class.

Narcissus "Ice Follies"

HEIGHT: 40 CM / 16 IN **FLOWERING PERIOD: EARLY MID SEASON**

"Ice Follies" features a wide, short **cup** that opens a brilliant yellow and soon fades to white in the sun. Probably one of the most vigorous-growing daffodils and also an excellent choice for a cut flower, "Ice Follies" is also great for naturalizing.

Narcissus "Tête-à-Tête"

HEIGHT: 40 CM / 16 IN **FLOWERING PERIOD: EARLY MID SEASON**

The many fragrant blooms atop short stems make this the most versatile and popular daffodil. "Tête-à-Tête" is excellent for containers, borders, rockeries or when interplanted with low ground covers. Be sure to get good-sized bulbs (12 cm+ / 5 in+ bulb minimum — the size of a large tulip bulb), as the smaller ones give only single blooms.

Fragrant Narcissus

Nothing says spring like a bouquet of daffodils, and the only way to improve upon this is to choose some of the sweetly fragrant varieties. In fact, these narcissi are such good cut flowers that it is worthwhile planting a few for the vase (or forcing), so you can enjoy their enticing fragrance indoors.

Narcissus "Carlton" — *pure yellow / large cup (45 cm / 18 in)*

N. "Cheerfulness" — *white to cream / double (40 cm / 16 in)*

N. "Baby Moon" — *yellow / miniature (20 cm / 8 in)*

N. "Thalia" — *white / multiple flowers per stem / (35–40 cm / 14–16 in)*

N. "Minnow" — *pale yellow with deep yellow cup / (15 cm / 6 in)*

N. "Geranium" — *white with short orange cup / (40 cm / 16 in)*

N. "Suzy" — *yellow with an orange cup / (35–40 cm / 14–16 in)*

N. "Hawera" — *dwarf yellow / (15–20 cm / 6–8 in)*

N. "February Gold" — *golden yellow, early / (30–35 cm / 12–14 in)*

N. "Yellow Cheerfulness" — *pale yellow, double / (40 cm / 16 in)*

*Those readers interested in the many new varieties that are continually being introduced and shown should visit the American Daffodil Society on the web at **www.mc.edu/ ~adswww/ads/info.html**

Specialty Bulbs

Stuart Bronson
Van Bloem Gardens
Delta, B.C.

At one time, if a bulbous plant was not a tulip or a daffodil, it fell into the category of a "minor bulb." Fortunately, with the proliferation of these plants on the retail market, they are no longer a "minor" item but a major source of design material for gardeners and landscapers alike. This chapter then renames these assorted true bulbs, rhizomes, tubers and corms as specialty bulbs.

Van Bloem Gardens is an international source of bulbs, perennials and aquatic plants, supplying a broad selection of standard and unusual ornamentals to both growers and retailers. All of their products display the Dutch *Keurmerk* or "quality mark," assuring the gardener that their plants are true to name and of the highest quality.

Acidanthera bicolor / Peacock Gladiolus (corm)

HEIGHT: 75 CM / 30 IN	ZONE: 10
FLOWERING PERIOD: MID-AUG–SEPT	

Although this member of the iris family appears quite exotic, it is quite easy to grow. Spring-planted corms will bloom mid-August to September with fragrant, creamy-white flowers contrasted with brown centres. *Acidanthera* is an excellent cut flower, but the bulbs will need to be lifted and stored in a dry, frost-free site over the winter.

Leucojum aestivum / Summer Snowflake (true bulb)

HEIGHT: 40 CM / 16 IN	ZONE: 4
FLOWERING PERIOD: LATE SPRING	

Summer snowflake is an unsurpassed naturalizer in the moist conditions it prefers. The nodding white flowers (tipped in jade green) are borne in late spring and are often mistaken for snowdrops at a distance. This is a good choice for planting pond- or streamside, but be sure to leave the bulbs undisturbed for at least three years before dividing.

Bletilla striata / Chinese Ground Orchid (pseudobulb)

HEIGHT: 30 CM / 1 FT	ZONE: 7
FLOWERING PERIOD: JUNE–JULY	

This is one of the easiest of the "terrestrial" orchids to grow and well worth the effort. The small *Cattleya*-like pink blooms are produced in early summer over pale green foliage. Plant in light shade with well-drained, humus-rich soil and watch a single plant quickly form an attractive colony. A white variety ("Alba") is also available.

Alocasia macrorrhiza / Upright Elephant Ear (tuber)

HEIGHT: 1.5 M / 5 FT	ZONE: 10
PRIMARILY A FOLIAGE PLANT	

This exotic foliage plant produces leaves of an enormous size, with stems arranged in a strong vase-like fashion. A specimen feature, it is well suited for both the formal "Victorian" setting of cast-iron urns or as a focal point in a modern "tropical" landscape. Start the tubers in early spring by planting in a moisture-retaining potting mix (with good drainage) and then "sweat out" the growing tip by keeping it in a warm, humid location in the dark. Once the growing point is 15–30 cm / 6–12 in above the tuber, gradually reintroduce it to the light over a week or so. *Alocasia* needs plenty of fertilizer once established and can be enjoyed as a houseplant over the winter or allowed to go dormant.

Eucomis bicolor / Pineapple Lily (true bulb)

HEIGHT: 45–60 CM / 1½–2 FT	ZONE: 7
FLOWERING PERIOD: JULY–AUG	

Pineapple lily is an easy plant to describe, as the flower heads resemble the body of a tropical pineapple — complete with a tuft of green leaves on top. This South African native is excellent in patio containers, where the large

Specialty Bulbs by Season:

Winter
Eranthis hyemalis / *Winter aconite*
Anemone blanda / *Greek Anemone*
Galanthus nivalis / *Common Snowdrop*
Cyclamen coum / *Winter Cyclamen*

Spring
Erythronium *"Pagoda"* / *Yellow Fawn Lily*
Chionodoxa luciliae / *Glory of the Snow*
Fritillaria imperialis / *Crown Imperial*
Puschkinia libanotica / *Striped Squill*

Summer
Galtonia candicans / *Summer Hyacinth*
Tigridia pavonia / *Tiger Flower*
Eremurus bungei / *Foxtail Lily*
Cardiocrinum giganteum / *Giant Himalayan Lily*

Autumn
Colchicum autumnale / *Autumn Crocus*
Schizostylis coccinea / *Kaffir Lily*
Sternbergia lutea / *Autumn Daffodil*
Dierama pendulum / *Wand Flower*

strap-like foliage and chartreuse-edged maroon blooms can best be appreciated. It thrives in sunny, well-drained sites but should be mulched if left in the ground over winter.

Canna "Wine and Roses" / Canna Lily (rhizome)

HEIGHT: 1 M / 3¼ FT	ZONE: 9
FLOWERING PERIOD: LATE JULY–EARLY OCT	

A new, self-cleaning cultivar, "Wine and Roses" bears huge blossoms of deep rose complemented with burgundy foliage, much resembling banana leaves. This is a highly adaptable plant that can be used in containers, annual beds or even on the marginal shelf of a fishpond. Canna lillies are generally lifted after a hard frost and stored in peat moss, in a frost-free area for the winter.

Allium bulgaricum / Flowering Onion (true bulb)

HEIGHT: 90 CM / 3 FT	ZONE: 5–6
FLOWERING PERIOD: MAY	

This member of the onion family carries strong stems with pendulous, tricolour blooms of olive green, cream and dark rose-pink. *Allium bulgaricum* is also reliably perennial, and the mature flowers can be cut for dried arrangements.

Zephyranthes candida / Zephyr Lily (true bulb)

HEIGHT: 30 CM / 1 FT	ZONE: 9
FLOWERING PERIOD: SUMMER OR EARLY FALL	

A marginally hardy bulb, the zephyr lily's large, crocus-like blooms of white to light rose are borne atop foliage reminiscent of chives. They are a native of the southern hemisphere, where they normally sprout after a long-awaited rain and flower quickly before the onset of drought. Zephyr lily prefers a sandy loam soil and is easily grown in containers — but should be stored in a frost-free site for winter.

Colocasia esculenta / Big Leaf Elephant Ear (tuber)

HEIGHT: 90 CM–1.5 M / 3–5 FT   ZONE: 9–10

PRIMARILY A FOLIAGE PLANT

This bold ornamental is widely grown in the tropics for its starchy, potato-like roots known as taro. *Colocasia* prefers full sun and fertile, wet soils but will easily adapt to life on the marginal shelf of a pond. The deeply sculpted leaves are reminiscent of an African tribal shield, and their lush character blends in well with an exotic garden design. It can be enjoyed as a houseplant during the winter, as it is not hardy outdoors.

Fritillaria meleagris / Checkered Lily (true bulb)

HEIGHT: 15–30 CM / 6–12 IN   ZONE: 3

FLOWERING PERIOD: APRIL

Fritillaria meleagris features delicate, nodding "checkerboard" flowers of white and bronze-purple. This is an excellent choice for the lightly shaded rockery, as it naturalizes quite well. Checkered lily thrives in moist, organic soil and should be planted in small clumps for the best effect. Pure white forms ("Alba") are also available.

Vegetables

I have spent most of my career dealing with ornamental plants, so when the idea of a vegetable section came up, I was less than enthusiastic. My primary concern was to create a comprehensive book that reflected the diversity of the many gardeners that I have met over the years. While pondering this, a bit of persuasion came to me in the form of my wife Pauline, who grew up on a farm and was quick to remind me that corn can be as attractive as canna lilies. In the end the idea prevailed, and the result is a short but fascinating section — rich in plant diversity and down-to-earth advice.

While I may be a novice in the vegetable garden, the harvested results are frequent ingredients in the few dishes I try my hand at. Fiery peppers bring life to a stir-fry, while plenty of pungent garlic and diced Roma tomatoes constitute the basis of my spaghetti sauce. The cooks among us will also appreciate the broad selection of edibles, including herbs, salad greens and such rare gourmet delights as cardoon — which is also quickly gaining popularity as a bold accent plant in the perennial border. After reading this section, you will agree that vegetables can be as beautiful as they are tasty.

Vegetables

Wes Barrett
City Farmer
Vancouver, B.C.

City Farmer is a non-profit society that has promoted the introduction of organic food gardens in urban areas since 1978. Their Web site at <www.cityfarmer.org> has been chosen as one of the top Internet sites on several occasions, and it also serves as the publishing format for their *Urban Agriculture Notes.* Since its inception, this small coalition has evolved into a multinational resource, with 1.2 million files being transmitted from their site to readers in 138 countries across the world during 1998 alone.

Wes Barrett is City Farmer's horticulturist or head gardener — he manages their organic food garden in Kitsilano, which now functions as the City of Vancouver's compost demonstration site. Many unusual as well as standard vegetables are grown there, but all crops are chosen for their nutritional value as well as their biodiversity. This unique criterion is directly responsible for Wes Barrett's interesting choices.

Bush Bean "Royal Burgundy"

This vigorous grower produces an abundance of tasty, deep purple pods on a compact plant. (The 12–15 cm / 5–6 in long purple beans change to a bright green once they are cooked.) "Royal Burgundy" will tolerate cooler soils, but in general, bush beans prefer warmer soil temperatures. Since this is a nitrogen-fixing plant, be sure to leave the roots in the ground after the tops have died back. "Purple Queen" (snap bean) and "Black Coco" (dry / snap bean) are also highly recommended.

Cardoon

Gardeners are more likely to find cardoon at the back of the perennial border than in a vegetable garden these days, but at one time it was considered a choice edible. This is a bold perennial with large, silvery-green leaves and an overall appearance of an enormous thistle (to 2 m / 6½ ft tall). It bears flower heads that resemble small artichokes, but the edible portions of this plant are the stems, in particular the fleshy bases of the leaves. These are prepared by removing the outer layer and steaming (or boiling) until they are tender. Try adding them to homemade soups.

Lettuce "Brunia"

This oakleaf-type lettuce is as good to look at as it is delicious to eat. This French variety features unusual green-tinged red foliage that is very slow to bolt, much like the other recommended lettuce, "Buttercrunch." "Brunia" has a reputation for quickly replenishing after harvest and producing over a long period of time.

Broccoli "Purple Sprouting"

This popular European vegetable is a non-heading broccoli that produces many individual purple **florets**. It is generally planted in the fall (start from seed in July), overwintered and ready for harvest in early spring. Several varieties are available, including "Early," "Late" and "Red Arrow." For more standard broccoli fare, try "Packman," a heavy producer that bears many side shoots once the main head is cut off.

Cucumber "Lemon"

At first glance, this hardly appears to be a cucumber — it grows in the shape of a small apple with bright yellow skin. "Lemon" is actually an old variety, with heavy yields

Good Compost = Good Vegetable Garden

Composting recycles many nutrients from organic waste that would otherwise be lost, and the resulting "black gold" serves as the primary ingredient in any successful garden. Good compost is not the result of a random pile tucked in the corner. Instead, with a little planning, even a small bin can create an abundance of this valuable soil amendment. Here is a condensed outline of some good composting practices:

1. Alternate thin layers (5–10 cm / 2–4 in) of green, nitrogen-rich material (i.e., grass clippings, fruit and vegetable scraps) and dry, brown, carbon-rich materials (i.e., leaves or straw).

2. The layers of green and brown materials should be in approximately equal proportions by volume.

3. Always cover the food wastes to avoid problems with rodents. This will mean adding a minimum of two layers at a time.

4. Mix the pile at least every two weeks.

5. Soil can be added at any time (up to one-third the volume of pile), but always add soil onto food waste before topping with brown material.

Compost Troubleshooting

Through operating the compost hotline, City Farmer has found that most problems with urban composting derive from two common mistakes.

1. Not enough dry brown material for carbon (i.e., leaves, straw, newspaper) is added.

2. Insufficient mixing and turning of the pile to provide air for the many creatures that participate in the decomposing process and help to dispel odours, which are usually the result of a pile that is too wet.

Salad Greens
In addition to lettuce, City Farmer also grows many different plants that add colour and zest to a salad, as well as provide excellent nutrition. They are quite easy to grow and, like lettuce, most are cool-weather plants that will overwinter easily in a cold frame. Here are a few of their favourites:

Arugula — also known as roquette, with a fine peppery to nutty taste

Sorrel — a staple in French cuisine with tart, lemony foliage

Cilantro — also known as coriander or Chinese parsley, sharp citrus flavour

Garden Purslane — succulent green leaves loaded with antioxidants

Oriental Greens — "Mizuna" is a finely cut, mild-flavoured salad green

Edible Chrysanthemum — also known as shungiku, cool weather produces mild flavour

Oriental Mustard — "Giant Red" features purple foliage with a sweetly pungent taste

and fruits that taste pleasantly mild and sweet. Just sow the seeds in slightly dished mounds, with plenty of well-rotted compost, and watch the plants grow out of control.

Radicchio "Palla Rossa Special"

Italian chicory (*Cichorium intybus*) thrives in cooler temperatures and may be overwintered in a cold frame or planted in late June for harvest in autumn. "Palla Rossa Special" features a rounded head of deep red leaves, with a distinctive tangy flavour that some may find slightly bitter, but it makes an excellent addition to a gourmet winter salad. This vegetable will appreciate having some mushroom manure worked into the soil, and be sure to hold back on high-nitrogen fertilizers, as they can cause bolting.

Shelling Pea "Maestro"

"Maestro" is a fairly compact plant reaching an average size of 60 cm / 24 in free-standing and only 1.2 m / 4 ft tall with some support. The slender 10-cm / 4-in long pods are filled with medium-sized peas that are sweetly flavoured and tender — quite similar to "Green Arrow." It has good disease resistance and is a consistently heavy producer, allowing for multiple pickings.

Kale "Winter Red"

Kale is perhaps the most nutritious member of the *Brassica* family, yet it is probably one of the least planted. "Winter Red" is a red Russian type with deeply cut, greyish-green foliage accented with purple stems, with the leaves changing to a reddish-purple after a touch of frost. This kale is tender and sweet enough for fresh use in salads, but be sure to incorporate some dolomite lime in the planting area for the best results. "Westland Winter" also comes highly recommended — it features extremely frilly green leaves.

Grain Amaranth

Amaranthus is an ancient **annual** that is best known as a grain in many parts of the developing world, although the edible leaves of some species allow us to include it here as a vegetable. Love-lies-bleeding (*Amaranthus caudatus*) is one of those dual-purpose plants, with both leaves (cooked like spinach) and seeds harvested for food in India. This exotic vegetable is often used as a specimen in annual borders and features showy flower spikes of various colours (golden-yellow and red), depending on the cultivar or species. These plants require only modest amounts of nitrogen for production, so good compost is usually sufficient as a fertilizer.

Garlic "Yugoslavian"

This *Rocambole* or **hardneck**-type garlic produces purple-striped, copper-coloured bulbs that average between nine and 14 cloves. "Yugoslavian" is a vigorous, dark green variety and has a spicy garlic flavour that mellows to a sweet aftertaste. "Spanish Roja" is another good choice, having been grown in the Pacific Northwest for well over 100 years. Wes plants the garlic at City Farmer's demonstration garden from mid-October to early November, for harvest the following July.

Crop Rotation

To prevent pest and disease problems, City Farmer recommends crop rotation among beds. This practice also takes advantage of different plant nutrient needs and can be generally stated as alternating between heavy and light feeders, followed by **legumes** — which literally add nitrogen to the soil, if the roots are left intact after harvest. Here are a few samples of each category.

Heavy Feeders —
broccoli, cabbage, lettuce, potatoes, cucumbers, tomatoes, kale, cauliflower

Heavy Givers (Legumes) —
peas, beans

Light Feeders —
beets, carrots, garlic, parsnips, turnip, peppers

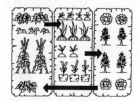

Raised Beds

For the best results in a vegetable garden, City Farmer recommends growing in raised beds. The advantages of this system are better drainage, earlier soil warming in spring and greater surface area for planting. Beds may be walled or left naturally mounded. Either way, all raised beds should be double-dug, which involves turning the soil to a depth of 60 cm / 24 in or two spade depths.

Tomatoes & Peppers

Mary Ballon
West Coast Seeds Ltd.
Vancouver, B.C.

Tomatoes and peppers hold a special place in the vegetable plots of many West Coast gardeners. Perhaps it is the obvious fact that they develop their brilliant fruit right before our eyes, rather than hiding beneath the earth. Whatever the reason may be for holding these vegetables in high esteem — pastas, pestos, salads and salsas would be sadly lacking without them.

Vegetables chosen for flavour and ease of culture using organic methods in the unique climate of the Pacific Northwest are the specialty of West Coast Seeds. From a small beginning behind Vancouver's first organic gardening store to an overflowing warehouse in Marpole, Mary Ballon has been encouraging people to grow as many of their vegetables as they can. Quite a few gardeners have limited growing space available, so Mary has chosen tomato and pepper varieties that are compact enough to grow in containers.

Tomatoes

The tomatoes developed for a West Coast climate are unique because they will set fruit well before any others — if they are placed out with a bit of protection, when the night temperatures are above 7°C / 45°F. They are called *parthenocarpic* because the fruit will form before the flower is fertilized.

"Siletz"

RIPENING PERIOD: 70–75 DAYS

"Siletz" is a great choice for containers (one plant per big white pail), as it grows only 90 cm / 3 ft tall and benefits from the support of a tomato ring. The first fruits are large and juicy with a rich flavour. This variety was developed at Oregon State University, specifically for a Pacific Northwest climate.

"Tumbler"
RIPENING PERIOD: 55 DAYS

This is *the* hanging basket tomato — with long branches that trail gracefully over the edge of the container. The large cherry tomatoes have a fine flavour and are always at "mouth level." Keeping these plants under the overhang of a porch or balcony ensures no blight problems, because the leaves never get wet.

"Oregon Spring"
RIPENING PERIOD: 75–80 DAYS

"Oregon Spring" was the standard of early ripening coastal varieties for many years. It produces large, slicing tomatoes with a fairly mild flavour. "Santiam" produces smaller fruits but ripens a bit earlier than "Oregon Spring."

"Kootenai"
RIPENING PERIOD: 70–75 DAYS

Another variety that looks lovely in containers, "Kootenai" features dark green leaves on a stocky, short plant with full-sized tomatoes. It will produce larger, more flavourful fruit if about two-thirds of the flowers are removed. Try planting a few "Johnny-jump-ups" around the containers for a touch of whimsy.

"Oregon Eleven"
RIPENING PERIOD: 60–65 DAYS

This cousin to "Siletz" is the first red tomato to ripen in West Coast Seed's trial gardens. Although the tomatoes are a little smaller, the richly flavoured fruits are an excellent balance of acidity and sweetness.

Beating the Late Blight
Every Pacific Northwest gardener wants to grow the perfectly ripe tomatoes they remember growing in other regions — where the sun warms the developing fruit and sugars, intensifying the flavour. We are challenged in our climate because our sunlight is not as strong and we have excessive moisture that will encourage the Phytopthera fungus late in the summer. "Late Blight," as the disease is called, will blacken a plant completely in one day if the spores land on a damp leaf and have 48 hours to spread. If the leaf can be dried off in less than 48 hours or if it never gets wet, the fungus will do no damage. Encouraging good air circulation around the plants, pruning excess leaves (and branches) and covering plants are tested strategies for preventing late blight. Another way to approach the problem is to grow early-maturing varieties that will fruit during the salad season of summer. Then, if the blight does not strike until September, these plants can be pulled out (and put in the garbage if they have blight), and the gardener will have lots of sun-ripened tomatoes without having to mourn the ending of a fine season.

Growing Peppers
In a really sunny exposure, pepper plants will need to grow a thick leaf canopy to protect the fruit from sunburn. Lots of rich compost and a handful of organic fertilizer for each plant should encourage good leaf development. When growing lots of pepper plants, let one or two of them mature their fruits all the way to red (or orange or purple or brown). The plant will not produce as many peppers, but the explosion of flavour from a fully ripened pepper is hard to beat. For gardeners wondering how hot a ripening pepper will be — here is a sampling of a few varieties available from West Coast Seeds:

Sizzling Hot
"Scotch Bonnet"
"Thai Dragon"

Very Hot
"Habañero"
"Long Thin Cayenne"

Hot
"Early Jalapeño"
"Surefire"

Mildly Pungent
"Ancho"
"Mulato Isleno"

Mild
"Banana Supreme"
"Red Bull's Horn"

Sweet
"Pimento Elite"
"Gourmet'

Peppers

Peppers are tropical plants like tomatoes and love the summer sun. They are easy to grow in containers and, with their many shapes and colours, delight the eyes as much as a choice flower or shrub. The added pleasure of their varied flavours make peppers stand-up favourites for the summer garden.

"Pimento Elite"

RIPENING PERIOD: 88 DAYS

This heart-shaped, thick-walled variety is wonderful for fresh eating —it turns red easily and can be munched like an apple. Fortunately, this pepper gets sweeter as it matures and will only develop into a hot pepper in regions with long, warm summers.

"Gypsy"

RIPENING PERIOD: 58 DAYS

"Gypsy" is the most reliable producer of long, fairly narrow, pale green peppers. They can be eaten in salads or cooked like the familiar bell peppers and are a good choice for cooler gardens. In the Pacific Northwest, "Gypsy" produces many more large fruit than any "bell" types.

"Surefire"

RIPENING PERIOD: 55 DAYS

This "hot wax" type pepper produces slender yellow to red, thick-walled morsels. "Surefire" thrives in marginal conditions and is one of the first peppers to mature in the Pacific Northwest.

"Long Thin Cayenne"

RIPENING PERIOD: 80 DAYS

This reliable coastal pepper produces slim green fruits that ripen to a deep red. This is a "very hot" pepper that is also suitable for drying.

"Pepperoncini"

RIPENING PERIOD: 75 DAYS

Despite the name and its appearance, this very slim Italian pepper is actually quite sweet. Its taste is like a sun-dried tomato, and it makes a lovely garnish on salads for fresh munching. This heirloom variety is also good for frying or pickling.

West Coast Seed's Demonstration and Research Garden

Good advice is always firmly grounded in experience, and Mary's tomato and pepper choices were already firmly rooted in her demonstration garden, long before they were chosen for this book. She has found that the only way to find vegetable varieties that will thrive in our climate is to grow them in our local coastal conditions and see how they fare. West Coast Seed's research garden is just a stone's throw away from the Georgia Strait and is located on the London Heritage Farm in Steveston, B.C. In this very "coastal" site, all Mary's seed offerings must endure foggy mornings, spring rain and cool summers — but through it all she manages to find a select few to offer in her catalogue.

Herbs

Erwin Gygli
Heimat (Homeland) Farms
Pitt Meadows, B.C.

The flavours, tastes and textures of herbs are as diverse as the people who use them. Every nationality has its favourites and, long before the widespread use of salt, pepper and MSG, people used herbs to enhance the taste of food. Even today, many people are returning to the natural flavour and healing properties of these plants, particularly in modern medicine.

Sharon and Erwin Gygli started down the herbal path with a small, lean-to greenhouse and a tiny backyard. When they started to use their neighbour's yard to plant their excess stock, they knew it was time to expand into a larger property. The focus for them today remains on quality first, with each year bringing them more knowledge in the field of growing herbs and unusual ornamentals.

Erwin has decided to concentrate on culinary herbs and has included specific cultural notes for each of his choices.

Rosmarinus officinalis / **Rosemary**

ZONE: 8

Anyone who has traveled through southern Europe has seen the lovely hedges of rosemary. In the Pacific Northwest, the climate is not ideal for large specimens, but this herb can still thrive in the right microclimate.

Rosemary thrives in hot sun and poor soil, provided some lime is added. The location should be well-drained and sheltered from cold winter winds. To save a young rosemary plant from year to year, dig it up in the middle of September and let it root in a pot for the next two months, preferably storing it in a frost-free environment with lots of light. Water very sparingly. Ideally, it is better to choose a sheltered outdoor site and leave it in the ground.

Levisticum officinale / Lovage

ZONE: 3

Lovage has fallen out of favour for some time and really needs to be back in the kitchen garden. Nothing brings flavour to soups, stew, sauces, stocks and vegetarian dishes like lovage — fresh or dried. All parts of this plant can be used, including the leaves, stems and roots.

Easy to grow, it should be placed in the back of the garden where it can reach heights of 2 m / 6½ ft. Lovage does not like overly wet ground, preferring full sun and rich soil. To encourage bushy growth, cut out the flower stalks as they appear. Divide every four years.

Coriandrum sativum / Cilantro, Coriander, Chinese Parsley

ANNUAL

Seldom has there been a herb that has divided public opinion so much. Love it or hate it — cilantro is already an integral part of cooking today.

Whether deciding to seed or transplant small starter plants, pick a site with some shade during the hottest part of the day. The only exception is when growing for the seeds, as these will develop quickly when planted in a hot, dry location. Otherwise, choose a cooler site with well-drained, rich soil. Cilantro will also self-seed.

Salvia officinalis / Sage

ZONE: 4–6

Thanksgiving and turkey filled with savoury sage stuffing go back a long way. This is a potent culinary herb and just a little does a lot of flavouring — so one plant is usually enough for the average gardener.

Sage gets quite woody after about three or four years and should be replaced. This is a wonderful herb for

Herbal Teas

Herbal teas may be enjoyed hot or chilled on ice, with endless flavour combinations possible. Growing a herbal tea garden is quite easy, as most of the plants listed below are robust growers, with ample foliage for fresh infusions or drying for winter use. As with any herbal tea, these infusions should be consumed in moderation.

Stevia rebaudiana / *Sugar Plant — used to sweeten tea*

Monarda didyma / *Bee Balm — Earl Grey Tea flavour*

Salvia elegans / *Pineapple Sage — pineapple*

Mentha x piperita citrata / *Orange Mint — citrus*

Matricaria recutita / *German Chamomile — calming effect*

Melissa officinalis / *Lemon Balm — lemon*

Agastache foeniculum / *Anise-Hyssop — licorice*

Mentha spicata / *Spearmint — Mint Julep ingredient*

Plectranthus amboinicus / *Cuban Oregano — use fresh, savoury tea*

Mentha suaveolens / *Applemint — fragrant tea*

savoury dishes, and pineapple or honeydew sage make fine teas. It prefers well-drained soil that is reasonably rich, and full sun.

Origanum ssp. / Oregano

ZONE: 5

Oregano means "joy of the mountain" in Greek — as derived from "oros" (mountain) and "ganos" (joy). *Origanum* as a perennial (*O. vulgare hirtum*) is the oregano we know and love, while the annual form (*O. majorana*) is better known as marjoram. While closely related, they are far apart in taste.

To get the best plant, buy from a nursery one that is labelled "Greek Oregano." By the end of summer it will have grown to 25–30 cm / 10–12 in wide (from a 10-cm / 4-in pot) — so there will be enough to dry for winter. Oregano is easy to grow in average soil and full sun.

Ocimum basilicum / Basil

ANNUAL

To a chef, there is nothing quite like the smell of fresh basil. It is like an aphrodisiac — overwhelming our tastebuds to the point that resistance is futile. Its varied uses are too many to list here, with sweet basil being ideal for salads, pizza and pasta. Other varieties such as "Dark Opal" make wonderful flavoured vinegar, "Genovese" is perfect for pesto and "Sweet Dani" will add a clean lemon flavour to any dish. One of the better methods to preserve basil for winter use is to freeze it firmly pressed in ice-cube trays that have been filled with water.

Do not plant basil too early — the soil needs to be consistently warm — and never water in the evening, only in the morning with tepid water.

Artemesia dracunculus sativa / Tarragon

ZONE: 4

Take care with French tarragon, as this truly great herb cannot be seeded — a plant must be purchased from your local nursery. The seeds sold are not worth wasting time on and should really be taken off the market. Seeded tarragon is much like grass and just as invasive, with no redeeming value.

French tarragon has survived in Heimat Farms' garden for 10 years and is still very productive. It needs a good frost for two weeks and then should be covered with leaves or boughs for winter. Tarragon requires rich, well-drained sandy soil and full sun to part shade

Thymus vulgaris / Thyme

ZONE: 5

As one of the classic ingredients in "bouquet garni," thyme has its place in the kitchen garden. Although it is considered by some to be a tender perennial, Heimat Farms has yet to lose a single plant, even in some severe winters.

As with sage, many varieties are available. The main species include *Thymus vulgaris* (English and French thyme) and *Thymus* x *citriodorus* (lemon thyme). The plant can be cut back hard (for drying) and will flush again quite easily. This herb may get woody in time and will self-seed. It requires dry, well-drained soil and full sun to part shade.

Petroselinum crispum var. crispum / Curly Parsley and *Petroselinum crispum* var. *neapolitanum* / Flat Leaf Parsley

BIENNIAL

Two common varieties of parsley are used primarily for their tasty foliage. The third, "Hamburg Rooted," is grown for its roots and sought after by many chefs for its great flavour in sauces and soups.

A **biennial**, parsley should be planted every year in order to make a continuous supply available. If grown in pots or containers, pay attention to the root space, as parsley roots grow from 45–75 cm / 1½–2½ ft deep. Plant in a moist, well-drained area with semi-shade to full sun.

Allium schoenoprasum /Chives and *Allium tuberosum* / Garlic Chives

ZONE 3

Like parsley, chives are a staple herb in the kitchen. They are used in both hot and cold dishes, as well as for plate decoration. Salads and sauces are also greatly enhanced by the addition of flowers (one flower head torn in pieces is usually enough) or chopped foliage. Garlic chives can be used where a gentle hint of garlic is needed.

These perennial herbs should be divided every three years. Plant in moist, moderately rich soil and full sun.

Fruits

There was a time when almost every backyard was stocked with at least a few fruit trees and a small berry patch of some sort. These "urban orchards" have since fallen victim to the demands of larger homes on smaller lots and the simple process of maturity and decline that occurs over the years. As well, as fewer and fewer fruit trees were left in some neighbourhoods, many of the remaining specimens started to produce very little or were left barren due to a lack of cross-pollinators, and as a consequence, most were removed.

While the skeptics may have declared the "age of the urban orchard" a lost cause, the next generation of gardeners began to reflect on their childhood memories of crisp apples and juicy pears picked from their own trees. The simple fact of the matter is that the fruit grown in our own backyards will almost always be fresher and taste better than its store-bought counterpart. Armed with modern fruit cultivars that emphasize disease resistance, compact growth habit and self-fertility, gardeners have brought the "urban orchard" back from extinction. In fact, gardeners have expanded on this concept with a greater interest in exotic fruits such as figs and kiwi. So whether gardening on acreage, a residential lot or even a condominium — there is always something in the realm of fruit to grow and enjoy for years to come.

Apples & Pears

Doug DeJong
Misty Meadow Nursery
Surrey, B.C.

Apples and pears are enjoying a resurgence of interest lately, partially brought on by the many delicious eating varieties available at our supermarkets. Unfortunately, not every apple bought at the store will thrive as a tree on the West Coast, as most are adapted to interior climates. The good news is that many of the recent cultivars have been bred for disease resistance and compact growth habit, making them ideal fruit trees for our largely urban landscapes.

Doug DeJong is one grower who has spent time researching and testing improved varieties at his Fraser Valley field nursery. Misty Meadow Nursery also grows a good selection of flowering and shade trees for retail nurseries across the province.

Apples

Malus "Florina"

FLOWERING PERIOD: MID SEASON

This European apple cultivar is not yet well known, but is probably one of the best coastal varieties to grow. It ripens in mid-October on the south coast of British Columbia and features very high quality fruit with a bright red finish. One bite of the firm, sweet apples will be enough to convince most gardeners that this tree belongs in their yards. "Florina" is also quite productive, branches freely and is European **scab** free.

Malus "King"

FLOWERING PERIOD: MID SEASON

This heritage apple was one of the first varieties planted during the Fraser Valley pioneer days. "King" is usually sought after for its delicious-tasting apples with a red finish — although it is not overly productive and is only moderately vigorous.

Malus "Liberty"

FLOWERING PERIOD: MID SEASON

"Liberty" is another scab- and mildew-resistant cultivar that has become the standard for disease resistance. This moderately productive apple bears firm, slightly tart fruit that has an attractive deep red finish, somewhat similar to "Spartan." "Liberty" ripens around mid-September in the Fraser Valley and is of medium vigour.

Malus "Pristine"

FLOWERING PERIOD: MID SEASON

"Pristine" is the best early season variety, which ripens to a full golden finish in early August. The firm apples are quite flavourful, but they are usually small due to heavy fruit set, with a two-year-old tree capable of producing up to 2 kg / 4–5 lbs of apples. "Pristine" exhibits a very flat branching pattern but tends to lose its central leader quite easily. The scab-resistant nature and excellent eating quality will certainly bring this new variety to a nearby garden centre.

Malus "Redfree"

FLOWERING PERIOD: MID–LATE SEASON

"Redfree" is considered one of the better early season red apples, with large fruit that matures in mid-August on the West Coast. This scab-resistant variety is moderately vigorous and quite productive. The bright red fruit is firm with good flavour — excellent for fresh eating or cooking.

Apple Rootstock Selection

Standard-sized fruit trees are not always desirable in the home garden except under very few conditions. Hence, dwarfing rootstocks are necessary to reduce tree size, increase yield and bring the tree to fruition earlier. Probably the best rootstock for Fraser Valley conditions (also for the average garden) is M26, which produces a tree 45 percent of the size of a standard apple. M9 produces a tree less than 40 percent of standard size but is sensitive to drought and poor soil conditions (i.e., coarse soils or high water tables). This rootstock is also weakly anchored and requires some support, which means an apple on M9 is basically more work. So under these circumstances, M26 is preferred, allowing an apple to reach an average height of 3–4 m / 10–15 ft and a spread of 1–1.5 m / 3¼–5 ft (at the base) in 10 years.

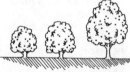

M9   M26   Standard

Apples and Pears for the Pacific Northwest

Apples

"Gravenstein" / old European variety

"Jonafree" / "Jonathan" type apple

"Golden Delicious" / scab-free

"Gold Rush" / matures late

"Redfree" / disease-resistant

Pears

"Bosc" / self-fertile

"Clapp's Favourite" / very juicy

"Bartlett" / good flavour

"Flemish Beauty" / very productive

"Conference" / good pollinator

Planting and Pruning
Always plant trees to the same depth as the soil in the nursery pot or, at most, 1–2 cm / ½–1 in deeper. Fruit trees require full sun to adequately develop fruit to maturity, with the degree of exposure affecting both the quality of the fruit as well as the size of the crop. Apples and pears prefer a sandy loam soil that holds adequate moisture during the summer — yet is well-drained during the winter. Never plant a fruit tree in an area with standing water — instead use raised beds to keep the roots above the high water table. At planting time, place a 2.5–3 m / 8–10 ft long support post (for M9 stock) in the ground before placing the tree to avoid root damage. Once the tree is planted, tie the post to the main leader where it is used for support (due to dwarfing rootstock) and training. Prune to achieve a central leader (i.e., leave one vertical leader) and use wooden spreaders to create horizontal branching. Fruiting spurs develop more readily on flat-angled branches, and the fruit matures better with the improved sun exposure. Always remove dead or diseased wood, especially canker.

Fertilizing Apples and Pears
Under Fraser Valley conditions, fruit trees require very little nitrogen fertilizer but benefit from the application of dolomite lime. Many fruit trees in the valley are too vigorous due to excessive organic decomposition and available soil nitrogen. In general, they should only be adequately fed to produce reasonable crops, as they are quite capable of producing higher yields under stress.

Malus "Gold Rush"

FLOWERING PERIOD: LATE SEASON

This late season variety bears firm, golden apples that usually ripen in early November. "Gold Rush" is a good keeping apple for storage, much in part to its late maturity. It is also scab-resistant.

Malus "Golden Sentinel"

FLOWERING PERIOD: EARLY–MID SEASON

One of the newer "columnar" apples, "Golden Sentinel" grows to a height of 3 m / 10 ft in 10 years under optimum conditions. It can also be grown on the patio in large containers — under these circumstances the ultimate size averages 2 m / 6½ ft tall and 30–40 cm / 12–16 in wide. This is a very productive apple that bears fruit along the main axis on short spurs. It features good quality fruit that is very similar to "Golden Delicious" and matures in early September. It is also scab-resistant.

Malus "Scarlet Sentinel"

FLOWERING PERIOD: EARLY–MID SEASON

"Scarlet Sentinel" is another of the columnar apples that was developed at the Summerland Research Station and, with "Golden Sentinel," was field evaluated at Misty Meadow Nursery for a period of five years. "Scarlet Sentinel" is slightly more compact than "Golden Sentinel," reaching an ultimate height of 2.5 m / 8 ft. It features a quality fruit that is firm and sweet, with a red finish over a yellow background. This cultivar matures in mid- to late October.

Pears

Pyrus "Harrow Delight"

This pear was introduced by Agriculture Canada in the early 1980s and was bred for resistance to fire blight. The juicy, flavourful fruit is of excellent dessert quality and is very similar to "Bartlett," but matures about two weeks earlier. "Harrow Delight " is a moderately vigorous, productive tree and is a good choice for coastal gardens in the Pacific Northwest.

Pyrus "20th Century"

FLOWERING PERIOD: EARLY–MID SEASON

One of the popular Asian pears, with a crisp, juicy fruit that tastes like a combination of apple and pear, "20th Century" is probably the best choice for the Fraser Valley. Doug has noted that it is more resistant to **bacterial canker** than other Asian pears. "Chojuro" is a good cross-pollinator for "20th Century" and, although it has done well in coastal conditions, it may be slightly more susceptible to the canker.

Dealing with Canker
Anthracnose and European canker are the most prevalent diseases of Malus (apples) under West Coast conditions. These diseases appear as **necrotic lesions** on the branches and trunk with visible symptoms of dead circular to elliptic forms in the bark and cambium occurring in early spring. As the rest of the tree begins to grow, these dead regions are made more prominent when callusing occurs around them. When infected bark is scraped away, the cambium tissue below will appear browned. To date, the only treatment is the removal of infected limbs by pruning, coupled with copper sprays.

Cherries, Plums & Peaches

Mike Lascelle
Amsterdam Garden Centre
Pitt Meadows, B.C.

As a kid, I spent most of my summer vacations at my grandmother's house, which just happened to be in the middle of orchard country in Westbank, in the Okanagan Valley of British Columbia. The first thing I would do when we arrived was climb into one of her Bing cherry trees and eat to my heart's content, despite my grandmother's repeated warnings. After a few days of recuperation, I was again ready to enjoy her plums, cherries and more than a few of the neighbour's peaches — so I can honestly say that I have been a "*Prunus* fruit" connoisseur since childhood.

Cherries, plums and peaches have been some of the most popular fruit trees in residential gardens for decades. Unfortunately, the days of every other yard having a convenient cross-pollinator are over — as many of these mature specimens are past their prime and have been cut down. This means that the next generation of gardeners will have to rely more heavily on self-fertile varieties or multigrafts, which provide their own pollination. The one exception would be peaches, which are totally self-fertile but sometimes difficult to grow under West Coast conditions.

"Rainier" (Sweet Cherry)

A newer introduction, "Rainier" bears unusual yellow fruit accented with a slight red blush. A superior cultivar when compared with older favourites such as "Royal Anne" and "Napolean," it features sweet-tasting, firm fruit. The best attribute of this variety is that the mostly yellow cherries seldom attract the birds as much as the standard red fruits do.

"Lapins" (Sweet Cherry)

SELF-FERTILE

This self-fertile sweet cherry was developed at Summerland, B.C., and was first introduced in 1984. "Lapins" was a deliberate cross of "Stella" and "Van" and produces dark red cherries of good flavour, which are resistant to splitting. This sweet cherry crops consistently and is very productive — making it the perfect choice for urban gardens.

"Schatten Morello" (Sour Cherry)

SELF-FERTILE

Many immigrants from Poland and Germany are already familiar with this variety and, when they go shopping for a cherry tree, this is the *only* one they want. Although "Schatten Morello" is a sour cherry, the deep reddish-black fruit are so flavourful (yet tart) that they are good eaten right off the tree. This virus-free cultivar is great for cooking or for preserves.

"Bing" (Sweet Cherry)

"Bing" has long been the standard variety due to its very sweet, purple-black fruit. Unfortunately, on the West Coast it is very susceptible to splitting in the rain or raids by ravenous birds such as starlings. It is a very large, upright tree, but a compact variety ("Compact Bing") is available. Pollinate with "Van" or "Stella."

Growing Peaches in Coastal Regions
There are only two obstacles to growing peaches and nectarines in coastal regions. The first is a lack of the hot summer temperatures that are necessary for ripening; the second is an abundance of rain, which causes a fungal disease called peach leaf curl. Both these factors can be negated by planting peach trees under the house eaves, on a south or west exposure. They can be grown espalier-style (flat); the eaves will protect them from rain and the sunny exposure (along with heat reflected from the house) will help to ripen the fruit. Another option is to try genetic-dwarf varieties, which grow only a few metres high and are easily kept in large containers. "Bonanza," "Empress" and "Golden Glory" will all bear peaches at a young age, while "Golden Prolific" produces medium-sized nectarines.

"Compact Stella" (Sweet Cherry)

SELF-FERTILE

Generally a small tree up to 4 m / 15 ft tall, "Compact Stella" tends to readily produce fruit spurs. It bears heavy crops of reddish-black cherries that are suitable for fresh eating or canning. "Compact Stella" is also a good universal pollinator for most cherry trees.

Italian Prune Plum (European Plum)

SELF-FERTILE

The very best plum to plant in the coastal B.C. gardens of the Pacific Northwest, the European plum is totally self-fertile and quite productive. The dark purple-blue fruits are egg-shaped with yellow flesh and may be picked for fresh eating a bit early (when they are slightly tart) or left to fully ripen (and sweeten) for dessert use. "Italian" prune plums may also be used for preserves or for dried fruit.

"Green Gage" (European Plum)

PARTIALLY SELF-FERTILE

This is a popular variety with gardeners from England, where it has long been a favoured plum. Despite its unusual greenish-yellow skin, "Green Gage" is actually quite sweet and may be used for fresh eating or cooking. Although it is self-fertile, it does not always set a heavy crop — so it might be a good idea to plant another European plum such as "Italian" or "Damson" to allow for some additional cross-pollination.

"Santa Rosa" (Japanese Plum)
SELF-FERTILE

The Japanese plums feature large, rounded fruit — much like the ones we buy in the supermarket. "Santa Rosa" in particular has deep red to purple blush fruits with excellent flavour. This cultivar is a good pollinator for another coastal variety of Japanese plum, "Shiro," which has yellow fruits.

"Damson" (European Plum)
SELF-FERTILE

"Damson" is an old-fashioned variety that is primarily grown for use in jams and cooking. It bears small, rounded dark blue plums that are a bit tart unless they are allowed to ripen fully, at which stage they are best used for preserves.

Peaches / *Prunus persica*
SELF-FERTILE

There really is no perfect peach to grow here in the Pacific Northwest — but a few varieties are tolerant of cooler temperatures and somewhat resistant to peach leaf curl. "Frost" is probably one of the best new cultivars, while "Pacific Gold" and "Renton" have been grown with satisfactory results. All peaches are self-fertile but may need to be hand-pollinated, as they often bloom early, before many of the bees are out.

A New Prunus *Fruit*

"Plumcots" are apricot-plum hybrids that have actually been around for quite some time, since they were originally crossed by Luther Burbank. More recently, two new fruits have been introduced with various percentages of both plum and apricot. "Pluots" have a smooth skin that encloses a very sweet flesh, with a slight aftertaste of apricot — these have a greater plum lineage. "Apriums" resemble apricots more strongly with their slightly fuzzy skin. Both these new hybrid fruit trees have been trademarked by their owner and are being grown commercially in California. While plumcots, pluots and apriums have yet to become readily available in our local market, work is currently being done to breed more hardy or tolerant varieties for regions across North America.

Exotic Fruit & Nut Trees

Sarah and George Kato
Kato's Nursery Ltd.
Abbotsford, B.C.

Exotic fruit and nut trees represent an increasingly important group of plants in the Pacific Northwest. Exotic fruits already have many admirers, among them landscape designers who covet their "tropical" foliage and homeowners who have experienced these fruits in other parts of the world. Nut trees, on the other hand, have a long history here but are only now regaining the popularity that they once held in residential landscapes.

Kato's Nursery Ltd. of Abbotsford is one of the few wholesale operations with a plant availability list comprehensive enough to currently include exotic fruit and nut trees. George and Sarah's knowledge of growing fruit has a long history, which began in 1952 when George, along with his parents and siblings, moved to the present site to operate a berry farm. In the late 1960s Sarah joined them and, together with George, they have built the business to the point of introducing their own "Touch of Nature" plant line. For more than 30 years, Kato's has been providing retail nurseries and landscapers with one of the largest selections of ornamental and edible plants in British Columbia.

Eriobotrya japonica

HEIGHT: 3–9 M / 10–30 FT	ZONE: 7

This is a handsome evergreen tree or large shrub much favoured by landscape designers for its glossy, dark green leaves (up to 30 cm / 12 in long), which lend an exotic touch to any landscape. The fruit resembles tiny, pale orange pears that are borne in small clusters. Unfortunately, loquat rarely comes to fruition in the cool West Coast climate. Although this native of southeastern China has adapted well in subtropical zones throughout the world, it can be grown in the Pacific Northwest when situated in well-drained soil (in part to full sun) with shelter from drying winter winds.

Diospyros kaki "Fuyu"

HEIGHT: 7.5–9 M / 25–30 FT	ZONE: 7

Persimmon is definitely one of those fruits that are an acquired taste, and "Fuyu" is the most popular **non-astringent** cultivar available. It forms an attractive, medium-sized ornamental tree with a distinct branching pattern that is prominent during the winter months. The deciduous foliage emerges pale lime, matures to a glossy, deep green and then turns rich gold to orange in autumn. This exotic tomato-like fruit will mature in warmer sites of the Pacific Northwest (i.e., Victoria) provided it receives full sun. "Fuyu" is self-fertile.

Ficus carica "Brown Turkey"

HEIGHT: 3 M+ / 10 FT+ (depending on pruning)	ZONE: 6

The edible fig has become quite fashionable lately and for varied reasons. Some people prefer its ornamental, smooth grey bark accented with large, deeply lobed leaves, while others simply want to grow fresh figs in their garden. "Brown Turkey" is the most tolerant cultivar, bearing purplish-brown fruits with a sweet strawberry-coloured pulp. *Ficus carica* produces two crops a year, but the second rarely matures in cooler climates. However, when given ideal conditions of sharp drainage, full sun and residual heat, a mature plant will bear more fruit than the average home gardener can consume.

A Selection of Edible Figs
"Brown Turkey" certainly is not the only edible fig grown on the West Coast — so here are a few others to try, if you consider yourself a fig connoisseur:

"Desert King" / many consider this the best Pacific Northwest fig — pale green with strawberry pulp

"Brunswick" / somewhat susceptible to early frosts — produces large purple fruit with good flavour

"Black Mission" / often grown here, but really needs a warmer clime — small, purple-black fruit

"Lattarula" / also known as the Italian honey fig — sweet yellowish-green fruit

"White Genoa" / sometimes disappointing without "hot" microclimate — very sweet, small fruit

Growing Kiwi

Available Species
Actinidia deliciosa — *Zone 7 /*
fuzzy, egg-shaped fruit
A. arguta — *Zone 3 / smooth,*
grape-sized fruit
A. *"Issai"* — *Zone 4 / self-fertile*
cultivar, small fruit
A. kolomikta — *Zone 5 / orna-*
mental variegated foliage

Pollination
All kiwis, except for the self-fer-
tile "Issai," will need both a male
and female plant in close prox-
imity (6–9 m / 20–30 ft) in order
for the female vine to bear fruit.
Even the ornamental A.
kolomikta will produce if a
female plant is available.

Morus alba "Tea's Weeping"

HEIGHT: 1.8–2.5 M+ / 6–8 FT+ (depending on graft and pruning)   ZONE: 5

This **pendulous** form of white mulberry has the overall appearance of an umbrella, depending on how high it has been grafted. With pruning, it forms a small tree and features luscious heart-shaped leaves that occasionally produce lateral lobes. The fruits are white in colour and mature to a reddish-pink, with a strong resemblance to raspberries. They are quite sweet, with a tart aftertaste, and make excellent jellies.

Feijoa sellowiana

HEIGHT: 5.5 M / 18 FT (in warmer climates)   ZONE: 8–9

Pineapple guava is a relative newcomer that is only marginally hardy, even in the mildest regions of the Pacific Northwest. This drought-tolerant, evergreen shrub (or small tree) has ovate foliage that is a glossy, dark green on top and silvery on the undersides. The unusual flowers are formed from edible, white-tinged purple petals that are almost buried in a huge tuft of bright red **stamens**. Fruits are an avocado colour on the outside with a soft pulp, vaguely reminiscent of pineapple. It is definitely worth overwintering in a greenhouse.

Vaccinium vitis-idaea

HEIGHT: 30 CM / 1 FT   SPREAD: 90 CM / 3 FT   ZONE: 5

Lingonberry is not really an exotic plant in the true sense of the word, as it is native of many temperate regions, including the Pacific Northwest. Rather, this fairly common broadleaf evergreen shrub is unusual for the fact that it is rarely grown for its abundance of edible, bright red berries, which make a wonderful preserve and taste much like cranberries. This handsome shrub features white to pale pink, bell-shaped flowers and is a good small-scale ground cover or underplanting for larger rhododendrons.

Actinidia deliciosa

HEIGHT: 36 M / 20 FT+	ZONE: 7

Many gardeners still have a hard time believing that kiwi fruit can be grown in the Pacific Northwest. These robust vines will need sturdy support (i.e., 10-cm / 4-in posts) and plenty of room to spread out. *A. deliciosa* has separate male and female plants and the garden needs both to ensure a crop of fruit, which is usually slightly smaller than the ones at the supermarket. For gardeners with limited growing space, try *A.* "Issai," a self-fertile vine with smaller leaves, grape-sized fruit and Zone 4 hardiness.

Castanea mollissima

HEIGHT: 18 M / 60 FT	ZONE: 5

Chinese chestnut forms an attractive shade tree with broad, sweeping branches and glossy, dark green foliage with **serrated** edges. The traditional roasted chestnuts used to be derived from the American species (*C. dentata*), which was nearly wiped out by a blight in the early 1900s. Fortunately, *C. mollissima* is resistant to this disease. These plants are only partially self-fertile, with single specimens bearing lightly at best — so plant at least two trees to ensure good cross-pollination.

Juglans regia

HEIGHT: 27 M / 90 FT	ZONE: 4

The best choice for its edible, thin-shelled nuts with superior flavour, English walnuts are self-fertile, but unfortunately the male and female flowers do not always bloom at the same time — so if you have the room, plant at least two varieties to ensure consistent pollination. It is also known as the Carpathian walnut.

Pests and Diseases
Kiwi is generally pest- and disease-resistant with the exception of the variegated A. kolomikta, *which seems to attract cats and may sustain damage to the stem.*

Growing Site
Fruiting kiwi prefers fertile, well-drained soils in part to full sun. During the growing season, adequate moisture is critical.

Fertilizing
Fertilize mature plants in March and early June with any "fruit tree" formulation.

Fruiting Habits
Kiwi begin to flower after five to six years, so expect to wait up to three or four years for flowers after planting a container specimen from a nursery. Fruit is borne on new shoots that develop from seasoned canes or laterals.

Initial Training
Single stems should be grown to about 2 m / 6½ ft tall (on support), then headed, allowing two dominant leaders to develop. Tie the stems to the supports rather than letting them twine. Allow an evenly distributed system of lateral branches to develop.

Corylus "Barcelona"

HEIGHT: 4.45 M+ / 15 FT+	ZONE: 6

Filberts or hazelnuts are enjoying a sort of renaissance as far as interest from the home gardener. These are probably some of the smallest nut trees, and with multi-grafts available, one tree may be all that is required. "Barcelona" is considered one of the best cultivars and is widely grown commercially — it features an abundance of large, rounded nuts. All filberts require another variety for production; "Royal" or Butler" would be good pollinators for "Barcelona." It may be trained as a standard tree or large multi-stemmed bush.

Blueberries

Joanne Freeman grew up on the same blueberry farm that she now operates with her husband and family in Pitt Meadows. Many of the plants on site are more than 50 years old — a testimony to their durability when good maintenance practices are applied.

Joanne Freeman
Freeman Farms
Pitt Meadows, B.C.

Most highbush blueberries were derived from selections of wild species such as *Vaccinium corymbosum*. Height and spread will vary, depending on pruning and soil conditions.

Blueberry "Bluecrop"

HEIGHT: 1.2–1.8 M / 4–6 FT	SPREAD: 1.2–1.8 M / 4–6 FT	ZONE: 4

This mid-season blueberry is the most widely planted of any cultivar in North America and is the leading commercial variety. "Blue Crop" is an easy plant to grow, with few cultural problems, and it tolerates spring frosts quite well. The vigorous, upright bushes produce heavy crops of large, light blue berries.

Blueberry "Duke"

HEIGHT: 1.8 M / 6 FT	SPREAD: 1.2–1.5 M / 4–5 FT	ZONE: 4

"Duke" features a strong upright, open growth habit with vigorous cane production and branches that are often laden with fruit. This is one of the most consistently productive varieties that Joanne has grown, and although it ripens early, the late blooming season minimizes the damage from spring frosts. The berries are large, light blue in colour and quite firm.

Blueberry "Dixi"

HEIGHT: 2.5–3 M / 8–10 FT	SPREAD: 1.8–2.5 M / 6–8 FT	ZONE: 4

An excellent choice for gardens in the Pacific Northwest, this plant bears large, medium-firm berries with a distinctive sweet, aromatic flavour. The fruit ripens late on this robust shrub, with a reputation for high yields. "Dixi" was introduced in 1936 and exhibits a spreading growth habit.

Blueberry "Northland"

HEIGHT: 1.2–1.8 M / 4–6 FT	SPREAD: 1.2–1.8 M / 4–6 FT	ZONE: 3

"Northland" is another heavy-producing variety that performs well in cold climates or where extremes of winter and summer temperatures may preclude other varieties. The branches are flexible and will bend under heavy snow loads. Medium-sized, dark blue berries that ripen in mid season are excellent for cooking because of their high sugar content.

Blueberry "Hardyblue" (1613-A)

HEIGHT: 1.8–2.5 M+ / 6–8 FT+	SPREAD: 1.2–1.8 M / 4–6 FT	ZONE: 4

"Hardyblue" is worth growing just as an ornamental in the garden, as it features spectacular autumn foliage of bright orange and dark red new wood during the winter. Couple that with an abundance of medium-sized berries that are superior in flavour and sweetness — and you have a real winner. The shrub itself is vigorous and quick to establish, with strong upright canes and an open growth habit. 1613-A is the proper name or designation for this plant, while "Hardyblue" has become the more common selling name of this cultivar.

Grapes

The Fraser Valley and the east coast of Vancouver Island are ideally suited to viticulture. The long growing season and, in particular, the summer conditions of hot days and cool nights all provide ideal circumstances for many varieties of grapes — especially those that can produce the popular German style white wines. Margaret and Jock Fairholm propagate a selective group of these cultivars in the central Fraser Valley and were gracious enough to share their unique perspective on growing grapes on the West Coast.

Vitis "Kerner"
HIGHLY RECOMMENDED

"Kerner" is a relatively new grape variety and is the result of intensive German vine breeding. This durable plant ripens reliably almost anywhere grapes can be grown, but prefers the longer growing season of the West Coast as opposed to a hot interior climate. "Kerner" is popular with growers as well as winemakers, as it is late budding and has good frost and disease resistance. This is a vigorous vine — so it will require careful summer pruning to prevent an unwanted canopy.

Vitis "Reichensteiner"
RECOMMENDED

This truly "European" grape was the result of cross breeding French, Italian and German grapes ("Müller- Thurgau" x "Madeline Angevine" x "Calahessen Fröhlich"). This vine thrives on well-drained sites with rich soil but is somewhat susceptible to **botrytis** and stem rot. Flower set is good even in a late or cool spring, and matures to an abundant crop of sound grapes, in loose bunches.

Margaret and Jock Fairholm
Abbotsford, B.C.

General Care
Before planting grape vines, a wise grower will do some research, to purchase the best varieties to suit the area (i.e., disease resistance or early ripening / growth habits). Planting the vines in a north- to south-direction is best, as they will receive maximum sunlight when oriented this way. While good soil conditions are a bonus, grape vines are vigorous growers and thrive under stress, with their long tap roots going down very deep in search of water and nutrients.

Pruning
Grape vines require judicious pruning, usually in February or March, when the plant is dormant. There are several different methods used to train the vines, but the gardener must know the idiosyncracies of each variety, to know which buds to remove and how many are required to produce a good crop.

Protecting Your Crop
Birds know exactly when grapes are ripening and they will come in great numbers to consume your crop. Protective netting to prevent bird damage is absolutely necessary — our practice is to put the nets on long before the grapes begin to ripen. Should the birds get a taste of ripe fruit before the nets are up, it then becomes an obstacle course and they will eventually get under your nets.

Vitis "Siegerrebe"

RECOMMENDED

This is a modern German grape that bears fruit with high sugar and a low acid content. It was bred from "Gewurztramminer" x with a red table grape and is not particularly productive — but with good weather during the flowering period, it is capable of high yields. "Siegerrebe" will not tolerate alkaline conditions or liming, and usually ripens around mid-September.

Vitis "Schonburger"

RECOMMENDED

This pink-coloured grape is a result of a cross of "Pinot Noir" x "Chasselas Rose" x "Muscat Hamburg." It adapts well to all soil conditions and is capable of good fruit set even with a cool, wet spring. "Schonburger" is a reliable producer, although additional irrigation will be required to ripen the fruit (and turn it pink) if the soil is dry.

Vitis "Dornfelder"

HIGHLY RECOMMENDED

"Dornfelder" embodies almost every important red wine grape grown in Germany and seems to have inherited most of their good qualities. This hybrid was bred for its deep red colour in 1956 and has subsequently proven to be resistant to disease and wood rot. The stocks are strong and vigorous, so this vine requires a good summer pruning to prevent a large canopy. "Dornfelder" produces large, full bunches of grapes with good ripening levels and high yields — but quality-conscious winemakers are careful to restrict its high production. It adapts extremely well to the Fraser Valley and east coast of Vancouver Island.

Cane Fruits & Strawberries

Most gardeners have experienced cane fruits and strawberries at one time or another — for me, they bring to mind childhood memories of picking wild strawberries in Saskatchewan or of earning junior high "pocket money" in the commercial raspberry fields of Chilliwack. Strawberries and raspberries are both good choices for beginner gardeners or for children, as these plants are easy to care for and often bear fruit in their first year.

As a landscape gardener, I have had the privilege of "sampling" many of my customers' small fruits and, as a nursery manager, I continue to help people choose the right varieties for their needs. Quite often, though, prospective customers are young couples looking to stock their yard with berry plants for their children to enjoy as they grow up. Others are looking to grow fresh berries to use in their preserves and baking — so a few of us "older kids" can enjoy them too.

Mike Lascelle
Amsterdam Garden Centre
Pitt Meadows, B.C.

Strawberry "Totem"

ZONE: 3

"Totem" has long been the favoured commercial variety for its large, dark red berries with firm texture. It has all the attributes a serious grower would be looking for — including disease resistance, winter hardiness and individual plant longevity. This is a June-bearing strawberry with consistent yields in early to mid summer. Some other good June-bearing varieties for the home gardener include "Rainier" or "Hood."

Pruning Raspberries

Summer-Bearing — fruits on old wood / after harvest, cut down all canes that have produced fruit to the ground / thin the new canes and tie to wire supports / head excessively tall canes in late winter

Fall-Bearing (Everbearing) — produces fruit on new wood / cut down all canes to the ground in late winter / tie new canes to wire supports

Unusual Berries

Loganberry (Zone 5) — A Canadian-bred raspberry x blackberry hybrid with juicy but tart, deep-red berries / good for preserves

Youngberry (Zone 5) — A loganberry x dewberry hybrid with nearly seedless purple berries that are sweet and juicy

Tayberry (Zone 5) — Another blackberry x raspberry cross with heavy crops of dark purple berries / fruit is large and quite sweet

Boysenberry (Zone 5) — Large reddish-black berries that are sweet with a tart aftertaste / a thornless cultivar is available

Marionberry (Zone 5) — Parentage is relatively unknown, but it features black fruit with a sharp loganberry flavour and thorny canes

Strawberry "Sumas"

ZONE: 3

For gardeners serious about strawberry production, consider the heavy-bearing "Sumas." Some people prefer its flavour to "Totem," although the flesh is soft and definitely lighter in colour. This June-bearing variety also matures slightly earlier then "Totem."

Wild Strawberry / *Fragaria vesca*

ZONE: 2

Wild strawberries are not high-yielding plants, but they are unsurpassed for flavour. The berries are small (about 1 cm / ½ in long) and a bit seedy, but the almost "bubble gum" aftertaste is quite fascinating. These are runnerless, everbearing plants that make good informal ground covers in partial shade. Cultivars such as "Alexandria" and "Yellow Wonder" (pale yellow berries) are available, but just the species is likely to be found.

Strawberry "Tristar"

ZONE: 2

This day-neutral strawberry produces modest crops of medium-sized berries in much the same way as everbearing varieties. It features good disease resistance, winter hardiness and is an excellent choice for hanging baskets or containers. Some other day-neutral strawberries to consider are "Hecker" and "Fern" — both are considered to have somewhat better flavour than "Tristar."

Strawberry "Quinault"

ZONE: 3

This everbearing strawberry was developed specifically for conditions in the Pacific Northwest. "Quinault" bears a modest early crop, followed by heavier production later in the season. It is a robust plant with good runner production, and the large berries have superb flavour, but can be a little soft.

Raspberry "Fallgold"

ZONE: 4

This is an unusual everbearing raspberry with attractive yellow fruit. Although "Autumn Bliss" (red berries) is often the recommended fall-bearing raspberry, "Fallgold" has far superior flavour and sweetness, with a true raspberry taste. These plants really love to grow — canes planted this past spring (in 4 L / 1 gal pots) put on 1.5 m / 5 ft of growth and produced a handful of berries each — and that is only about three months after planting. One concession to "Autumn Bliss," though — the yields of "Fallgold" are only modest in comparison.

Raspberry "Boyne"

ZONE: 2

This tough raspberry comes out of the Agriculture Research Station at Morden, Manitioba. Its Zone 2 hardiness makes it ideal for most gardeners on the prairies or in northern communities. "Boyne" is a vigorous summer-bearing type, featuring medium-sized, dark red berries of good quality. For gardeners looking for consistency in harsh climates, this is the raspberry to choose.

Raspberry "Tulameen"

ZONE: 5

For gardeners who really love eating fresh raspberries with cream, all the flavour ever dreamed comes with "Tulameen." Add to this the large berry size, its remarkably long fruiting season, the high yields and good plant vigour, and "Tulameen" is a real winner. This is a great choice for the Pacific Northwest — gardeners in colder

Strawberry Types
June-bearing — Most produce a heavy single crop (June–July) of good quality large fruit / productive lifespan is about three years
Everbearing — Most produce two crops (June and late summer) with some interim fruiting. / smaller berries / productive lifespan is about two years
Day Neutral — Fruit production is not affected by day length / similar to everbearing, with slightly larger fruit / productive lifespan is about two years
Alpine — Most produce very small, flavourful berries continually from summer to fall / no runners are produced

regions will just have to visit to be able to enjoy them first-hand. "Qualicum" and "Chilliwack" are two other summer-bearing raspberries worth considering.

Raspberry "Meeker"

ZONE: 4

This raspberry is perfect for gardeners who want large quantities of good quality fruit for preserving, be it juice or jam. "Meeker" has long been grown commercially for those same purposes, as the deep red berries with high sugar content lend themselves to this use. This summer-bearing cultivar has very robust canes (they tend to lean over) and some tolerance for poor soils.

Blackberry "Black Satin"

ZONE: 4

For gardeners who hate battling thorny blackberry thickets just to get that one cluster of berries lingering beyond reach, there is some relief. "Black Satin" will give an abundance of large, flavourful berries without all the thorns. It produces a bit earlier than most blackberries, often starting to ripen in late July to early August — depending on the weather.

Specialty Plants

The specialty plants in this section fulfill a specific purpose in the landscape or they are included in a group of special interest plants. The latter is well represented by bonsai and fragrant shrubs, as both are much sought after for their aesthetic rather than practical qualities. Others, such as exotic and winter-flowering plants are geared toward a particular landscape design rather than a utilitarian purpose.

The more practical individual plants included here fulfill some of our basic landscape needs, such as hedging for privacy or as low-maintenance ground covers for erosion control. Specific problem situations, including limited soil moisture or landscape covenants requiring the use of native plants, are also addressed in this section. One chapter, "UBC Plant Introductions," encompasses both the aesthetic and the practical with some representation of ornamental shrubs, native plants, ground covers and drought-tolerant species — so it truly can be said that there is a plant for every landscape in this section of the book.

UBC Plant Introductions

Bruce Macdonald
UBC Botanical Garden
Vancouver, B.C.

The UBC Botanical Garden's Plant Introduction Scheme was first set up in 1980 to allow commercial access to its collection of more than 15,000 plants. Some emphasis was placed on indigenous plant material that was primarily collected in the field by Wilf Nichols, resulting in many natives of the Pacific Northwest (*Vaccinium ovatum* "Thunderbird" and *Ribes sanguineum* "White Icicle") gaining wide acceptance in residential gardens. Other introductions, such as *Genista pilosa* "Vancouver Gold" and *Viburnum plicatum* "Summer Snowflake," have proven their worth and gone on to become industry standards in the landscape trade.

Bruce Macdonald is the Director of the University of British Columbia Botanical Gardens, and overseeing the Plant Introduction Scheme is just one of his many duties. Along with consultants and nursery production staff, Bruce is constantly working behind the scenes promoting the garden's next introduction. Judging by their track record, these plants are bound to be successful.

Aronia melanocarpa "Autumn Magic"

HEIGHT: 2 M / 6½ FT	SPREAD: 2 M / 6½ FT	ZONE: 3
FLOWERING PERIOD: MAY		

This seedling selection of eastern chokeberry has much to offer — beginning with glossy, dark green leaves and sprays of fragrant white flowers in May. As the name implies, autumn finds this shrub flaunting a brilliant combination of scarlet and purple foliage accented with large clusters of shiny, black, edible berries. This is an excellent shrub for mass planting, as it is not affected by any serious pest or disease problems.

Sorbus hupehensis "Pink Pagoda"

HEIGHT: 10 M / 33 FT	ZONE: 5–6
FLOWERING PERIOD: MAY	

This unusual mountain ash features flower clusters in spring followed by an abundance of bright pink fruits that whiten by mid winter. The compound leaves are bluish-green in colour and are borne on contrasting red **petioles**. Autumn brings attractive shades of orange and vermilion to the foliage.

Lonicera "Mandarin"

HEIGHT: 6 M / 20 FT	ZONE: 3–4
FLOWERING PERIOD: MAY–JUNE (sporadic blooms throughout the summer)	

This hybrid honeysuckle has a parentage that includes the venerable *Lonicera x brownii* "Dropmore Scarlet." The tubular flowers combine pale apricot inside with deep salmon outside to create an overall effect of intense orange — guaranteed to attract local hummingbirds. This vigorous vine is prairie hardy, and its rapid growth rate makes it an ideal candidate for screening on a trellis, arbour or fence.

Artemesia stelleriana "Silver Brocade"

HEIGHT: 15–30 CM / 6–12 IN	SPREAD: 75 CM / 30 IN	ZONE: 3
PRIMARILY A FOLIAGE PLANT		

A distant relative of dusty miller, "Silver Brocade" is technically a **sub-shrub**, although it will most likely be found in the perennial section of the local nursery. The low, spreading foliage is composed of deeply lobed, silvery-white leaves that are completely herbaceous in colder climates. Consider this a textural rather than a flowering plant, as the small yellow blooms are not significant and should be sheared after they fade. "Silver Brocade's" cascading foliage is the perfect foil for pink or blue summer flowers in patio containers or large hanging baskets.

How the Royalty Program Works

The UBC Botanical Garden offsets the cost of its Plant Introduction Scheme by selling stock plants and by collecting a modest royalty on each rooted cutting. Wholesale growers who wish to participate in the program must first be members of the British Columbia Landscape and Nursery Trade Association and the Canadian Ornamental Plant Foundation (COPF). The latter organization oversees the financial end of this scheme by monitoring propagation reports and collecting royalty fees from the wholesale nurseries on behalf of the botanical garden. Most growers pass the royalty costs down to the retail level but, when the quality of the UBC introductions is considered, the extra cost is not an issue (from the consumer's point of view).

Microbiota decussata

HEIGHT: 20 CM / 8 IN	SPREAD: 3–4 M / 10–13 FT	ZONE: 2

Siberian or Russian cypress was discovered in Siberia in 1921, thriving in exposed sites well above the timberline. This low, spreading evergreen resembles juniper and is a good substitute for juniper in residential or commercial landscape applications. The bright green foliage turns a copper brown during winter.

Ribes sanguineum "White Icicle"

HEIGHT: 3 M / 10 FT	SPREAD: 2 M / 6½ FT	ZONE: 6–7
FLOWERING PERIOD: EARLY SPRING		

This cultivar of our native flowering currant blooms in early spring, about two weeks earlier than most of the red forms. The pure white flowers are held in pendulous **racemes**, which appear just as the leaves are emerging. This large, deciduous shrub is tolerant of full sun to light shade and is particularly effective when interplanted with the species.

Penstemon fruticosus "Purple Haze"

HEIGHT: 20 CM / 8 IN	SPREAD: 60 CM / 2 FT	ZONE: 3–4
FLOWERING PERIOD: MAY–JUNE		

This semi-evergreen **sub-shrub** is native to dry regions of Southern B.C. A profusion of mauve-purple blossoms literally envelops the foliage in late spring. "Purple Haze" is an excellent companion plant for other low, spreading alpines, such as *Aubrieta, Iberis* and *Arabis*, on well-drained slopes in full sun.

Clematis chiisanensis "Lemon Bells"

HEIGHT: 2–3 M / 6½–10 FT		ZONE: 6
FLOWERING PERIOD: MAY–JUNE (sporadic blooms throughout the summer)		

This selection of a little-known South Korean species shares many attributes common to species clematis — unusual foliage, abundant flowers and persistent silky seed heads. The **pendulous** blooms are predominantly pale yellow with a deep wine base, although the latter feature is diminished when planted in shade. As "Lemon Bells" is not as aggressive as some of the better known species of clematis (e.g. *C. tangutica*), it is ideal for clambering through medium-sized shrubs.

Viburnum plicatum "Summer Snowflake"

HEIGHT: 2 M / 6½ FT	SPREAD: 1.5 M / 5 FT	ZONE: 4
FLOWERING PERIOD: MAY–FROST		

It is hard to believe that any shrub could be low maintenance, tolerate full sun to partial shade and bloom all summer long. "Summer Snowflake" meets all these criteria, bearing white **lacecap** flowers from May through to frost and thriving in a wide range of growing conditions. This deciduous viburnum also has an attractive tiered-branching habit.

Anagallis monelli "Pacific Blue"

HEIGHT: 15 CM / 6 IN	SPREAD: 75 CM / 2½ FT	ZONE: 7–8
FLOWERING PERIOD: LATE MAY–FROST		

This Mediterranean native features beautiful gentian-blue flowers from late May until frost. "Pacific Blue" is an ideal choice for perennial borders, alpine gardens or containers — provided they are in full sun — as the flowers do not open in the shade. Pair this herbaceous perennial with yellow strawflower or trailing *Bidens* to create an elegant hanging basket.

A New Introduction Timeline

Ardent gardeners often complain that new introductions seem to take a long time before they are available to the public at the retail level. To give some appreciation of this sometimes long process, a brief timeline of the production stages involved in creating Lonicera "Mandarin" is presented:

1989 — Lonicera tragophylla and Lonicera x brownii "Dropmore Scarlet" crossed by Dr. Wilf Nichols

1990 — the seeds from this intentional hybrid are sown

1992 — plants from this cross begin to flower

1993 — this new honeysuckle is shown to the horticulture industry

1994 — plants are sent to research stations in Canada and the US

1996 — enough stock plants are propagated to distribute to wholesale growers

1998 — Lonicera "Mandarin" is available to the public for the first time

Zone 4 Hardy Plants

Raymond LaForest
Van Vloten Nurseries Ltd.
Pitt Meadows, B.C.

A chapter on hardy plants may seem a little out of place in a book for the Pacific Northwest — but considering the many gardeners with "out-of-town" resort property, it makes perfect sense. Those cabins at Whistler or in the interior require cold-tolerant shrubs, which will have to look good with minimal maintenance. Although many cold-tolerant plants are sold locally, few gardeners are aware of their hardiness and subsequent potential in recreational landscapes.

Van Vloten Nurseries started in 1962, when Walter Van Vloten rented a small piece of land to begin his fledgling nursery. Since then, this Pitt Meadows-based wholesale operation has expanded to 76 hectares / 190 acres of both container and field stock. They specialize in hardy plant material and ship much of their stock to eastern Canada and the central United States.

Rhododendron "Northern Starburst"

HEIGHT: 90 CM+ / 3 FT+	SPREAD: 90 CM+ / 3 FT+	ZONE: 4
FLOWERING PERIOD: EARLY SPRING		

This newer cultivar is part of the "Genesis" series by Briggs Nursery of Washington, which is working on developing hardier plant varieties. "Northern Starburst" is an improvement on the "PJM Compact" rhododendron — with larger, more pink flowers and deep purple-black winter foliage. The new leaves flush a bright apple-green on this robust plant.

Potentilla fruticosa "Pink Beauty"

HEIGHT: 90 CM / 3 FT	SPREAD: 1.2 M / 4 FT	ZONE: 2
FLOWERING PERIOD: EARLY SUMMER–OCTOBER		

An unusual potentilla that was developed by the University of Manitoba, it features clear pink, semi-double flowers that fade slightly in the heat of summer. "Pink Beauty" forms a mounded shrub of bright green foliage and blooms for an extended period of time.

Juniperus horizontalis "Blue Prince"

HEIGHT: 15 CM / 6 IN	SPREAD: 90 CM–1.5 M / 3–5 FT	ZONE: 3

This intensely coloured juniper has powder blue foliage that requires little pruning to retain its shape. "Blue Prince" was selected from the wild in Alberta by Casey Van Vloten, and has proven to be hardy to Zone 3.

Prunus "Evans"

HEIGHT: 3.5–4.25 M / 12–14 FT	SPREAD: 3.5 M / 12 FT	ZONE: 2–3

Imagine a fruiting cherry tree that could withstand bone-chilling winter temperatures of -45°C / -49°F , which only a northern city such as Edmonton could provide. The "Evans" Cherry has thrived there since 1923 and produces up to 22 kg / 50 lbs of flavourful (yet tart) fruit on mature specimens. This self-fertile tree comes into bearing only four years after planting.

Rhododendron "Lemon Lights"

HEIGHT: 1.25–1.5 M / 4–5 FT	SPREAD: 90 CM–1.2 M / 3–4 FT	ZONE: 4
FLOWERING PERIOD: SPRING		

Another outstanding deciduous azalea from the "Northern Lights" series, this was developed at the University of Minnesota. "Lemon Lights" features nearly bicolour blooms, with light yellow outer petals accented with a gold throat. This cultivar is also resistant to powdery mildew and has maroon-coloured fall foliage.

Since most of the selections happened to be in the shrub category, it might be more comprehensive to include a few additional lists of Zone 4 hardy plants.

Zone 4
Hardy Ornamental Trees

Aesculus glabra / *Ohio Buckeye (Zone 3) — creamy-yellow flowers*

Prunus virginiana "Schubert" / *Schubert Chokecherry (Zone 2) — purple foliage*

Malus "Royalty" / *Flowering Crabapple (Zone 2–3) — reddish blooms-purple foliage*

Crataegus "Toba" / *Toba Hawthorn (Zone 3) — pink flower clusters*

Syringa reticulata "Ivory Silk" / *Japanese Tree Lilac (Zone 3–4) — creamy-white blooms*

Acer ginnala / *Amur Maple (Zone 3) — scarlet-red fall foliage*

Elaeagnus angustifolia / *Russian Olive (Zone 3) — silvery foliage*

Quercus macrocarpa / *Bur Oak (Zone 3) — corky, ridged bark*

Populus tremula "Erecta" / *Swedish Aspen (Zone 2–3) — distinct columnar form*

Prunus padus commutata / *Mayday Tree (Zone 2–3) — fragrant white flowers*

Andromeda polifolia "Blue Ice"

HEIGHT: 27.5 CM / 15 IN	SPREAD: 27.5 CM / 15 IN	ZONE: 3
FLOWERING PERIOD: EARLY SPRING		

This extremely attractive cultivar of the native bog rosemary was introduced by Van Vloten Nurseries. A broadleaf evergreen shrub, it features steel blue foliage and an abundance of pale pink, bell-shaped flowers in spring. It prefers full sun, acidic soil and is tolerant of well-drained to almost bog-like conditions.

Physocarpus opulifolius "Diabolo"

HEIGHT: 1.8 M / 6 FT	SPREAD: 1.8 M / 6 FT	ZONE: 3
FLOWERING PERIOD: EARLY JUNE		

This new selection of ninebark has deep purple-black foliage that is the perfect foil for bright shrubs such as golden mock orange or the closely related *Physocarpus* "Dart's Gold." The leaves are somewhat similar to maple, and it bears small white flowers in early summer. Since this is primarily a foliage plant, keep it pruned back to ensure that there is always a heavy flush of new leaves.

Syringa patula "Miss Kim"

HEIGHT: 1.5–1.8 M / 5–6 FT	SPREAD: 1.5–1.8 M / 5–6 FT	ZONE: 3
FLOWERING PERIOD: MAY–JUNE		

A compact, deciduous shrub with deep green foliage and an overall rounded appearance, "Miss Kim" is extremely hardy and produces an impressive display of fragrant, violet-purple blossoms in late spring. Excellent autumn tones of deep burgundy can also be expected.

Sambucus nigra "Madonna"

HEIGHT: 2–2.5 M / 6½–8 FT	SPREAD: 2–2.5 M / 6½–8 FT	ZONE: 4
FLOWERING PERIOD: SPRING		

An ornamental European elderberry that produces little fruit, "Madonna" more than makes up for it with attractive, deeply cut leaves that are edged in cream. "Madonna" also features white flower clusters in spring that contrast well with the compound foliage. Use this variegated shrub to brighten up "green zones" in the garden.

Rosa rugosa **"Therese Bugnet"**

HEIGHT: 1.5–1.8 M / 5–6 FT	SPREAD: 1.5–1.8 M / 5–6 FT	ZONE: 2
FLOWERING PERIOD: JUNE (intermittently during summer)		

This is perhaps one of the finest rugosa roses ever introduced. "Therese Bugnet" combines good disease resistance with fragrant, double blooms of an unsurpassed shade of lilac-pink. It also features attractive deep red stems and orange-red **hips** during the winter.

Zone 4
Hardy Fruit Trees and Shrubs

Amelanchier alnifolia / *Saskatoon Berry — Zone 2*

Prunus tomentosa / *Nanking Cherry — Zone 2*

Vaccinium *"Northland"* / *Blueberry — Zone 4*

Malus *"Goodland"* / *Goodland Apple — Zone 2*

Prunus *"Brookcot"* / *Brookcot Apricot — Zone 3–4*

Pyrus *"Ure"* / *Ure Pear — Zone 3*

Ribes nigrum / *Black Currant — Zone 3*

Malus *"Dolgo"* / *Dolgo Crabapple — Zone 2*

Prunus *"Pembina Plum"* / *Pembina Plum — Zone 3*

Ribes uva-crispa / *Gooseberry — Zone 4*

Native Plants of the Pacific Northwest

Paulus Vrijmoed
Linnaea Nurseries Ltd.
Langley, B.C.

Until fairly recently, less than 200 years ago, people from other continents visiting the Pacific Northwest found a natural landscape that was stunning in its pristine beauty. The plant material they found in the mountains, forests and swamps was almost all new to them and of a beauty equalling the surroundings. These are the trees, shrubs and perennials that are called native plants today.

Linnaea Nurseries and its staff have been involved in native plant production as a wholesale propagator for the past 20 years. Long before indigenous plants gained popularity in the urban landscape, they were already used extensively in the restoration of sites disturbed through various types of development, such as mining, roads, forestry and gas line corridors. More and more, native plants are now finding their way into home gardens and parks — with the following being preferred for their natural beauty, as well as their ease of care.

Ferns

Blechnum spicant / Deer Fern

HEIGHT: 45–60 CM / 18 IN–2 FT   SPREAD: 45–90 CM / 18 IN–3 FT   ZONE: 3

This evergreen fern forms a tuft of spreading deep green foliage from the base, followed by fertile **fronds,** which darken as they mature. This is a very useful landscape plant, which features a high shade tolerance and better hardiness than sword fern. It prefers a rich, humus soil.

Polystichum munitum / Sword Fern

HEIGHT: 1 M / 3 FT	SPREAD: 1.2 M / 4 FT	ZONE: 5

This large evergreen species is much less fussy about its growing conditions than deer fern. The new fronds are quite erect in spring, which is also the best time to prune out any foliage that was damaged during the winter. Sword fern prefers partial sun to shade.

Perennials and Ground Covers

Cornus canadensis / Bunchberry

HEIGHT: 15 CM / 6 IN	SPREAD: 20–30 CM / 8–12 IN	ZONE: 3
FLOWERING PERIOD: MAY–JUNE		

This low, carpet-forming ground cover retains much of its foliage during the winter. It has lovely white dogwood-type flowers, followed by bright clusters of red berries in fall. Bunchberry works well in combination with native ferns, which also share its preference for a humus-rich soil.

Mahonia nervosa / Dull Oregon Grape

HEIGHT: 60 CM / 2 FT	SPREAD: 90 CM / 3 FT	ZONE: 5–6
FLOWERING PERIOD: APRIL–MAY		

This lower-growing cousin of the tall Oregon grape (*Mahonia aquifolium*) features bright yellow flower clusters that mature to dark blue berries, with a whitish bloom. It thrives in a variety of conditions — from moist to dry — and is one of the few plants that will grow below red cedars.

Linnaea borealis / Twinflower

HEIGHT: 10–15 CM / 4–6 IN	SPREAD: 30–60 CM / 1–2 FT	ZONE: 3
FLOWERING PERIOD: MAY–JULY		

Linnaea Nurseries' namesake is a delightful evergreen ground cover that tolerates diverse conditions — ranging from dry to moist, and shade to full sun. Its trailing stems carry small, shiny leaves and pink trumpet-shaped fragrant flowers in pairs. Twinflower also does well in the rock garden.

Fragaria chiloensis / Coastal Strawberry

HEIGHT: 15 CM / 6 IN	SPREAD: extensive due to runners	ZONE: 4

This easy-to-care-for ground cover has shiny, dark green foliage and white flowers. It prefers dry, sunny conditions, as does the closely related *Fragaria virginiana* (wild strawberry), which produces very tasty small strawberries.

Allium cernuum / Nodding Onion

HEIGHT: 50 CM / 20 IN	SPREAD: 30–60 CM / 1–2 FT	ZONE: 3
FLOWERING PERIOD: JUNE–JULY		

This native perennial has varied uses. The nodding pink flower clusters are an attractive addition to dry, sunny spots in the landscape. It can also be grown in containers both inside the home and outside in the garden, where the narrow green leaves can be cut for culinary use, much like chives or green onion.

Shrubs

Amelanchier alnifolia / Saskatoon Berry

HEIGHT: 1–5 M / 3–15 FT	SPREAD: can form dense colonies	ZONE: 2
FLOWERING PERIOD: EARLY SPRING		

This attractive multi-stemmed shrub bears fragrant clusters of small white flowers, resembling star magnolia blooms in miniature. Saskatoon berries are much favoured by the birds, so for gardeners looking for enough fruit to make a pie, be sure to pick them as soon as they have ripened. It prefers a sunny location with well-drained soil.

Rosa nutkana / Nootka Rose

HEIGHT: 1–2.5 M / 3–8 FT	SPREAD: 1–2 M / 3–6½ FT	ZONE: 7
FLOWERING PERIOD: MAY–JUNE		

This vigorous, deciduous shrub tolerates a wide range of conditions, from moist to dry. Nootka rose features very fragrant, large pink single blooms (4–8 cm / 1½–3 in across) borne from May to June — followed by purplish-red **hips** that last well into the winter. Do not be afraid to use pruners on this one.

Vaccinium ovatum / Evergreen Huckleberry

HEIGHT: to 3 M / 10 FT	SPREAD: 1–2 M / 3–6½ FT	ZONE: 7

This ornamental shrub is a must for any coastal garden. *Vaccinium ovatum* has lustrous, dark green foliage with clusters of pale pink, bell-shaped flowers. These eventually produce shiny, purplish-black edible berries, which ripen in the fall and become sweeter after a few frosts. The University of British Columbia has introduced an improved variety called "Thunderbird."

Ribes sanguineum / Red-Flowering Currant

HEIGHT: 1–3 M / 3–10 FT	SPREAD: 1–2 M / 3–6½ FT	ZONE: 5
FLOWERING PERIOD: APRIL–MAY		

One of our earliest-flowering shrubs, *Ribes sanguineum* does not take up too much space in the garden. It thrives in more exposed, well-drained, sunny locations but will still bloom in partial shade. Its distinctive rose-red flower clusters are absolutely irresistible to hummingbirds.

Historical Context

Many native plants were a traditional source of food, medicine or building materials for the native peoples of the Pacific Northwest. Here are a few examples of indigenous species and their particular use in the past. Modern medicinal or culinary use of these plants is not recommended without adequate knowledge.

Fritillaria lanceolata / *Chocolate Lily — bulbs were eaten*

Lysichiton americanum / *Skunk Cabbage — leaves used as "wax paper"*

Philadelphus lewisii / *Mock Orange — hard wood used for tools*

Rubus spectabilis / *Salmonberry — berries and new sprouts eaten*

Juncus effusus / *Common Rush — stems used for weaving*

Arctostaphylos uva-ursi / *Bearberry — dried leaves smoked like tobacco*

Cornus nuttallii / *Pacific Dogwood — bark used in medicines*

Picea sitchensis / *Sitka Spruce — pitch chewed like gum*

Salix hookeriana / *Hooker's Willow — bark used to make rope*

Pteridium aquilinum / *Bracken Fern — leaves used for protection in fire pits*

Trees

Acer circinatum / Vine Maple

HEIGHT: to 6 M / 20 FT	SPREAD: Variable	ZONE: 5
FLOWERING PERIOD: LATE APRIL		

Every garden should have at least one specimen of this lovely tree. It certainly equals Japanese maple (*Acer palmatum*) for beauty — yet is probably less demanding when it comes to growing conditions. Vine maple is also quite variable in form, exhibiting upright branching in full sun and an arching habit when grown in the shade. The tiny spring flowers are a welcome sight, but its true beauty is best expressed in the yellow to bright red autumn foliage.

Crataegus douglasii / Black Hawthorn

HEIGHT: to 8 M / 25 FT	SPREAD: 3–5 M / 10–15 FT	ZONE: 6
FLOWERING PERIOD: MAY		

This is the perfect small tree (or large shrub) for people wanting to attract birds, as it is a favoured nesting site and the abundant clusters of blackish-purple berries are a valued food source. Black hawthorn features white spring flowers and prominent thorns — so it also makes a good choice as an informal hedge to keep unwanted guests out. It prefers a moist location in either sun or partial shade.

Rhamnus purshiana / Cascara

HEIGHT: to 8 M / 25 FT	SPREAD: to 3 M / 10 FT	ZONE: 6

Historically, cascara was an important source of medicinal bark for natives of the Pacific Northwest. It features dark green, glossy foliage with deep veining and radiant orange autumn tones. This small, erect species is quite tolerant of diverse conditions but is commonly found in the wild as an understory tree.

Ground Covers

Ground covers may be anything from herbaceous perennials and ornamental grasses to small broadleaf evergreens. Many are useful in areas where it may be difficult to establish turf grass, including steep banks, dry locations, deep shade and gaps between paving stones. Although ground covers may require some initial care and attention in order to establish themselves, in the long run they are the best low-maintenance alternative.

Ground Effects is a Langley-based business that has focused on growing broadleaf evergreen ground covers. Owned and operated by Neil Bylenga, this wholesale nursery is now producing up to 100 different varieties. Although all of the following selections are good performers in their own right, many of them are also some of Neil's personal favourites.

Neil Bylenga
*Ground Effects Wholesale
Nurseries Ltd.
Langley, B.C.*

Arctostaphylos uva-ursi "Vancouver Jade"

HEIGHT: 15 CM / 6 IN	SPREAD: 90 CM / 3 FT	ZONE: 4
FLOWERING PERIOD: APRIL–JUNE		

"Vancouver Jade" is probably one of the most popular ground covers, and for good reason — it features glossy evergreen foliage, attractive pale pink bell-shaped flowers and good disease resistance. This West Coast native was selected out of the wild and introduced by the University of British Columbia's Botanical Garden. To achieve maximum growth, plant bearberry in sunny, well-drained sites with slightly acidic soil and good air circulation.

Ground Covers for Nature

While many people view ground covers as utility plants, they should also be thought of as beneficial to wildlife — capable of furnishing both food and shelter. Here is a selection of Pacific Northwest native perennials, shrubs and ferns that make attractive ground covers and provide a source of food for wildlife.

Fragaria chiloensis / *Coastal Strawberry* — *small hairy berries*

Pachistima myrsinites / *False Boxwood* — *browse for deer*

Mahonia nervosa / *Low Oregon Grape* — *berries / browse for elk*

Arctostaphylos uva-ursi / *Bearberry* — *red berries for birds*

Cornus canadensis / *Bunchberry* — *foliage and berries for deer*

Gaultheria shallon / *Salal* — *foliage and berries for deer*

Dicentra formosa / *Pacific Bleeding Heart* — *attracts hummingbirds*

Blechnum spicant / *Deer Fern* — *winter food for deer*

Vaccinium uliginosum / *Bog Blueberry* — *berries for bears*

Linnaea borealis / *Twinflower* — *nectar for hummingbirds*

Ceanothus gloriosus "Point Reyes"

HEIGHT: 45 CM / 15 IN	SPREAD: 3 M / 10 FT	ZONE: 7
FLOWERING PERIOD: EARLY SPRING–EARLY SUMMER		

Although this is a relatively unknown ground cover, *Ceanothus gloriosus* is a wonderful creeping shrub with a modest growth rate. "Point Reyes" has somewhat fragrant lilac-blue flowers that appear in abundance from early spring through to early summer. This plant prefers a sunny, well-drained site and must be sheltered from extremely cold winters, making it a good choice for coastal gardens in the Pacific Northwest.

Pachysandra terminalis "Japanese Spurge"

HEIGHT: 24 CM / 10 IN	SPREAD: 30 CM / 12 IN	ZONE: 3

Japanese spurge is a reliable, dense ground cover for deep shade that tolerates wet soils and also some drought once established. It slowly matures to form a mat of dark green evergreen foliage that even some of the toughest weeds cannot penetrate. This plant is very useful under tree canopies or along the edges of buildings, where it makes a good low-maintenance foundation planting.

Thymus doerfleri "Bressingham"

HEIGHT: 2.5 CM / 1 IN	SPREAD: 20 CM / 8 IN	ZONE: 4
FLOWERING PERIOD: LATE SPRING–SUMMER		

Thyme is the finishing touch to any landscape, and "Bressingham" in particular features a superior flower display. The clear pink blooms envelop the attractive greyish-green foliage from late spring through to the end of summer. This particular cultivar is well suited to sunny, well-drained sites such as rock gardens or between stepping stones.

Genista pilosa "Vancouver Gold"

HEIGHT: 20 CM / 8 IN	SPREAD: 60–75 CM / 2–2½ FT	ZONE: 5
FLOWERING PERIOD: MAY–JUNE		

Another superior introduction from the UBC Botanical Garden, this shrub is very durable and immensely colourful when flowering. The bright yellow flowers appear in the latter part of spring and remain until early summer. Once established, "Vancouver Gold" forms a dense, low-profile mat with excellent erosion control and weed-repelling capabilities. Although it will tolerate most soil conditions, choose a sunny, well-drained location for optimum growth.

Lithodora diffusa "Grace Ward"

HEIGHT: 15 CM / 6 IN	SPREAD: 50 CM / 20 IN	ZONE: 7
FLOWERING PERIOD: MAY–SEPT		

An outstanding flowering ground cover, this evergreen plant will begin to show its intense gentian-blue flowers in late spring and will continue to produce them throughout the summer. *Lithodora* should be planted early in the year to allow it some time to establish itself before winter. "Grace Ward" is rather short-lived in colder climates (where it can be used as an annual), but seems to thrive in the acid soils of the West Coast. This is an ideal specimen for a well-drained rock garden in full sun.

Hedera helix "Hahn's"

HEIGHT: 15–18 CM / 6–7½ IN	SPREAD: 60–75 CM / 2–2½ FT	ZONE: 6

With so many hardy ivies to choose from, it is sometimes hard to make a choice. "Hahn's" ivy features medium-sized evergreen foliage that is self-branching and may be used as a creeper or a climber. This cultivar is a great substitute for the much overused and vigorous English ivy species (*Hedera helix*). The best quality of this particular ground cover is that it can be grown anywhere from partial shade to full sun and is tolerant of most soil conditions.

Points on Establishing Ground Covers

Carefully clear the planting site of all weeds, as the invasive types (e.g., creeping buttercup) will nearly be impossible to remove after the fact.

If necessary, amend the soil to allow the ground cover to establish quickly. Pocket planting in poor soil rarely leads to satisfactory results.

Choose a ground cover that will thrive in the growing site. This means assessing exposure, drainage and soil types.

When planting, place the ground covers close enough so they will be able to cover the entire soil surface within two years.

Water newly planted ground covers regularly until they are established. Water deeply to promote strong root growth.

Established ground covers can be fertilized in spring with standard granular fertilizers (with modest nitrogen). Be sure to water afterward to avoid foliage burn.

Gaultheria shallon "Salal"

HEIGHT: 30 CM+ / 1 FT+	SPREAD: 60 CM+ / 2 FT+	ZONE: 6
FLOWERING PERIOD: MAY–JUNE		

Salal is a native of the Pacific Northwest and is already used extensively throughout that region. This evergreen shrub is also quite adaptable, with cultivated plants reaching maximum height in wet-shaded areas, yet remaining low-growing in sunny, well-drained sites. The glossy foliage is often collected as greens for the flower industry and is a perfect foil for the pale-pink, bell-shaped flowers, which are followed by edible blue-black berries.

Vinca minor "Bowle's Variety"

HEIGHT: 15 CM / 6 IN	SPREAD: 60–75 CM / 2–2½ FT	ZONE: 5
FLOWERING PERIOD: APRIL–JUNE		

Periwinkle is a very popular and well-known shade ground cover, and "Bowle's Variety" has been used in gardens for decades. This selection features glossy, dark green rounded foliage (more vigorous than the species) and large, brilliant blue flowers that appear in early spring. *Vinca minor* tolerates moist soil conditions and is best used in mass plantings or in areas where it can naturalize and take care of itself.

Cotula squalida "Brass Buttons"

HEIGHT: 5–6 CM / 2–2½ IN	SPREAD: 30 CM / 1 FT	ZONE: 5
FLOWERING PERIOD: EARLY SUMMER		

Cotula squalida is another ground cover ideally suited for medium shade to full sun. Since it can tolerate moist soil conditions, it may be used as a lawn substitute around a pond or water garden. It features fern-like foliage that has a soft texture but is durable enough to walk over. In early summer, small flowers reminiscent of tiny brass buttons appear among the foliage.

Exotic Plants

Although this chapter is a bit of a departure from the regular format, I thought the best way to introduce the average gardener to exotic plants would be to suggest a few sample landscapes. Some of the most effective gardens use themes to bring attention to the bold architectural beauty and fragrance of these plants. So this chapter explores four different gardens — each with a brief introduction, plant list and detailed descriptions of the most important components mentioned.

Ray Mattei
Tropic to Tropic Plants
Delta, B.C.

Ray Mattei has been growing and experimenting with all of the plants and landscape designs listed in this chapter, for about 18 years now. While he follows no set rules, he has found through trial and error that certain plants really bring out the character of each garden theme. As the owner of Tropic to Tropic Plants, Ray is constantly working to introduce as many new exotic species and cultivars to the nursery trade as possible.

The Mediterranean Garden

Creating a Mediterranean garden is fairly easy. Terra cotta and earthen tones usually dominate the landscape and are incorporated into the garden through the use of brick, crushed rock and bark mulch for pathways. Large specimen rocks and strategically placed driftwood will add character — while lawn grass is kept to a minimum. This garden loves sunshine, and the ideal exposure is southeast to southwest, with well-drained soil a necessity. Most of the plants listed are evergreen and require minimal maintenance — with many of the smaller selections (i.e., ornamental grasses and yuccas) making attractive container specimens for clay pots along the paths.

Plant List
Trachycarpus fortunei, Chamaerops humilis / Hardy Palms
Blue Fescue / Ornamental Grasses
Arbutus menziesii / Arbutus
Cytisus battandieri / Atlas Broom
Euphorbia characias wulfenii / Evergreen Spurge
Ficus carica / Fig Trees
Albizia julibrissin / Silk Tree
Yuccas
E. archeri, E. debeuzevillei, E. neglecta / Eucalyptus

Eucalyptus debeuzevillei / **Janama Snow Gum**

HEIGHT: 7.5 M / 25 FT	SPREAD: 4.5 M / 15 FT	ZONE: 7

This is the most hardy eucalyptus in the world, enduring temperatures as low as -20°C / 0°F. It is extremely ornamental, with snow-white young branches and trunks that develop grey, tan and white mottling with age. This evergreen tree produces 20-cm / 9-in long, kidney-shaped leaves that are dusty-blue with maroon margins. In full sun it grows to its maximum height and width within eight years.

The Oriental Garden

The Oriental garden makes use of the shadier, damper side of the landscape. Water features, such as small ponds and creeks, add dramatic Asian character and ambiance. The most important component of this theme garden is the largest of all grasses — exotic bamboo — of which several hundred varieties will thrive in our Pacific Northwest climate.

Plant List
Hosta cultivars / Plantain Lily
Fatsia japonica
Acer palmatum dissectum / Weeping Japanese Maple
Helleborus niger / Hellebore
Ornamental Mushrooms
Chamaecyparis / Dwarf Conifers
Phyllostachys, Fargesia, Thamnocaiamus / Bamboo

Thamnocalamus tessellatus / South African Bamboo

HEIGHT: 5 M / 15 FT	SPREAD: 2 M / 6 FT	ZONE: 8

This hardy mid-size species from South Africa is unique. It is the only bamboo from this region and grows very tall, eventually developing 5 cm / 2 in diameter **culms**. An extremely ornamental plant, South African bamboo forms a tightly bunched clump of canes, with attractive beige sheathing. This rare, clumping bamboo is highly recommended for all gardens.

Phyllostachys aurea "Koi" / Golden Bamboo

HEIGHT: 9 M / 30 FT	SPREAD: Running	ZONE: 6

This beautifully coloured, running bamboo needs to be available to all gardeners. It features golden-yellow **culms** with green horizontal banding, with canes eventually reaching a diameter of 4 cm / 1½ in. Compacting knots growing near the base of the older **culms** are said to resemble stacked "Buddha bellies." This cultivar grows to its maximum height in six years and can be easily contained with bamboo barrier or root pruning.

The Jungle Garden

The jungle theme is perhaps the most dramatic during the summer-through-fall period. It is best expressed with bold, lush foliage that has vivid variegation or leaf colour, and with spicy, fragrant blooms. Creating a jungle garden in a temperate climate will require some extra winter protection, but is well worth the effort. Choose a sheltered southern exposure out of strong winds with rich, well-drained soil. Complete this garden with the rambling vines of *Passiflora* and evergreen clematis, to soften the hard features.

Plant List

Gunnera manicata / Giant Gunnera
Actinidia / Kiwi Vine
Magnolia macrophylla / Big Leaf Magnolia
Canna Lily Cultivars
Hedychiums / Hardy Gingers
Passiflora incarnata / Passion Flower
Datura / *Brugmansia* / Angel Trumpets (all parts of this plant are highly toxic if ingested)
C. armandii / Evergreen Clematis
Musa "Basjoo" / Hardy Banana

Musa "Basjoo" / Japanese Fibre Banana

HEIGHT: 7.5 M / 25 FT	SPREAD: 1.8–2.5 M / 6–8 FT	ZONE: 8

This giant is perhaps the most impressive of all the plants included in the jungle garden — of the more than 400 species of bananas in the world, this is the hardiest. *Musa* "Basjoo" doubles in height every year and can reach its maximum height with winter protection. A 1.5-m / 5-ft stalk protection is recommended for overwintering, as this will produce a full 3-m / 10-ft high plant the following year — with the potential to produce ornamental bananas in three or four years. Dozens of 5–10 cm / 2–3 in fruit are borne on a 1-m / 3-ft long stalk, which terminates in a football-sized, maroon flower.

Passiflora incarnata / Maypop Passion Flower

HEIGHT: 5.5 M / 18 FT	ZONE: 7–8
FLOWERING PERIOD: SUMMER	

The hardiest of the passion flowers, Maypop is root hardy to -15°C / 0°F and can remain evergreen through a mild winter, although in colder exposures it is considered herbaceous, dying back to ground level. It is fast-growing and can reach full height in a single season. *Passiflora incarnata* produces hundreds of intricate white, pink and purple tricolour blooms up to 8 cm / 3 in wide. They have an unusual scent of bubble gum and can potentially produce yellow, egg-shaped fruits that are edible.

Hedychium gardnerianum "Tara" / Kahili Ginger

HEIGHT: 1.8–2.5 M / 6–8 FT	SPREAD: 60–90 CM / 2–3 FT	ZONE: 7
FLOWERING PERIOD: LATE AUGUST–FROST		

This lovely orange variety of the Hawaiian kahili ginger is superior in every way. Hardy to Zone 7 with a winter mulch, it features large blue-green leaves borne on thick stalks. The fragrance it emits is unsurpassed and is best described as a spicy-to-sweet gardenia scent. This hardy ginger grows exceptionally well in full sun on our temperate West Coast. It was formerly known as *H. coccineum* "Tara."

Variegated Canna Lily / Canna "Tropicanna"

HEIGHT: 1.25–1.8 M / 4–6 FT	SPREAD: 90 CM–1.5 M / 3–5 FT	ZONE: 8*
FLOWERING PERIOD: SPRING–FALL		*Tender

A must for the exotic garden, "Tropicanna" features dazzling variegated foliage of maroon leaves accented with stripes of deep red, pink, orange and yellow. This prize-winning canna is a **sport** of "Wyoming" and features red flowers from late spring to fall. Protect the **rhizomes** from freezing by lifting after the first frost or mulching in protected sites.

The Desert Garden

The desert theme is the most recent trend in exotic gardening. This type of landscape makes use of dry, inhospitable sites that may be hard to find in parts of the Pacific Northwest. That being said, many south-facing foundation beds (under overhangs) provide this exposure — as do microclimates on southern Vancouver Island, the Sunshine Coast, the Gulf Islands and the San Juan Islands. Start by creating a suitable environment for these plants with raised gravel beds for drainage and rock borders, which help to retain the sun's heat. Accent the desert garden with sand mulches, large specimen rocks and even gnarled pieces of weathered driftwood.

Plant List

Opuntia / Prickly Pear Cactus
Echeveria / Hens and Chicks
Callistemon / Bottlebrush
Sedum / Low Stonecrop
Delosperma cooperi / Hardy Ice Plant
Agave
Yuccas
Arctostaphylos manzanita / Manzanita
Puya / Bromeliads
Aloes

Opuntia fragilis / Brittle Prickly Pear Cactus

HEIGHT: 15 CM / 6 IN	SPREAD: 30 CM / 1 FT	ZONE: 5
FLOWERING PERIOD: SPRING		

This small cactus with easily broken, rounded pads, grows in clumps. Bright yellow flowers are borne in spring on this North American native, which ranges from the Great Plain, to the B.C. interior to the San Juan Islands.

Delosperma cooperi / Hardy Ice Plant

HEIGHT: 5–10 CM / 2–4 IN	SPREAD: 50 CM / 20 IN	ZONE: 6
FLOWERING PERIOD: JUNE–SEPT		

This emerald-green succulent grows like a carpet, flowing over rocks. It produces a profusion of magenta-purple, star-shaped flowers from early summer until fall. Full sun and sharp drainage will allow this species to be a "maintenance-free" plant. It is excellent for containers.

Agave parryi / Mescal Agave

HEIGHT: 45 CM / 18 IN	SPREAD: 45 CM / 18 IN	ZONE: 6

Found in regions from New Mexico to Arizona, this medium-sized succulent forms a rosette of thick blue leaves in five to 10 years. Use this plant as an architectural feature in the desert garden or plant it on steep rockeries.

Bonsai

Keith and Becci Russell
Stone Tree Nursery
Courtenay, B.C.

The term "bonsai" comes from the Japanese and literally means "a tree in a shallow container." Of course, it is much more than a potted tree, as the process of keeping a healthy specimen in a container for a long period of time also stunts its growth. Careful pruning and placement in a complementing bonsai pot can create a beautiful work of art, while wiring the branches seasonally when the plant is young will speed the process of making an immature tree look old.

Keith and Becci Russell run Stone Tree Nursery on a beautifully landscaped one-acre property in Courtenay, B.C. In addition to bonsai specimens and supplies, you will also find a broad selection of ornamental plants, garden pottery and seasonal cut flowers on site. Their choices of both indoor and hardy outdoor bonsai plants will be of interest to gardeners throughout Canada and the US, regardless of site limitations.

Acer buergeranum / Trident Maple

ZONE: 6

A beautiful deciduous tree that is native to both China and Japan, the trident maple features glossy, dark green leaves with three distinct lobes and foliage that tends to reduce in size when grown in a bonsai pot. This is a very long-lived species with spectacular fall colours of red, orange and yellow.

Rhododendron impeditum / Dwarf Rhododendron

ZONE: 4–6

This hardy species rhododendron is readily available at most garden centres and is well known for its dense, grey-green foliage, which is smothered in mauve to violet-purple blossoms in spring. Actually, many dwarf rhododendrons are suitable bonsai specimens but almost all will require humus-rich, slightly acidic soil. The flower colour is really the gardener's choice, but be sure to choose one with finely textured foliage, as the smaller leaves usually end up looking better in bonsai applications.

Malus sargentii / Sargent Crabapple

(other varieties as hardy as Zone 2)   ZONE: 4

One of the lowest-growing crabapples, *sargenti* has tiny, pure white fragrant blooms (1.5 cm / ½ in across) followed by long-lasting pea-sized red fruit. A pink ("Rosea") flowering form is also available, but many other crabapples make particularly fine bonsai. This group of small trees provides year-round interest, although a slightly deeper container (and fertilizer) is required to ensure flowering and fruit set.

Carpinus koreana / Korean Hornbeam

ZONE: 4–5

This rugged, architectural tree develops handsome **exfoliating** bark. The foliage has pronounced deep veins and brilliant fall colours of scarlet, orange and yellow. This hornbeam responds well to pruning and can become a very nice bonsai in a short time.

Tsuga mertensiana / Mountain Hemlock

ZONE: 2

This British Columbian native has many good qualities, including short, blue-green needles and small cones, which provide a good sense of scale for a bonsai. The slow growth rate and good response to pruning also make this conifer an ideal candidate. A slightly rich, organic soil on the acidic side seems to suit this species well.

Fertilizing Bonsai

During spring and summer when the bonsai is growing, it will need to be fertilized. Any organic or water-soluble fertilizer will be fine, but look for one with trace elements for the best results. Dilute the fertilizer to half the recommended strength and apply it to a bonsai that has just been watered. During winter dormancy, fertilizing is unnecessary and can actually be harmful.

Alternate Bonsai Specimens

Vaccinium vitis-idaea minus / Mountain Cranberry — evergreen

Ilex crenata "Mariesii" / Dwarf Japanese Holly — evergreen

Acer palmatum "Red Pygmy" / Japanese Maple — deciduous

Chaenomeles japonica / Japanese Quince — flowers, fruit

Ilex verticillata / Winterberry — berries with pollinator

Chamaecyparis obtusa "Nana" / Dwarf Hinoki Cypress — conifer

Gardenia jasminoides / Common Gardenia — indoor/flowers

Tsuga canadensis "Jervis" / Dwarf Eastern Hemlock — conifer

Zelkova serrata / Japanese Zelkova — deciduous, fall colour

Cryptomeria japonica "Compressa" / Pygmy Japanese Cedar — conifer

Pinus parviflora / Japanese White Pine

ZONE: 5

Japanese white pine is the classic bonsai tree that is depicted on some blue willow china patterns. There are actually 800-year-old *Pinus parviflora* bonsai in existence today. This five-needled pine has short, bluish-green foliage with white stripes on the underside. Set the Japanese white pine, like all pines, in a gritty, fast-draining soil. Prune **candles** in the spring to create good branch **ramification.**

Juniperus chinensis sargentii / Shimpaku Juniper

ZONE: 3–4

The evergreen foliage on this variety is grey-green (i.e., "Glauca"), depending on the cultivar. It features interesting **exfoliating** bark with a red tinge underneath. The branches also respond well to wiring and regular pruning. This is a good choice for beginners, as an aged-looking tree can be achieved with just a few years of training.

Ficus species / Ornamental Figs

ZONE: Indoor

The tropical species of ornamental figs make excellent indoor bonsai. *Ficus salicifolia* or willow leaf fig has small, elongated leaves and will eventually develop aerial roots, giving it an exotic appearance. All *Ficus* tolerate lower levels of light (but not deep shade) and prefer to dry out between watering. This is one of the best beginner trees for indoor use — both "ZigZag" and "Natasha" are suitable cultivars of *Ficus benjamina* for bonsai use.

Punica granatum "Nana" / Dwarf Pomegranate

Indoor use for Bonsai ZONE: 8

Dwarf fruiting pomegranate has single, orange-red flowers and small fruits that are only about 4 cm / 1½ in wide. Several other dwarf cultivars are also available, including "Chico," which has double red blooms and no fruit. This plant benefits from an outdoor exposure during the summer and prefers higher light levels indoors.

Olea europaea / Olive Tree

Indoor use for Bonsai ZONE: 9–10

This Mediterranean native comes in many cultivars, including dwarf forms (i.e., "Skylark Dwarf"). It is actually a broadleaf evergreen with supple, leathery foliage and smooth, grey juvenile bark that becomes gnarled with maturity. An olive tree prefers high light levels and likes to dry out between watering — a gravelly, well-drained soil ensures its success. With a bit of luck, it may even produce some fruit for you.

Repotting Your Bonsai
Occasionally a bonsai will need to be repotted. This should be done at the end of dormancy, just before the new spring growth begins. After removing the tree from the pot, trim off some of the old, thick roots and replace a portion of the spent soil — never remove any more than 25 percent of the root mass. The replacement soil should be porous and free-draining, not just soil from the garden. Once the root pruning is done, the bonsai can be put back in the same pot, but it may need to be wired in place

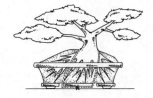

Drought-Tolerant Plants

Brian and Kishori Hutchings
Cusheon Creek Nursery
Salt Spring Island, B.C.

Although the West Coast is often thought of as a rainforest, much of the inner South Coast, San Juan and Gulf Islands and eastern portions of Vancouver Island are more accurately described as a Mediterranean climate, with wet winters and dry summers. Many drought-tolerant plants are ideal for these conditions, wanting only adequate drainage during the winter. With watering restrictions becoming more common in urban areas, dry gardens offer us spring-to-fall beauty with minimal maintenance.

Cusheon Creek Nursery grew out of a love of gardening, sparked by an early interest in cacti for Brian and vegetables for Kishori. The purchase of 5 acres on Salt Spring Island allowed this passion to expand into full nursery status. With their specialty being drought-tolerant plants and their hands-on experience with dry summers, Brian and Kishori's suggestions will prove invaluable to other gardeners who are dealing with the same conditions.

Gaura lindheimeri

HEIGHT: 90 CM–1.2 M / 3–4 FT	SPREAD: 60–90 CM / 2–3 FT	ZONE: 5
FLOWERING PERIOD: JUNE–OCT		

This member of the evening primrose family rewards the grower with endless clouds of small white flowers from June to late October. Wanting only sun and good drainage, gaura will thrive for many years. Wet winters tend to shorten its lifespan, but this is easily remedied by the species' tendency to self-seed — so replacement plants are always nearby. Several cultivars are available, including "Whirling Butterflies" (compact), "Siskiyou Pink" (deep-pink flowers) and "Corrie's Gold" (creamy-yellow variegation).

Spartium junceum / **Spanish Broom**

HEIGHT: 3 M / 10 FT	SPREAD: 3 M / 10 FT	ZONE: 6
FLOWERING PERIOD: JULY–FALL		

Spanish broom is a large shrub that begins flowering just as the smaller brooms finish, and continues into the fall. Bright green, rush-like stems bear fragrant golden-yellow pea blossoms in abundance. Unlike the Scotch broom (*Cytisus scoparius*), it rarely self-seeds in our climate and is a good choice for seaside gardens.

Perovskia atriplicifolia

HEIGHT: 90 CM–1.5 M / 3–5 FT	SPREAD: 50 CM / 20 IN	ZONE: 4
FLOWERING PERIOD: JULY–SEPT		

Wonderful spires of lavender-blue flowers from silvery-white buds and stems grace this erect shrub. Russian sage is a member of the mint family, with attractive sage-scented, grey-green foliage that works well in combination with bold perennials such as rudbeckia. This is a deer-proof plant that dislikes wet winter weather.

Elaeagnus angustifolia

HEIGHT: 2.5–7 M / 8–23 FT	SPREAD: 4 M / 13 FT	ZONE: 2
FLOWERING PERIOD: EARLY SUMMER		

Russian olive is a small deciduous tree with distinct silvery-grey foliage and dark brown, shaggy bark. It may be grown as a small specimen or trained to form a medium-height hedge, which is made more effective by the occasional thorn. The small yellowish flowers borne in early summer are highly fragrant and followed by fruits that resemble miniature olives. This is an extremely hardy plant that thrives in cold winter regions.

Preparing the Dry Garden

With the wet winters of the Pacific Northwest, the primary considerations for a dry garden are drainage and sun exposure. While sun exposure is simply a matter of placement, heavy soils will need to be amended with some coarse drainage material (i.e., gravel or fir bark) or, in the case of **subsoils**, a drain tile may be necessary. Another possibility is to build raised beds with up to 30 cm / 12 in of sandy soil, to keep the roots above the high water table during winter. Remember that soils from dry climates are often alkaline or near neutral, so add liberal amounts of dolomite lime to compensate for our acid conditions. Many of these plants are also adapted to poor soils, so fertilize sparingly to produce stronger, longer-lived perennials and shrubs.

Geranium sanguineum var. *striatum*

HEIGHT: 10–15 CM / 4–6 IN	SPREAD: 50 CM / 20 IN	ZONE: 5
FLOWERING PERIOD: LATE SPRING–SUMMER		

This wonderful little hardy geranium is at home when grown on dryish, sandy soils in full sun. It forms a mound of dark green, glossy foliage that is covered with pale pink flowers (**striated** in dark crimson) in late spring followed by occasional blooms all summer. This versatile perennial spreads moderately by underground runners and features red leaves in autumn.

Cistus x *corbariensis*

HEIGHT: 1 M / 3¼ FT	SPREAD: 2 M / 6½ FT	ZONE: 6
FLOWERING PERIOD: EARLY SUMMER		

This evergreen shrub was the result of a natural cross (*C. populifolius* x *C. salviifolius*), which produced a more compact and fairly hardy plant. It bears single white "roses" (5 cm / 1½ in across), which are highlighted with yellow **stamens** and produced in profusion during early summer. Rock rose can be somewhat sprawling in the border, but is quite effective over a rock wall or down an embankment. The dark green foliage takes on a reddish tinge during the winter.

Epimedium x *versicolor* "Sulphureum"

HEIGHT: 30 CM / 1 FT	SPREAD: 45 CM / 18 IN	ZONE: 5
FLOWERING PERIOD: APRIL–MAY		

Dry shade is a difficult obstacle to overcome in any garden — fortunately barrenworts such as "Sulphureum" (pale yellow blooms) provide the perfect solution. The yellow- or white-flowered varieties (i.e., *E.* x *youngianum* "Niveum") are preferred because the blooms show up well in dark areas, but red and pink forms are also available. The semi-evergreen, heart-shaped foliage persists until spring in mild winter regions, although it can look a little tired — so some gardeners cut them back at this time in order to appreciate the multiple sprays of tiny flowers.

Cotoneaster dammeri

HEIGHT: 15–30 CM / 6 IN–1 FT	SPREAD: 60–90 CM / 2–3 FT	ZONE: 5
FLOWERING PERIOD: MAY–JUNE		

This lovely evergreen ground cover has something for every season — shiny dark green foliage all year-round, white flowers in late spring and showy red berries remaining well into winter. Most forms are prostrate, with strong horizontal growth that is ideal for covering banks or cascading over a wall. Bearberry cotoneaster is not particularly a fast grower in drier conditions, so it's quite easy to keep within bounds. It requires no additional water once it is established.

Catananche caerulea / Cupid's Dart

HEIGHT: 60 CM / 2 FT	SPREAD: 30 CM / 1 FT	ZONE: 4
FLOWERING PERIOD: JUNE–AUG		

Cupid's Dart has attractive silvery buds that produce periwinkle-blue or white "cornflowers" all summer long. This lover of light, dry soils is alleged to be short-lived, but experience shows that at least a six-year lifespan can be expected under the right conditions. The seed heads are quite useful for dried arrangements.

Sempervivum species / Hens and Chicks

HEIGHT: 10 CM / 4 IN	SPREAD: 30 CM / 1 FT	ZONE: 2
FLOWERING PERIOD: SUMMER		

With an overwhelming selection of species and hybrids available, this extremely hardy, evergreen succulent can be appreciated by all. *Sempervivums* are well adapted to shallow soils over rock, tiny crevices or container culture. Established colonies of different varieties can create a fascinating mosaic of colour and form, with the added attraction of starry flowers during the summer. Although hens and chicks will survive severe drought, occasional watering will keep them looking good.

Adjusting New Plants

Most nursery stock receives regular to heavy watering, so the small root systems are usually sufficient to support the plants. Before abandoning new plants to a low-maintenance drought zone, be sure to water occasionally while they are adjusting and rooting into their new environment.

Plants for Dry Shade

Even in the midst of "rainforest country," it is not uncommon to have a dry spot under the canopies of huge cedars or Douglas firs. While the following plants will need some water to become established, they will tolerate dry shade once they have settled in.

Mahonia repens /
Creeping Oregon Grape

Ruscus aculeatus /
Butcher's Broom

Euphorbia robbiae /
Wood Spurge

Buxus sempervirens /
English Boxwood

Gaultheria shallon / *Salal*

Endymion non-scriptus /
English Bluebell

Ribes sanguineum /
Red-Flowering Currant

Bergenia cordifolia / *Pig Squeak*

Geranium macrorrhizum /
Bigroot Cranesbill

Aucuba japonica / *Japanese Aucuba*

Fragrant Plants

Glenn Lewis
Fragrant Flora
Roberts Creek, B.C.

Scent is the ethereal element of any garden — adding sophistication to the varied colours and forms of the flowers that surround us. Fragrant plants have long been valued, with the centuries-old Egyptian and Phoenician cultures being some of the first to create extracts for perfume. Even in a contemporary landscape, scented shrubs and perennials bring life to the home garden by attracting bees and butterflies for pollination and our enjoyment.

Glenn Lewis originally trained as a fine artist but, after travelling the world to photograph gardens for a Canada Council project on the "origins of paradise," he decided to settle down and create a unique nursery. The Sunshine Coast soon became the home of Fragrant Flora, a mail-order and retail nursery specializing in scented flowers and foliage.

Magnolia grandiflora

HEIGHT: 6.3 M+ / 21 FT+	SPREAD: 2.75 M+ / 9 FT+	ZONE: 7

A medium-sized evergreen tree, its large, glossy dark green leaves give it a very exotic appearance. The sumptuous flowers are cup-shaped (to 25 cm / 10 in across) with a scent reminiscent of lemon to jasmine, and are borne from late spring to mid summer, with a few sporadic blooms later in the season. Some of the better cultivars include "Edith Bogue" (very hardy), "Little Gem" (compact), "St. Mary" (large, bushy shrub) and "Samuel Sommer" (large flowers to 35 cm / 15 in across).

Syringa vulgaris "Krasavitsa Moskvy"

HEIGHT: 5.5 M / 18 FT	SPREAD: 4.5 M+ / 15 FT	ZONE: 4

Although there are hundreds of cultivars of the common French lilac to choose from, "Krasavitsa Moskvy" is one of the very best. The jonquil-scented, double blossoms emerge from pink buds to form large, conical **panicles** of pale lavender-pearled white. This large upright shrub has a suckering habit and features attractive heart-shaped leaves.

Ptelea trifoliata / Hop Tree

HEIGHT: 4.5 M / 15 FT+	SPREAD: 3.5 M / 12 FT	ZONE: 5

An upright deciduous shrub or small tree, the hop tree has strongly aromatic, compound leaves (three leaflets) and bark. It bears sweetly scented greenish-white (hop-like) summer flowers that are rather inconspicuous and are followed by rounded, pale green winged fruit. This is possibly the most fragrant of any tree, and it prefers a well-drained site in sun or dappled shade. A golden cultivar ("Aurea") is also available, with leaves that emerge a beautiful bright yellow in spring.

Rosa "Constance Spry"

HEIGHT: 5.5 M / 18 FT (as a climber)	SPREAD: 3 M / 10 FT	ZONE: 4–5

The first of David Austin's modern English roses, "Constance Spry" sparked a great deal of interest when it was introduced back in 1961. This vigorous climbing rose features heavily myrrh-scented, large pink blossoms, which are borne in early summer. Another rambler worthy of note is "Treasure Trove," with large trusses of strongly scented creamy-apricot blooms, which fade to a blush pink.

Glenn's Favourite Lavenders

Lavandula "Sawyers" — bluish-purple

L. angustifolia "Hidcote" — compact

L. "Goodwin Creek Grey" — rich texture

L. angustifolia "Jean Davis" — very pale pink

Lavandula stoechas — French Lavender

L. angustifolia "Munstead" — blue-purple

Lavandula "Fred Boutin" — violet

L. angustifolia "Lodden Blue" — compact

Lavandula "Richard Gray" — felted leaves

L. angustifolia "Twickle Purple" — purple

Caring for Lavenders

Lavender has been used as a herbal remedy and source of fragrance for centuries, with the early Romans scenting their bath water using sprigs of this plant. They form small shrubs that thrive in well-drained, poor to moderately fertile, light soils. Lavender requires full sun and will not perform well in poorly drained or very rich soils. They are useful in herb gardens, rockeries, perennial borders or as an informal hedge along a path. For the best effect, they should be planted in threes (or more) and allowed to grow together into a single mass. To keep this shrub in best form, be sure to lightly shear it after flowering or rejuvenate it with a harder pruning in early spring.

Lilium "Star Gazer"

HEIGHT: 90 CM / 3 FT	SPREAD: 30 CM / 1 FT	ZONE: 4

This oriental hybrid lily has crimson blooms spotted with deep pink, and a spicy, exotic fragrance in late summer. Some may find this perennial bulb a little garish, but this 90-cm / 3-ft high beauty really stands out, whether it's in the perennial border or in a container. For a more subtle Oriental lily try "Casablanca," which features pure white, textured flowers.

Daphne caucasica

HEIGHT: 1.2 M / 4 FT	SPREAD: 1.2 M / 4 FT	ZONE: 6

A relatively unknown shrub, this daphne has narrow, lance-shaped foliage and a very long blooming period. It bears deliciously scented, white tubular flowers held in clusters during spring and intermittently until frost. *Daphne caucasica* is one of the parents of the better known hybrid *Daphne* x *burkwoodii,* which has produced many fine cultivars, including "Somerset" (purplish-pink blooms), "Carol Mackie" (leaves edged yellow) and the newer "Brigg's Moonlight" (creamy-white leaves edged with green).

Lavandula x *intermedia* / Lavendin

HEIGHT: 75 CM / 30 IN	SPREAD: 75 CM / 30 IN	ZONE: 5

This hybrid evergreen shrub is a cross between English lavender (*L. angustifolia*) and *Lavandula latifolia,* a native of Mediterranean regions. Also known as lavendin, many of the cultivars such as "Grosso" (large dark-violet flower spikes) and "Provence" are used commercially in the fragrance industry. Another variety, "Grappenhall," bears purple-blue flowers on a robust framework often reaching a size of 1 m / 3 ft tall by 1.5 m / 5 ft wide.

Philadelphus hybridus

HEIGHT: 1.5–2.5 M+ / 5–8 FT+ SPREAD: 1.5–2.5 M+ / 5–8 FT+ ZONE: 5

Many of the hybrid mock orange provide the expected flowers, sweetly scented with a hint of citrus, but with a slight twist on the form or colour. "Belle Etoile" bears single cup-shaped blooms with pale purple centres, while "Bouquet Blanc" features pure white, semi-double to double flowers. "Beauclerk" has a slightly arching habit with large, single white blossoms flushed pink in the centre.

Osmanthus x burkwoodii

HEIGHT: 1.25–2 M+ / 4–6½ FT+ SPREAD: 1.25–2 M+ / 4–6½ FT+ ZONE: 7

A dense evergreen shrub, this *Osmanthus* hybrid bears glossy, dark green foliage that makes an excellent informal hedge or topiary subject. The tubular white blooms have a jasmine-like fragrance and are borne in profusion from mid to late spring. A hybrid of *O. decorus* and *O. delavayi*, it prefers alkaline soil in sites sheltered from cold winter winds.

Viburnum carlesii

HEIGHT: 1.5–1.8 M / 5–6 FT SPREAD: 1.8 M / 6 FT ZONE: 5

For sheer beauty and scent, it is hard to resist this Korean native. *Viburnum carlesii* forms a dense, deciduous shrub with oval, dark green foliage that often turns red in autumn. The small, pale pink flowers are held in domed terminal clusters, which emerge in spring before the leaves and are strongly clove-scented. Several cultivars are available, including "Aurora" (copper-tinted foliage), "Charis" (vigorous) and "Compactum" (dwarf).

The Four Seasons of Fragrance

Winter
Hamamelis mollis /
Chinese Witch Hazel
Viburnum x bodnantense
"Dawn"
Sarcococca ruscifolia /
Christmas Box

Spring
Wisteria sinensis /
Chinese Wisteria
Paeonia *"Bowl of Beauty"* /
Peony
Magnolia stellata /
Star Magnolia

Summer
Buddleia davidii /
Butterfly Bush
Cosmos atrosanguineus /
Chocolate Cosmos
Helichrysum angustifolium /
Curry Plant

Autumn
Perovskia atriplicifolia /
Russian Sage
Caryopteris clandonensis /
Blue Spiraea
Clematis paniculata /
Sweet Autumn Clematis

Hedges

John Blok
*Canadian Green
Nurseries Ltd.
Maple Ridge, B.C.*

While hedging material may not seem like much of a fashionable garden topic, it is certainly a necessity for privacy in any newer residential development. Despite the prevailing sentiment that pyramid cedars are the only hedging available, there are actually many plant options out there, including various cedar cultivars and broadleaf evergreens. Compact hedging is also becoming a very popular addition to any landscape where foundations or borders may need to be defined or softened. With the diversity of material available, there is no reason why a utility hedge could not also serve as a beautiful backdrop to the rest of the garden, as well as providing privacy.

Hedging material is one of John Blok's specialties, and his Canadian Green Nurseries certainly produces its fair share. John was also growing trees, shrubs, perennials and topiary specimens in Pitt Meadows for many years but has recently relocated to an east Maple Ridge site that includes a retail nursery outlet. He has chosen to present his choices in size categories, which is usually the most important criteria when choosing a hedge for a specific location.

The height and spread of all hedging plants will vary considerably, depending on pruning practices and local soil conditions.

Large Hedge Material

Settings: acreage, industrial parks, condominium perimeters
Uses: property boundary, specimen trees

Thuja plicata "Excelsa"

HEIGHT: to 20 M / 66 FT	SPREAD: 4–8 M / 13–26 FT	ZONE: 5

This selection of western red cedar grows very quickly and features dense, deep green foliage. "Excelsa" has a narrow, pyramidal form that is ideal for large-scale hedging, and it is more resistant to **keithia** blight than other cultivars. Although this conifer tolerates a wide range of soil conditions, it prefers moist, well-drained soil.

Thuja occidentalis "Pacific Jade"

HEIGHT: 5–8 M / 16–26 FT	SPREAD: 1.5–2 M / 5–6½ FT	ZONE: 3

This broader form of *T. occidentalis* grows slightly more slowly than the "Excelsa" cedar. "Pacific Jade" features light to mid-green foliage and a narrow, conical form. For gardeners looking for a hedge plant in between a pyramid (columnar) and red cedar (conical), this would be an ideal choice.

Photinia x *fraseri*

HEIGHT: to 5 M / 16 FT	SPREAD: 2–3 M / 6½–10 FT	ZONE: 7

Photinia has a lush, exotic look and is surprisingly easy to grow when planted in the right location. This broadleaf evergreen features bright copper-red new growth that fades to a deep green as the summer progresses. While it does provide a nice variation in colour, *Photinia* should receive at least six to eight hours of direct sun a day and be sheltered from northeast winter winds.

Drainage
Poor drainage is perhaps one of the major causes of dieback in hedging plants, due to a lack of oxygen to the roots and possible stem rot. Here are a few pointers to help you assess your new planting site.
1. Always check for soil compaction.
2. Never assume that a lack of surface water means good drainage below.
3. Soils tend to be heavily compacted in newer developments — so it may be necessary to create a planting berm.

Watering
Watering is probably the most important maintenance task in the first year, after planting a hedge. If nothing else, water hedging plants well during dry periods — this will mean soaking the root balls (a soaker hose works well) and not just using a sprinkler, which usually allows water to run off. Remember also, when planting under the overhang of any building, careful attention will need to be given to watering.

Fertilizer
Since most hedging plants are primarily foliage, a slow-release fertilizer such as 18–6–12 or 17–7–11 is recommended. Conifers can be fertilized twice during the growing season (March and September), while broadleaf evergreens should be fertilized only once in early spring (March), as the fall flush is not always as winter hardy. If a hedge extends below a larger established tree, an additional feeding may be necessary within that tree's drip line — as it will compete with the hedging for nutrients and may cause stunting in that section.

Planting Depth
A large hedge of any species is usually an expensive investment — so proper planting techniques should be used to help avoid any losses. Here are a few tips.
1. Never plant any deeper than the top of the root ball, and be careful when backfilling that no soil is worked up on the stem.
2. Balled and burlapped specimens should be placed in the planting hole intact — then the top string (around the stem) should be cut and the burlap peeled down. This keeps the lower root hairs from being disturbed and will allow your plant to establish more quickly.
3. Caged balled and burlapped specimens do not have any string immediately around the stem and will need to be left intact until the tree is rooted in (usually about one year).
4. Containerized plants should be placed at a depth equal to the height of the root ball, after being taken out of the pot.

Prunus lusitanica

HEIGHT: 5 M / 16 FT	SPREAD: 4 M / 13 FT	ZONE: 7

Another fine broadleaf evergreen that makes a great informal hedge, Portuguese laurel has glossy, dark green leaves that are held on contrasting red **petioles**. It will bear fragrant, creamy-white flowers in June (followed by black fruit) if clipped lightly — but still makes a good formal hedge, if it is sheared more often to promote density.

Medium Hedge Material

Settings: residential lots, townhouse developments, urban commercial sites

Uses: property boundary, screen existing fences, accent business signage

Thuja occidentalis "Brandon"

HEIGHT: 3–5 M / 10–16 FT	SPREAD: 1–1.25 M / 3¼–4 FT	ZONE: 3

This prairie-hardy cultivar of the pyramid cedar has mid-green foliage and a narrow, cylindrical form. This particular variety is also less prone to unsightly heavy seed production, which can occur when plants are under stress. "Brandon" tends to be flat-topped over time and has dull green winter foliage.

Thuja occidentalis "Smaragd"

HEIGHT: 3–4 M / 10–13 FT	SPREAD: 1 M / 3¼ FT	ZONE: 3

Emerald green cedar is probably one of the most popular hedging plants, and for good reason. It features fine sprays of bright green foliage that retains its colour throughout the winter months. "Smaragd" is also slower growing than "Brandon" and more conical than many *T. occidentalis* cultivars.

Thuja occidentalis "Europe Gold"

HEIGHT: 3–5 M / 10–16 FT	SPREAD: 1.5 M / 5 FT	ZONE: 3

This brilliant golden-yellow form of *Thuja occidentalis* is guaranteed to brighten any landscape. "Europe Gold" is squat and pointed when young — but matures to a more upright, cylindrical form with age. It may be a bit hard to find but is well worth the effort.

Compact Hedge Material
Settings: residential lots, condominium patios
Uses: foundation plantings, patio and sidewalk edges

Taxus x *media* "Hicksii"

HEIGHT: 1.5–3 M+ / 5–10 FT	SPREAD: 50 CM–2 M / 20 IN–7 FT	ZONE: 4

This shade-tolerant plant is quite columnar when young but definitely broadens with age — intensive shearing will help to keep this handsome hedge in top form. Hick's yew features the darkest green needles, multiple upright stems and is quite tolerant of heavy pruning to maintain size. Gardeners with young children should note that the red berries are particularly poisonous when ingested.

Buxus microphylla "Winter Gem"

HEIGHT: 50 CM–1.2 M / 20 IN–4 FT	SPREAD: 50 CM–1.2 M / 20 IN–4 FT	ZONE: 5

Unlike English boxwood, "Winter Gem" has glossy, emerald green foliage that retains its colour during the winter months. This broadleaf evergreen has a tidy, compact habit, making it a good choice for low hedges on patio perimeters. As with most boxwoods, it will tolerate heavy shearing during the growing season and thrives in light shade to full sun.

Pruning
In general, all of the conifers mentioned can be pruned any time from early spring to early fall — pruning at other times of the year should be avoided as it exposes tender foliage to cold and wind burn. Broadleaf evergreens should be pruned to keep them in form but at least some of the new growth should be retained. As with conifers, these plants will suffer if pruned in late autumn or winter.

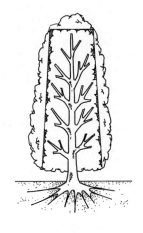

Some Alternate Plants for Hedging

Juniperus scopulorum *"Wichita Blue"* — *upright juniper*

Prunus laurocerasus */ English Laurel*

Viburnum tinus *"Spring Bouquet"* — *informal hedge*

Thuja occidentalis *"Danica"* / *Dwarf Globe Cedar*

Pinus mugo / *Mugo Pine* — *informal hedge*

Ligustrum ovalifolium / *Privet* — *semi-evergreen*

Euonymus japonicus *"Aureo-marginatus"* / *Euonymus*

Spiraea "Anthony Waterer" — *informal deciduous hedge*

Ilex crenata "Convexa"

HEIGHT: 2 M / 6½ FT	SPREAD: 2 M+ / 6½ FT+	ZONE: 5–6

This slightly hardier form of Japanese holly has been around since 1919. It features tiny, **convex** leaves that are quite shiny and, unlike other hollies, it bears small black berries. "Convexa" is an excellent substitute for boxwood where a slightly faster growth rate is needed and tolerates partial shade.

The Winter Garden

Despite the short days and inclement weather, the winter garden can offer some unexpected pleasures that are not available at any other time of the year. Quite often, it is a persona of bark texture, berries and brightly coloured branches rather than a display of flowers — but even these features are greatly enhanced with a simple touch of frost. While not every winter plant need bloom to earn respect, those that do bring joy and quite often fragrance, warming the gardener's heart on even the darkest days of the season.

I can't think of a more qualified person for this chapter than a landscape gardener, especially one who incorporates a winter element into almost all of his designs. For Kim Kamstra, this is both the first and last portion of the gardening year, and he has found that there can be as much beauty in dormancy as there is in spring flowers

Kim Kamstra
Kamstra
Landscaping Service
Maple Ridge, B.C.

Helleborus niger / **Christmas Rose**

HEIGHT: 30 CM / 1 FT	SPREAD: 40 CM / 16 IN	ZONE: 4
FLOWERING PERIOD: DEC–FEB		

There are so many beautiful hellebores to choose from that it is difficult to pick just one. Christmas rose is the first to bloom (white fading to bronze) and thrives in partial shade with moist, well-drained soil. It is particularly effective when planted in drifts and is a good companion for larger rhododendrons and pink dogwood.

Gaultheria procumbens / **Wintergreen**

HEIGHT: 15 CM / 6 IN	SPREAD: 30 CM / 1 FT	ZONE: 3–4
FLOWERING PERIOD: JUNE–AUG		

Many gardens have unwanted partial shade conditions that can be difficult to plant — wintergreen is the perfect

A Few Hellebores

Since Kim had such a difficult time choosing just one hellebore for the list, here are a few other worthy choices.

Helleborus x hybridus "Royal Heritage Strain" — white-pink-red-maroon flowers

H. foetidus (Stinking Hellebore) — green-edged purple blossoms

H. purpurascens "Red Power" — deep maroon flowers from Feb–May

H. argutifolius (Corsican Hellebore) — green flowers / leathery foliage

H. f. "Wester Flisk" — grey-green foliage with red veins, stems

H. a. "Pacific Frost" — white marbled variegation / green blossoms

solution. Although it is not widely known for its pale pink flowers, the bright scarlet berries borne in fall and winter are quite ornate. This evergreen ground cover is great for small pockets between aucuba, ferns or even *Fatisa japonica.*

Crataegus "Autumn Glory" / Hybrid Hawthorn

HEIGHT: 4.5–5.5 M / 15–18 FT	SPREAD: 2.75–4.5 M / 9–15 FT	ZONE: 5
FLOWERING PERIOD: SPRING		

This small tree produces a profusion of single white flowers in spring, followed by a heavy crop of glossy fruit. It is an excellent choice for planting among mugo pines or *Leucothoe*, where the bright red fruits can contrast with the evergreen foliage below. As soon as the leaves have fallen and winter sets in, this hawthorn will seem to have a life of its own.

Hamamelis japonica / Japanese Witch Hazel

HEIGHT: 3.5 M+ / 12 FT+	SPREAD: 3.5 M+ / 12 FT+	ZONE: 5
FLOWERING PERIOD: FEB–MARCH		

This species of witch hazel is not very common, but is well represented as the parent of many *H.* x *intermedia* hybrids such as "Arnold's Promise." Walking past this large shrub in flower, one might think that the hyacinths have come into bloom early — but the mildly sweet fragrance is actually emanating from small clusters of twisted yellow blooms. Japanese witch hazel needs lots of room to grow, but its vibrant yellow-red autumn foliage and late winter flowers add interest to any garden.

Corylus avellana "Contorta" / Corkscrew Hazel

HEIGHT: 3.5 M / 12 FT	SPREAD: 1.8–2.5 M / 6–8 FT	ZONE: 4
FLOWERING PERIOD: FEB		

Twisted and "bent out of shape" are about the best terms to describe this large, deciduous shrub. Florists often use the most spiralled stems in arrangements — but be warned that this genetic trait also causes the foliage to appear crumpled. Corkscrew hazel is at its best during winter, when the contorted branches and pale yellow male catkins are most visible.

Callicarpa bodinieri g. "Profusion" / Beauty Berry

HEIGHT: 1.8 M / 6 FT	SPREAD: 1.5–1.8 M / 5–6 FT	ZONE: 6
FLOWERING PERIOD: JULY–AUG		

Dense clusters of small pink flowers during the summer give way to an abundance of lilac to bright purple berries. This shrub really does not stand out until the leaves fall and so is best not obscured by trees or other large shrubs. Rather, give it some sun and a background of dark green foliage and be prepared for brilliant berries, which often last until Christmas in milder regions.

Betula papyrifera / Paper Birch

HEIGHT: 18 M+ / 60 FT+	SPREAD: 6 M / 20 FT	ZONE: 2

This North American native is often overlooked for Himalayan birch (*B. jacquemontii*) and, as a consequence, has become less available in some areas. Many a garden situation calls for some type of tree that will tolerate high soil moisture yet still provide some visual focus in the landscape. Be it standard or clump form, paper birch, with its peeling white bark and tolerance of wet soils, is an ideal choice for winter interest.

Cryptomeria japonica "Elegans" / Plume Japanese Cedar

HEIGHT: 7.5 M / 25 FT	SPREAD: 5 M / 16 FT	ZONE: 6

Every time Kim plants this conifer, he gets a phone call in late autumn from customers worried about their "dying tree." He calmly tells them that they did nothing wrong and that the colour change from grey-green to bronze-plum

---

The Winter Yellows

For some reason, the season from winter to early spring seems to be dominated by many shrubs with bright yellow flowers. Here are just a few of the species or cultivars available — along with their respective hardiness zones.

Corylopsis spicata / *Spike Winter Hazel — Zone 5–6*

Mahonia bealii / *Leatherleaf Mahonia — Zone 6*

Forsythia x intermedia / *Border Forsythia — Zone 4*

Chimonanthus praecox / *Winter Sweet — Zone 7*

Hamamelis mollis / *Chinese Witch Hazel — Zone 5*

Stachyurus praecox / *Japanese Stachyurus — Zone 6*

Corylus a. "Contorta" / *Corkscrew Hazel — Zone 4*

foliage is quite normal. Aside from that, this evergreen features very soft-textured foliage and makes an attractive informal hedge.

Cotoneaster frigidus / **Himalayan Cotoneaster**

HEIGHT: 3.5–5.5 M / 12–18 FT	SPREAD: 3M / 10 FT	ZONE: 6–7
FLOWERING PERIOD: JUNE		

When sprayed up against a wall in full view of a casual glance, the winter display of brilliant red berry clusters is extremely eye-catching. This is one of the fastest-growing cotoneasters that can also be used to form a tall, open shrub or small tree. Try growing this semi-evergreen to deciduous plant among fine-needled conifers for the best contrast.

Viburnum grandiflorum

HEIGHT: 1.8–3 M / 6–10 FT	SPREAD: 1.8–2 M / 6–6½ FT	ZONE: 6
FLOWERING PERIOD: DEC–APRIL (main bloom period in early spring)		

Given room to grow, this fine deciduous shrub sheds dense orange leaves in autumn, then starts blooming sporadically from early winter through to spring. This species is closely related to *V. farreri*, but it has larger blooms that are usually a slightly deeper pink. Place this large shrub near a walkway, where the passersby can appreciate its fragrant flowers. As a side note, this is also one of the parents of the popular cultivar, *Viburnum* x *bodnantense* "Dawn."

Glossary

AARS: All-America Rose Selection

aerial roots: a root that develops above the soil level

annual: a plant that completes its growing cycle within a single growing season

anthers: the male flower organ that produces pollen grains

APS: American Peony Society

axil: the area between the stem and the upper leaf stalk

axillary: side buds that can remain dormant until the terminal bud is removed

bacterial canker: a bacterial disease that causes blackening of the wood and dead tissue on Asian pears and Prunus species

balled and burlapped: root ball is dug, covered with a sheet of burlap and tied together with heavy string

beard: the fuzzy, brightly coloured strip in the centre of the falls of an iris flower

berm: a raised planting bed

biennial: a plant that finishes its growth cycle in two seasons

black spot: a fungal disease that typically shows as black, circular spots on the foliage

bloom: a whitish coating found on some fruit

botrytis: a fungal disease, commonly known as "grey mould"

bract: a modified leaf that often looks like a flower petal

Brassica: an important genus of edible plants that includes cabbage, kale, cauliflower, turnip and broccoli

caliper: refers to the width of a tree trunk

calyx: the outer portion of a flower, composed of sepals

cambium: the layer of actively growing cells just beneath the bark of trees and shrubs

candles: the young, unopened shoots of a pine

chlorosis: a yellowing of the foliage due to a lack of chlorophyll

conifer: a plant that bears cones and is usually evergreen (i.e., cedar, pine and spruce)

conker: slang for the fruit of some horse chestnuts

convex: curving, much like the surface of a ball

cordate: a leaf shape, much like the outline of a heart

corm: an enlarged stem base covered with the lower portion of dried leaves from the previous year

corona: the trumpet portion of a daffodil flower

crozier: the crown of unfurled new fronds

culms: the stems of bamboo

cultivar: a cultivated variety

deadheading: the act of removing the seedhead or spent flowers

deciduous: a plant that loses all of its leaves during winter

ephemerals: plants that are active for a short, transitional period

exfoliating: peeling

eyezone: a splash of colour above the centre throat of the flower

F1: an intentional hybrid between two unique plants resulting in strong, uniform offspring

falls: the three lower petals of an iris flower

fertile frond: a separate frond that carries the spores

filament: the stem that supports the anther

florets: smaller flowers that make up the head of a bloom

floribunda: a class of rose that produces a large number of smaller flowers in clusters, usually a bushy plant

friable: a soil that can easily be crumbled in the hand

frond: the leaf of a fern

genera: the plural for genus

genus: a group of related species

glaucous: covered with a waxy bloom that can appear grey or bluish

grandiflora: a class of rose that produces single or long-stemmed clusters of flowers borne on tall shrubs

hardneck: a type of garlic with excellent flavour and loose skins, but a short storage life

herbaceous: a plant composed of soft tissue that generally dies back to the ground in winter

hip: the fruit of a rose that contains the seed

humus: decomposed organic matter present in many soils

hybrid tea: a class of rose with large flowers usually produced on a single stem

indumentum: a hairy covering found on some rhododendron leaves

inflorescence: a flower shoot composed of multiple bloom clusters

internode: the space between the nodes, found on bamboo stems and other plants

keithia: a fungal blight that causes the foliage to drop

lacecap: a bloom with large sterile flowers surrounding small fertile blossoms, creating a lacecap effect (plate-like)

legume: members of the pea family (*Leguminosae*), including beans, peas, peanuts and soybeans

liner: a small, rooted starter plant

loam: a soil composed of sand, silt and clay

marginal: a plant that thrives with submerged roots and foliage above the water's surface

mophead: a generic term for large, rounded hydrangea blooms (i.e., *H. macrophylla* / Hortensia)

mycorrhiza: a group of beneficial soil fungi that attach themselves to plant roots

necrotic lesions: a localized area of dead plant cells

nonastringent: the fruit has little or no sharp aftertaste

ovate: oval shaped

oxygenator: usually submerged plants that use carbon dioxide and excess nutrients in the water

palmate: a leaf shape, much like the outline of an outstretched hand

panicle: a flower cluster composed of multiple branches

parthenocarpic: capable of setting fruit without pollination

pendulous: weeping; hanging down and drooping

perianth: the outer portion of the flower, both petals and sepals

petaloid: flower organs that *appear* to be petals

petiole: the stalk that attaches the leaf to the plant

picotee: a narrow, contrasting marginal zone on flower petals

pinnae: the individual fern leaflets

pinnate: leaflets attached on both sides of a common stem

plicata: stippled margin colour on a white background

powdery mildew: a fungal disease that typically shows as a white, powdery cast on the foliage

pseudobulb: a thickened, modified stem of many orchids

pubescent: covered in short hairs

quartered: a shape of rose flower with a quartered rosette in the centre of the bloom

raceme: a flower cluster in which individual blooms are attached with short stalks along the stem

ramification: causing branch formation, to divide or spread out

reticulated: refers to leaves that are dark veined with light green interspaces

rhizomatous: spreading by means of rhizomes or underground stems

rhizome: a thickened stem that grows horizontally, below or at the soil surface

rosarian: a person devoted to the cultivation of roses

scab: a fungus prevalent in wet regions, damaging foliage and fruit

scape: the flower stem

scree: an alpine bed composed of crushed rock with a thin layer of soil (drains quickly)

sepal: a part of the flower that surrounds the inner flower bud

serrated: having notched edges, much like those of a saw

silica: a micronutrient used in the production of Bamboo stems

spathe: a structure or bract that covers the flower spike

spores: the reproductive structure of the fern

sport: a naturally occurring mutation

spurs: short, lateral branches that flower and produce the fruit

stamen: the male portion of the flower, best described as a thin stem (filament) with a grain-like structure (anther) on the end

standards: the upper petals of an iris flower

stolon: an above-ground horizontal plant stem that can root as it spreads

striated: striped

style: an elongated stem that connects the stigma to the ovary

sub-shrub: a small plant with a woody stem base and upper growth that dies back in winter

subsoil: the layer of soil just below the fertile topsoil, usually mineral-based with no organic matter

systemic: designed to be absorbed by the plant tissue, allowing the whole shrub to be protected

terminal: forming at the ends of the branches or stems

trifoliate: compound leaf with three leaflets

true bulb: a flower embryo surrounded by fleshy scales, which are held together with a basal plate

trumpet: a long, narrow corona

truss: a flower cluster

tuber: a swollen underground stem with irregular growing points

tuberous roots: a swollen root that has growth buds located at the base of the old stems

umbel: a flower cluster with individual blooms arising from one point at the tip of a stem

undulata: wavy leaf margins

Contact Information

WHOLESALE CONTRIBUTORS

The wholesale contributors included in this book supply landscapers, retail garden centres and other wholesale nurseries exclusively with large quantities of plant material. Generally, the **do not** deal with the public directly due to safety concerns and the time limitations of assembling and shipping such large orders. The best place to find the plants mentioned in this book is at your local garden centre or one of the following retail contributors.

RETAIL CONTRIBUTORS

While many of our retail contributors had difficulty choosing only 10 plants to write about, I am sure they would welcome the opportunity to show you the vast array of other botanicals that they offer to the public at their nurseries. As well, many also provide descriptive catalogues (for a nominal fee) and a mail-order service, for those who may not be able to visit in person.

Brentwood Bay Nurseries Ltd.
1395 Benvenuto Ave.
Brentwood Bay, BC V8M 1J5
phone (250) 652-1507
fax (250) 652-2761
retail nursery / mail order

Cusheon Creek Nursery
175 Stewart Road
Salt Spring Island, BC
V8K 2C4
phone (250) 537-9334
fax (250) 537-9354
retail nursery

Erikson's Daylily Gardens
24642 — 51 Avenue
Langley, BC V2Z 1H9
phone (604) 856-5758
mail order / retail nursery in season

Ferncliff Gardens
8394 McTaggart Street
Mission, BC V2V 6S6
phone (604) 826-2447
fax (604) 826-4316
mail order /
retail nursery in season

Fragrant Flora
RR 22, 3741 Sunshine Coast Hwy.
Robert's Creek, BC V0N 2W2
phone and fax (604) 885-6142
mail order /
retail nursery in season

Fraser's Thimble Farm
175 Arbutus Road
Salt Spring Island, BC
V8K 1A3
phone and fax (250) 537-5788
mail order /
retail nursery in season

Hansi's Nursery
27810 — 112th Avenue
Maple Ridge, BC V2W 1P9
phone (604) 462-8799
fax (604) 462-8042
retail nursery in season

**Hawaiian Botanicals
and Water Gardens**
6011 No. 7 Road
Richmond, BC V6W 1E8
phone (604) 270-7712
fax (604) 271-2433
retail nursery

The Heather Farm
Box 2206
Sardis, BC V2R 1A6
mail order only

Made in the Shade Nursery
4586 Saddlehorn Crescent
Langley, BC V2Z 1J7
phone (604) 856-2010
fax (604) 856-0049
retail nursery in season

Old Rose Nursery
1020 Central Road
Hornby Island, BC V0R 1Z0
phone (250) 335-2603
fax (250) 335-2602
mail order / retail nursery

The Perennial Gardens
13139 — 224 Street
Maple Ridge, BC V4R 2P6
phone (604) 467-4218
fax (604) 467-3181
retail nursery in season /
mail order

Phoenix Perennials Ltd.
4153 Yuculta Crescent
Vancouver, BC V6N 4A9
phone (604) 267-0266
landscape design

The Plant Farm
177 Vesuvius Bay Road
Salt Spring Island, BC
V8K 1K3
phone and fax (250) 537-5995
mail order / retail nursery

Select Roses
22771 — 38 Avenue
Langley, BC V2Z 2G9
phone and fax (604) 530-5786
retail nursery in season

Stone Tree Nursery
2271 Lake Trail Road
Courtenay, BC V9N 9C3
phone and fax (250) 338-9785
retail nursery in season

Wrenhaven Nursery
16651 — 20 Avenue
South Surrey, BC V4P 2R3
phone (604) 536-7283
retail nursery

FEATURED PARKS
If a picture is worth a thousand words, then a visit to one of our featured botanical or demonstration gardens should prove to be an enlightening experience. Be sure to bring your camera and suitable outdoor clothing, as many of them contain extensive plant collections and exhibits.

VanDusen Botanical Garden
5251 Oak Street
Vancouver, BC V6M 4H1
phone (604) 878-9274

UBC Botanical Garden
6804 SW Marine Drive
Vancouver, BC V6T 1Z4
phone (604) 822-4529
(garden shop)

Park & Tilford Gardens
440 — 333 Brooksbank
Avenue
North Vancouver, BC V7J 3S8
phone (604) 984-8200 fax
(604) 984-6099

Queen Elizabeth Park
33rd Ave. & Cambie Boulevard
Vancouver, BC
phone (604) 257-8584
(conservatory)

Queen's Park
1st Street & 3rd Avenue
New Westminster, BC

**West Coast Seeds
Demonstration Garden**
6511 Dyke Road
Richmond, BC V7E 3R3
phone (604) 482-8800
fax (604) 482-8822
best from July–September

**Vancouver Compost
Demonstration Garden**
2150 Maple Street
Vancouver, BC V6J 3T3
phone (604) 736-2250
(compost hotline)

Index